# The *Vast* Difference between the African American and the American Negro

## A Novel

Martin J. Lee

PAGE PUBLISHING, INC.
New York, NY

First originally published by Page Publishing, Inc. 2017

ISBN 978-1-68409-578-0 (Paperback)
ISBN 978-1-68409-579-7 (Digital)
ISBN 978-1-63568-233-5 (Hardcover)

Printed in the United States of America

A good tree cannot produce bad fruit . . . Nor can a bad tree produce good fruit . . . Every tree that does not bear good fruit is cut down and thrown into the fire . . . So then you will know them by their fruits.

—Matthew 7:18–20

# PREFACE

"When all else has failed to organize the people, then conditions will" (Mr. Marcus Garvey). Well into the twenty-first century can conditions be any more ripe for change for black people in America than they are now? Between 28 percent to 30 percent of all black males will be arrested, jailed, or imprisoned in their lifetime, most before they reach manhood. Of all the black children, 70 percent of all black children are being raised by a single parent (most only by mothers). The jails and prisons in America are populated by an inordinate amount of black males and females, many for nonviolent crimes. Today there are more blacks in correctional control (in prison, probation, or parole) than were enslaved in 1850. That's a decade before the Civil War began.

Many serve time primarily because they are poor. The charges of the nonviolent detainees aren't enough to keep any person of means locked up more than twenty-four hours. However, most blacks and other minorities stay locked up far longer than Caucasians because they just don't have bail money. Blacks are still being gunned down during traffic stops and/or profiled and harassed just because they are black. Still, the absolute worst part of black folks' condition in America is the pain we cause ourselves, the lack of respect we have for one another, the jealousy that exist between us, how much we covet what others have, the violence we as a people inflict upon one another, how much we yearn to see anyone of our people who have been successful fall flat on their faces.

Instead of hoping that the talented amongst us get better so that all our lots can improve, some of us behave like we want to personally bring about their demise. This is not a subject matter that black people like or want to hear about. We will call one another traitors, sellouts, or Uncle Toms if we speak the truth of how poorly we coexist. Until we accept what we do and/or how we treat one another as a reality, our so-called cohesiveness will continue to erode, and we will not move forward.

If anyone from any other ethnicity or race wrote or spoke about what you are about to read, then their feet would be held to the fire. However, these are the words of a black man about black people. I'm an African American in America who, through my literature, is sharing with you, my readers, the current state of the goings-on in the black community in America. No matter what we have to deal with to improve, we must undertake the endeavor as soon as possible, to come together, to become a cohesive lot trying to help one another improve, to work with one another for progress, to educate one another, to live amongst ourselves in relative peace, to stop killing one another, to truly try to love one another.

I have witnessed some great strides as well as some drastic backsliding by my people because of a dichotomy. A *vast* difference in the mind-set exists amongst black Americans. There is a portion of my people that are figuratively and literally killing us, undermining the great accomplishments black leaders and activist have given their lives for, only to find ourselves back on a rollercoaster of doom.

I have decided to pen this novel to enlighten all who read it about the happenings in our world. The two main evils that afflict black people in America are (1) racism and (2) the throwback American Negro. Depending on the day or week or year, 1 sometimes changes places with 2. Sometimes we are our number-one worst problem. I have put in words through the protagonist, Claude M. N. Paine, what it is like to be black in America and have to tolerate racism and, more importantly, to have to tolerate the mind-set of some of my own people who despise their own wretched lots. They despise their lot so much that all they want to do is make the life of someone else who looks like them, someone who comes from where they come from and has had to endure the same hardships *all* black people have to endure, as miserable as theirs.

"Who the fuck those niggers think they are?" they reason. "If they're black like me and I'm miserable, then I'll be damned if they're going to be happy when I'm not, if they are talented when I'm not, if they have means, wherewithal, and money when I don't, if they chose to get an education when I didn't want one. Shucks! Even if I can't espouse it aloud, but I'll be damned if those niggers do better than me. I just won't have it."

African Americans are on the move and have been upwardly mobile for just under two hundred years. Still, save for racism, our worst impediment lives amongst us and even looks like us. It's what I call the throwback American Negro. As you read the story of Claude Paine and the Paine family, draw your own conclusion, for this is reality-based fiction based on my lifelong experience as an African American interacting with other black and white folks in America. As you read through this novel, try to base the opinion you glean from my literature on your own personal life and equate it with your own experience. Please, just don't deny the truth; then perhaps we can rise above the existence of our worst detractors, some of our own people—the throwback American Negro.

Perhaps then we can even bring them aboard our vehicles of progress and, in the process, most importantly, give all black folks *hope*. Sincerely, I thank everyone who undertakes the endeavor to read my literature. I really hope it educates and enlightens everyone who reads it.

There is no passion to be found in settling for
a life that is less than the one you are capable
of living.

—Mr. Nelson Mandela

———— ❦ ————

# CHAPTER 1

The one thing that irritated Claude Paine most of all was his inability to experience peace of mind whenever interacting with the true-to-life, modern-day, throwback American Negro (heretofore referred to as T.A.N.). The T.A.N.s he encountered had no use for principles. Apparently, absolutely nothing is sacred to them. They appear to be totally lacking a sense of self and oh so quick to disrespect adults and the elderly. One would tend to think "Who the heck raised you?" or "Where the hell do you come from?" when interacting with a T.A.N..

These were the folks who Claude would hear talk racial pride all the time, but Claude continually saw how baffled a T.A.N. looked when you asked him or her who Dr. Charles Drew or Dr. Daniel Hale Williams were. "Wasn't Bessie Coleman a singer?" they'd ask. Who Gabriel Prosser was and what did he do? They'd say stuff like "The Harlem Renaissance—wasn't that a team in the Negro leagues?" Benjamin Banneker was an A.A. Inventor. Most blacks that Claude grew up with don't know that. So they might say, "Benjamin Banneker, what team does he play for? How can anyone expect folks to have pride, self-respect, and/or vision when they know and want to know very little about their own heritage, their own history and the very rich history it has?

To Claude, sometimes it's frightening interacting with some of the young T.A.N.s (or any T.A.N. for that matter). There is no direction and not an inkling of hope in their eyes—just blank, like premature death. It is very similar to beholding a sinister smirk, a surreptitious sneer, or a great white shark's death glare during a feeding frenzy.

One day, during a lengthy conversation with one of Claude's dearest and most respected friends, Danielle, a psychologist, he mentioned what a glorious childhood he had.

She then stated, "That's the difference in yourself and some of my patients who are T.A.N.s. Most of my T.A.N. patients have had a terrible childhood experience."

Claude then said, "I understand, and I realize how debilitating that can be, but isn't that the kind of experience that could be used to motivate oneself?"

"Sure," said Danielle, "as long as the youngster believes there is a God and doesn't give up on themselves—ever. However, he or she has to be taught that. Sometimes that's easier said than done when a child is rudderless, when their life is governed by someone who has neither the interest nor desire to invest the time in teaching their children anything."

This lack of parental guidance is what Claude felt could be where the black child begins to develop (or evolve) into what eventually becomes the throwback American Negro. Our African American community and American society are inundated with these pariahs. As Claude made his way through life, he began to see the anger, the vitriol, the immense self-hate for their own people these T.A.N.s had. It was a true impediment for the African American community and society as well. And as Claude saw so many times, what was even more evident was their abject fear of Caucasian Americans.

Oh so quick they were to wreak havoc among their own kind, (Claude himself was the victim of a blood curdling Armed Robbery in a Chinese takeout) to aggressively disrespect or ignore African American adults and the elderly, to steal an elderly African American woman's purse, to shoot one of their own brethren (they really like doing that), to sell one of their *own* people a used car and turn back the odometer to fifty, seventy, or a hundred thousand miles, to break into a hard-working African American neighbor's house to burglarize it and rob someone who has less than they have themselves, to accept a contracting job in their own neighborhood with their own people and try to take them for every dime they can, to steal some personal information from them while they're working in their house, to go to work and do *whatever* they can to cost other African Americans their jobs in an effort to ingratiate themselves with their bosses.

And oh lord, the jealousy. You hadn't seen jealousy until you'd seen a T.A.N. get jealous. All one had to do was do well or be admired by someone more than they were admired, and they could watch the jealousy brew up in their eyes and then ooze out of their pores or emanate from their foul-smelling mouths with their words. But when Claude saw that same T.A.N. in a predominately Caucasian setting, they became frozen in fear and indecision, conflicted. It seemed like the victims they were used to harassing usually looked like themselves.

"Don't take that shit to no white neighborhood. Shucks, you might get killed!" they reason. "If you screw your own kind, more than likely, at worst, you'll only go to jail. Shit, jail ain't no spooky place, ain't nothing there but other black folk." When things got too rough, when it was too difficult to maintain, then at least in jail, one could get three meals a day, and there would even be a bed. Also, there was always someone there weaker to get one's shit off on or to take advantage of.

Claude read the book *Subliminal Seduction* by Mr. Wilson Bryan Key, and he believed the media has already drilled that and other negative things into their psyche subliminally. To Claude, it was what the rapper Jeru da Damaja was referring to when he said, "Subliminal hypnotism and colonialism leaves most niggers dead or in prison." So what Claude came to believe, based on his own inter-active experience with them, was that the T.A.N. really only wanted to upset the apple cart among their own kind. It was safer. They (T.A.N.s) are a creation, an aberration, truly lost and astray.

It was like when Claude saw the character actor Mr. Vic Morrow state, referring to slaves, in his role as an overseer in the classic mini-series *Roots*. It is a statement that is analogous to the conditioning of the modern-day T.A.N.. He said, "Niggers are made—they are *not* born!" To Claude, the saddest thing about this whole scenario is that, what they do seem like it is all they know. That is what all their friends seem to know, so sadly, that is all they want to know—how to fuck one another figuratively and literally because they sure do.

Obviously to Claude, this is their goal in life, if you'd want to call it that. He saw no sense of pride in self, family, race, or country—totally lacking in shame. Like the old saying goes, "Show me your friends, and I'll show you your future."

# CHAPTER 2

> "You should hear things in your spirit that contradict what you hear with your ears. You got to be willing to be criticized because you hear things on a level that other people don't hear. You are seeing things they don't see and building for things they don't understand because it hasn't happened yet. Neighbor you don't have to believe in my dream. I don't have time to wait— time for you to figure out who I really am. To understand my true heart—to take into account how I was raised or what I've been through."
>
> —Bishop T. D. Jakes

Claude wanted an education to learn all he could about carpentry and plumbing, and he eventually wanted financial security. He was told all through his young life that those (save for lottery winners) who wanted riches and who weren't born into wealth would have to work for it and that most of the wealthy had to work to maintain their wealth. "You gotta work! Son, you gotta work!" As a child, he kept hearing things like "Oh, this nigger thinks he's Einstein" or "Ain't you a dreaming delusion of grandeur, nigger? Shit, we went to elementary school together. You ain't never was an A student."

Claude knew that if he was going to accomplish anything productive, he would have to do it in spite of their draining evaluations about his character while trying to avoid the company of folks who spoke like that. Claude experienced most of the aforementioned at the hand of the T.A.N.s in his immediate neighborhood. His grandmother's home was robbed by T.A.N.s. His brother and uncle were shot by T.A.N.s. A T.A.N. contractor working at his dad's home stole his father's social security number and destroyed his dad's credit. His brother bought a car that had 210,000 miles on it, but the odometer was turned back to read 90,000 miles. These were all done by his own people, his neighbors, right on his people. Black power????

However, these creeps who never had an encouraging word to say were only the tip of the iceberg of the T.A.N.s Claude would have to interact with as he grew older and entered the working world. One of the things that really unnerved him was the issue with people of color who were still in the twenty-first century being gunned down in the street like they were the prey, the victims of a fox hunt, the way Claude had read about how the early settlers in America killed buffalo and left their carcasses in the prairie to rot in the sun just for sport! He read and had been told that the Native Americans who killed buffalo for meat, hide, and fur had never seen anything like that prior to the American frontier settlers.

This fact was brought forth in Native American author Mr. Dee Brown's book *Bury My Heart at Wounded Knee* and the great movie *Dances with Wolves* starring and produced by Mr. Kevin Costner. Similarly, people of color in the twenty-first century are being gunned down and murdered for the most minor of traffic stops and other minor infractions of the law and then given to their bereaved, distraught families. The culprits then are truly disgusted that so much noise is made when all they did was kill a nigger!

Although he never mentioned it, Claude believed they're despondent that they couldn't mummify or stuff (at least sever and stuff the head for it to be mounted above their mantles) and keep their black corpses as trophies or, at the very least, leave their dark bodies in the street to rot, like they did the buffalo. Claude thanks God for CNN and other news networks who are bringing us this news immediately. Within hours of the events, this information age we're living in affords the entire world the opportunity to view the barbaric treatment of dark people on American soil. Claude felt the darker-hued folks warred with one another, killed one another at alarming rates, and are dumbfounded when other "Americans" killed or demeaned and disrespected them. To Claude, it looked like one of the reasons they are so wantonly dispatched, most of the time with impunity, is partially due to T.A.N. behavior.

Through his interaction with his Caucasian friends and the things they said, Claude believed many Caucasian Americans systematically murdered black people because of the subliminal anti-black training many of them received at home, from the media, and/or from their parents when they were very young. It was on T V, in movies, and in the airwaves as referred to earlier with subliminal seduction. That, coupled with the fact that the blacks' behaviors tended not to deter this Pic Nic behavior (pick a nigger to shoot, like the word *picnic* was originally derived from a lynch party), which was slang for pick a nigger to lynch.

After church one Sunday morning, while buying a Sunday paper at the neighborhood WAWA, Claude overheard a Caucasian kid no more than thirteen or fourteen years old say to one of his buddies that his dad told him anyone from a country that ended in *stan* (Kazakhstan, Uzbekistan) was probably a terrorist. Just like the old saying "Charity begins at home" was true, apparently, so did racism.

The horrific way blacks are now (sometimes subtly, sometimes overtly) typically portrayed and, more importantly, the way they behaved or comported themselves socially in public. The more Claude was involved in debates about the current state of and the goings-on in our country, the more Claude believed most black folks had their opinion given to them or they conformed quickly to what is popular. This demeaning subliminally seductive portrayal of blacks coupled with what some of our behaviors said to others about them is vividly illustrated on the law enforcement shows *US Marshals* and the long-running TV series *Cops*. From what Claude could see, both shows made the viewers of these shows think the predominance of criminals in America are black. This "beware the black crook" mindset stays with its viewers no matter what their ethnicity.

An example of this was made manifest in Claude's life one day while he was hurrying to work. Claude was running a little late, and he wanted a newspaper and a hot cocoa. He pulled up in front of the one-stop mini market he frequented. Quickly, he jumped out and ran into the store. No sooner did he open the door and try to make his way to the counter than this frightened young African American woman, seeing a black man moving quickly, immediately pulled down the bulletproof window and locked the register. This was the kind of thing that made Claude come to the conclusion that her subliminal training kicked in.

*Why not?* she must have thought. *Any black man moving that quickly had to be up to nothing positive, just like those aforementioned TV shows.* She seemed to actually be reacting according to the subliminal training she received from the TV shows and news she watched from time to time.

The odds of this black man, or any black man, moving quickly and being a criminal were very high, she felt, so she'd better play it safe! The only thing Claude was trying to do was make his purchase and get to work in time. For one quick minute, he actually thought he was just an average hard-working American. He forgot he was black and was moving fast.

Now, this was an African American woman who behaved this way, *not* a T.A.N.. Could it be that her subliminal subconscious training, unbeknownst to her, was the reason she had been wary of this fast-moving dark man? Perhaps interacting with T.A.N.s, who were *always* manipulative, had also been instrumental in rendering her wary and uncomfortable in this situation. This was the effect of dealing with T.A.N.s could have on anyone. Actually, this young lady felt horrible that for an instant, she had become what she had beheld. This African American woman *knew* amends had to be made. She looked forward to seeing this man again so that she could apologize for her less-than-savory interactive behavior with an African American male that didn't deserve her angst.

Obviously, this woman hadn't been privy to or read the infamous Willie Lynch letter. It might have helped her—at least the part that says, "You must use the female verses the male." It goes on to say, "If used intensely for one year the slaves themselves will remain perpetually distrustful of one another." Maybe, just maybe, if she had been aware of that letter or just be open-minded enough to believe this kind of mind-set possibly swayed her opinion or reactions, then maybe she would be wary of what this society duped her into believing about how terrible the black man was.

Perhaps then she will take each interaction with any male no matter what their color, race, or ethnicity individually. From Claude's experience, he came to believe that T.A.N. women obviously realized that black men were at the bottom of the American social order psychologically, and they took full advantage of this. They knew all they had to do was make the allegation, *any* allegation, and whoever will come running to behold the black savage culprit who was more than likely demeaning or battering or, at the very least, mistreating someone.

Claude experienced this first-hand when, years later, his girlfriend was angry because she suspected Claude was cheating on her. (And he was!) She had spent the night with him, and while he slept, she thumbed through his cell phone and rummaged through his pants pocket until she found what was to her evidence. Pissed off again, this time, she called the police on him. When they came to the door, pounding and damn near beating it down, he went to the door once awakened from his slumber by the noise to check out why they were there. When he made his way to the door, his girlfriend, who was visibly angry at him (for what, he really didn't know at the time since her taut face and rigid blow-out-of-her-coat posture had become habitual, especially when she heard the word *no* or suspected something fishy), starting yelling, "Stop hitting me, Claude!"

The police now demanded he open the door immediately, and of course, without hesitation, Claude complied. Upon entering, the police could see this was a ruse. Thank God the cops that came were experienced in T.A.N. women's bullshit behavior and smelled a rat as soon as they entered. Then he explained that he was asleep and didn't know what the hell his girlfriend was doing. Not seeing any ocular or physical evidence, the police (there were two) chided and berated her for her attempt to use the police to get Claude hurt, killed, or at the very least, arrested all because she was angry. Now the entire world had to react to her self-centered anger.

This was commonplace with T.A.N. women who loved manipulating circumstances to get their way no matter *who* got hurt in the process. Claude had seen some T.A.N. women even sacrificing their children's safety, especially if the focus of their anger was a black man. Conversely, Claude continually saw that African American women, in his opinion and based solely on his experience, had empathy for all people, *especially* black people. Their empathy made them reluctant to involve any kind of authority figure in any verbal (nonphysical) altercation with their spouses and/or mates, which were a part of most relationships from time to time. Thus, they were less likely to turn on black men or demonize them to all who would listen.

When he told real African American women no, if he wouldn't cajole or appease them or didn't do what they so badly wanted him to do or think he should do, they might get angry or annoyed but would never be vindictive. They seemed to know how quickly these things could escalate when an authority figure of other ethnicities or a T.A.N. cop or an ignorant T.A.N. friend or relative bought the T.A.N. woman's bullshit and got involved. African American women, from what Claude had seen, deplored the abusive treatment of all their people, and they refused to be complicit in the demise of not only African American men but also any other African American person, period. African Americans were already crippled by the racism that existed in society, and then they were criticized for limping. Hurting, paralyzing, and killing one another would only add insult to injury.

Claude Maxwell Norris Paine hated racism, and he hated even more the vicious way T.A.N.s treated African Americans. He understood the infamous Willie Lynch letter and the effect that kind of philosophy could still possibly have on his people. It was a kind of lingering indoctrination. He was bright enough to know what *all* of his people had to endure (and still had to endure) was enough to adversely affect any race or ethnicity's growth or lack thereof. Infighting, most of which was promoted, was sometimes by design and kept black folks oppressed. Notwithstanding, whatever black folk, T.A.N.s, and African Americans alike had to overcome had to be achieved no matter what the odds. If not, then being brutalized, disrespected, and socially undermined would continue.

To Claude and his family, obviously this was the message Minister Farrakhan and the other organizers tried to spread when they organized the Million Man Marches. In 1995 and again twenty years later: it is time to atone, to ask for forgiveness for our indiscretions, to come together and to try to do the right thing, to stop hurting ourselves.

Claude's doctor recently told him that he had to lose weight or his health would continue to deteriorate and that death at a young age was imminent unless he did so. When Claude replied, "Doc, you know I'm a diabetic, and I have to eat four to five times a day. That itself makes losing weight extremely difficult," his doctor replied, "I know. So?" The old saying that Claude first heard when he was in high school, "Excuses are tools of incompetence that build monuments to nothing, and those who specialize in excuses are seldom good at anything else," really held true for the forward progress of black folk.

From the things Claude had seen and read growing up, the reasons for the wretched existence of most black folks were understandably valid. What black folks in America had to endure would have adversely affected *any* ethnic group or race. Still, the task of getting better and stronger is not an insurmountable task. That, however, was the current lot of black folks in America. It didn't have to be the future!

Claude knew that T.A.N. behavior, in order to be vacated, first had to be accepted as a flaw, a reality, and at times, it seemed like a Don Quixote task. To be rid of it, the T.A.N. culprits had to first own up to it, then they could move away from it. But if they were not interested in change, then how the hell could you do that? Claude could see that it was a spiritual and social malady that had to be addressed as soon as humanly possible. If not, all of Claude's and most of his people's remaining days on this earth would be spent dealing with some of his own people who continued to keep his race's forward progress stymied!

# CHAPTER 3

Claude was recently hired at the pharmaceutical company Johnson & Johnson in Metuchen, New Jersey, as a laborer in the maintenance department. He could now use his carpenter and plumbing skills and be paid handsomely for them. He was pleased to land a high-paying job with such a prestigious Fortune 500 company. However, he was not aware of what awaited him: the competition and backstabbing among his own people, the racism that would test his adherence to any of the principles that had been instilled in him in his youth by both his parents and loved ones and by the African American celebrities, educators, and activists he so respected.

During orientation, he met a guy at work named Garry Foreman. During a conversation at lunch on his third day on the job, Garry told him that in his high school, the predominance of students were Caucasian. During a debate about which retired major league baseball pitcher was better, Bob Gibson or Roger Clemens, a guy (Ted) said he believed Clemens was much better than Gibson.

"Why?" said Garry. Bob Gibson held the record for ERA (earned-run average) over the course of a full season and the World Series record for strikeouts in a game.

Ted then said, "Oh, Garry, you just like him because he is black."

"Well, sure, I like that too," said Garry.

Ted then said, "Well, fuck that black shit, Garry! Show me the man."

This appalled Claude, but being new to these surroundings, he kept his feelings concealed while Garry continued to talk. Then much to Claude's chagrin, the weasel-dick, ball-less Garry said, "Hey,

Claude, when the guy said that, I really respected it. After all, race is the last refuge of a scoundrel, and I shouldn't have said I was happy he was black or involved my feelings about race at all."

"Huh," said Claude inadvertently. "You mean you're sorry one of your heroes is black? I don't understand, Garry." It was at this point that Claude felt it was best to withdraw, to bow out gracefully. He could sense that any further involvement of conversation with this Garry guy could only lead to a heated debate.

Being new to the position, Claude didn't want to develop a reputation of being a rabble-rouser. So Claude stopped talking about the pitchers and decided to switch the subject to the current status of each other's favorite baseball team. Garry's words was the kind of denial of his people's own racial or ethnic pride, which disgusted Claude. How immediately T.A.N.s would automatically, when out in society and among other races, in particular Caucasians, downplay or understate any affection for their own kind or show any appreciation for the voluminous extraordinary historical deeds African Americans had accomplished. They tried to not show a strong love for their own in certain situations *because* they were black. One could actually see the resignation, the trepidation in their eyes as if to say "I love my heritage" or "I love what my people can do" would bring disgust from other ethnicities. It was like they were responding to lackey training and behaving like the shuffling Negroes of the past.

When Claude left work later that day, he stopped at a one-stop convenience store and gas station for a cold soda and to play some lottery numbers. While at the window, playing his number, a woman quickly darted in the store and, feigning an emergency, quickly blurted out that her truck was almost empty of gas and asked if Claude give her gas money.

"You don't even have to give me the cash, sir. Just tell the guy to put whatever you're going to give me on pump 7."

Claude looked through the window at the truck in question and saw a guy waiting at the pump. The woman seemed to be very hyper and was a bit disheveled. Claude surmised that this was a ruse, something fishy, straight-up monkey business. It seemed the duo were trying to get as much gas as possible for free so they could keep their own money to buy drugs or spend it wherever.

Claude immediately decided he wanted no part of this. He then said, "No, miss, I think I'll pass on this one."

"Why?" said the now anxious woman, clearly agitated at Claude's assessment of the situation and his expedited no answer.

"Because to be honest with you, miss, I don't trust you," retorted Claude.

"Yeah, okay," said the woman. "I can understand that—things being the way they are today. Still, sir, I need the gas, and all you have to do is put the gas on pump 7 without giving me any money. Just give the money to the guy at the window for me."

Claude stated, "I think I already answered you, miss. Could you please back away and let me complete my business? You're crowding me."

The woman now raised her voice and demanded some gas. The lottery guy as well as the attendant at the window were really surprised at this woman's arrogance and lack of shame. How determined she was to force this stranger (Claude) to adhere to her demanding, obnoxious will. Just then a black female (African American or T.A.N.?) walked in and noticed that a patron was annoyed with this big black man. She looked Claude up and down and immediately (erroneously) surmised that the big black African American male must be the instigator.

After grimacing at the sight of Claude, she jumped in, saying, "What's the problem, dear?"

"Well," said the ignorant gas money demander, "I ran out of gas, and I only have a dollar. This man is acting funny, like I did something. Could you give me a couple of bucks for gas, please? I only have a dollar."

"Okay, here," said her new ally, who immediately bought the woman's bullshit.

As Claude had seen so many times in his young life. Another black person had observed a situation and instantly decided that the black male involved in a spat needed to be opposed immediately and jumped in to contradict him ASAP.

Claude thought to his now disgusted self, *Geez, it's hard enough dealing with racism in America and having to deal with everyone else cutting off my balls every day. Now I gotta put up with my own people's bullshit. That makes me more uncomfortable than racism sometimes.*

One could see racism coming. From elementary school age, most African Americans already knew what racism felt like, tasted like, and smelled like. However, T.A.N.s had a way of getting close enough to screw someone, especially when they were black. Until one had been around them for a while, if you were black, their bull-shit could be difficult to detect. Claude had heard them use words like *beloved brother, my man, brother man, bro, my sister, sis, fam* or *family, homey, blood, homeboy, ock.* Many of these words were often shortened and mispronounced, so one should listen carefully. And their favorite catch word was *God!* Yes, if all else failed, one should use *God,* they figured.

What Claude had grown to learn in his life's experiences was that true evil didn't hide where one would expect it to hide. It hid behind God and in places you'd never expect to find it. It was what spawned the saying "The greatest lie the devil ever told was that he doesn't exist." That was why that pussy in Charleston, South Carolina, who said he wanted to start a race war, then commenced to shooting nine unarmed African Americans in a church (a church, mind you) or why that flaming ass-wipe former journalist shot those newscasters near Roanoke, Virginia. Both events were in 2015, and they chose those places to commit those heinously, cowardly, dastardly acts.

Likewise, it was also why the Philadelphia Eagles wide receiver said, "I'll jump this fence and kick every nigger's ass in here." And it was also why the hilarious comedian D. L. Hughley said, "He said that crap at a Kenny Chesney concert." It was populated with predominately Caucasians. Mr. Hughley went on to say quite poignantly, "He would've never said that at a Little Wayne concert! Oh no, don't go where you might find someone to contest you, stand up to you, or perhaps shoot back. Go do your tough shit where the odds are stacked in your favor, like a real coward does! Use what's referred to as a soft target."

Claude came to realize that *true* evil was a total absence of God. So whenever Claude heard anyone, beside a clergy person espousing God ad nauseam, he became wary of them. God could be seen in a person's actions, in his or her behaviors, in his or her walk. Anyone could say anything at any time. Just because someone said it, that didn't make *it* so. If those aforementioned catch words (which were also frequently spoken by real African Americans) didn't get you, then they wouldn't stop. They'd just keep asking you for anything or doing what they want, swear they were not begging or crossing your boundaries, and when you'd had enough and you got angry and either yelled at them or demanded they left you alone, from what Claude had experienced, the T.A.N. women would tell everyone *you* know that you didn't know how to talk to people.

If, while talking, one witness happens upon you, they'd behave like they'd just been verbally abused by you, unprovoked. The T.A.N. men would try to get gangster and be ready to fight. "Who da fuck you talking to like that, motherfucker [or nigger]?" It'd be like you had initiated or started an altercation with them. It would be altogether your fault! It made Claude feel like a man deserted on an island with no support. It brought on feelings of hopelessness and made Claude wary a lot of times—in particular, when in the company of some of his own people!

# CHAPTER 4

When Claude came to these spiritual roadblocks, he knew it might be time again for him to seek understanding or at least solace from the one book that always, 100 percent of the time, gave him the *basic instruction before leaving earth* (BIBLE), which he continually sought. If, after consulting this book of information, he was still somewhat confused, he was always, at the very least, rendered serene and comforted by the inspirational words he had just devoured.

During his prepubescent days, Claude was taught to respect his elders, that they should be treated with reverence in most cases and that, when the *C* blues were upon him (being *conflicted, confused,* or *curious*), it was always a good idea to consult an elderly relative or friend of the family for advice and/or direction. It was not a bad idea to befriend an old-timer in order to have a continual sage source to consult when in a pinch.

He had developed a close relationship with Mr. Bernard, once a neighbor of his whom he ran errands for in his youth. The only person, outside of family members that Claude told about the recurrent dreams he has about the night he was robbed at Gunpoint. Mr. Bernard, after a twenty-year stint, retired from the army at thirty-eight years old. He once told Claude that when he retired from the army, he wanted to see the world, so he traveled through Europe, Africa, and Asia from the age of thirty-nine to forty-nine. He had interacted not only with black people all over the world but with every other ethnicity Claude could think of. It was during these years that Mr. Bernard came to several realizations based on his own personal experiences, no theories.

One basic truth for sure was that devils came in all colors, in all races and ethnicities. The African Americans he came to know worldwide were capable of unsavory behavior just like T.A.N.s were as well as every other ethnicity outside his race. That once-in-a-while poor behavior afflicted everyone's life. Being flawed and having even a small level of fucked-up-ness was a human condition. The *difference* was that real African Americans were interested in and capable of contrition. The ones he knew accepted that they were flawed, and like Claude, they were continually seeking ways to get better to become less self-destructive and less repulsive to others. When a real African American hurt *anyone*, especially their own people, guilt came over them, which they knew would have to be addressed in order to try to feel better about themselves, to give themselves hope, to try to become an asset not only to their family but also to their community as well. African Americans had a conscience.

In his opinion and based on his interactions, the (folks Claude called) T.A.N. didn't care about contrition or accepting guilt, not when it comes to being apologetic to the black people they have hurt, crossed, or annoyed. They believed or were taught that the only way to act at a time like this was to get tough, yeah, to show the other black person that they had just hurt, insulted, or fucked over the gangster in them. He also felt that neither did the T.A.N. care about community. From what he saw, they continually suppressed any inkling of a conscience and tamped down any notion of guilt by developing a way of releasing any ownership of their own wrongdoing. No matter what the situation, whether they themselves initiated the confrontation or not, it was apparently, to them, always someone else's fault.

Mr. Bernard further stated that, from what his experience had also taught him, when it came to unity, the only thing that T.A.N.s set out to unify was themselves and money, be it their money or someone else's. They behaved like they had no idea that the *ultimate* currency was respect! Over and over, whenever he saw T.A.N.s involved in an altercation, especially with their own people, they appeared to have stored up so much vile and inner hatred that the best way for them to deal with it was to try to destroy the reputation of, kill, or severely hurt one of their own. From what he saw, they tended to go at their own with a vigor that didn't exist or couldn't be drummed up if their adversaries were other than black. Mr. Bernard felt that since T.A.N.s felt like they were America's and the world's ultimate victims (and for a great deal of blacks, T.A.N.s or not, that was difficult to argue), then everyone was fair game to them, especially their own people. After all, like the old saying went, "The people closest to you are capable of carrying the knives that cut you the deepest."

An old acquaintance of Mr. Bernard's from his neighborhood in his youth, a Mr. Connie Limb, a former gang member, some forty years later (well into his sixties) was still bragging about how his gang had more "bodies" than any other gang in the city. Now he was not talking about white, brown, yellow, or red bodies. Unwittingly, the dumbass was bragging about making black mothers bereaved that they had to bury their sons. He was bragging about killing black men and putting a notch on his gun. And oh so proud he was to belong to the gang that did this more than the other gangs.

Good Lord, could he get any more ignorant than that! He and the likes of him should be adored by the Ku Klux Klan, Skinhead, and Nazi movements. As the old saying went, "There's no fool like an old fool," and Connie Limb fit that mold to a *T*.

Mr. Bernard stated finally that he believed Claude should continue to seek direction, the one true source of continual *good orderly direction*, which to him God was, and that he should pray for the ability to assess his own walk, like the great actress Ms. Jody Foster said in the movie, *The Silence of the Lambs*. She responded to (Mr. Anthony Hopkins) Hannibal Lectore's assessment of who she really was and where she was originally from, what really actually led to her total development, her makeup as a person. As she stood in front of him, the two separated by a transparent glass cell door, she stated, "It would be real nice if you could use some of that high-powered perception on yourself!" Self-evaluation—what was more productive than that?

Mr. Bernard stated, "Who *you* are, Claude, and what *you* do are the most important concerns you'll ever have! Always remember the wheels of reciprocity, young man."

"Why the laws of reciprocity, sir?" said Claude.

"Oh, young man, you can figure that out," Mr. Bernard continued. "If you believe you'll get back what you put out, you tend to tread forward a little more carefully. You become less reckless. Those folks you always complain about—what do you call them again . . . errr . . . T.A.N.s? Yeah, that's it. Those T.A.N.s don't give two shits about reciprocity. Just watch them. It's made manifest in their behavior. They behave as if they are above reproach. Don't fall in that hole with folks like that, Claude, please."

"Okay, sir," said Claude. "I gotta get going."

"Well," said Mr. Bernard. "Last week, I watched Anthony Bourdain interview Questlove, the drummer from the musical group the Roots. When Mr. Bourdain asked Questlove what his job title was, he responded, [paraphrased] 'Well, actually I have about nine different projects or jobs.' That made me think about you and to tell you what I think about self-definition.

"Claude, my young friend, as you go through life and mature, never allow anyone to make you believe you are anything but what you aspire to be. When you voice aloud about your dreams or your endeavors or your purpose and you're in the company of detractors or, as you call them, T.A.N.s, you prompt them to weigh in as to how successful you're *not* going to be. It's kind of an unconscious defense mechanism of theirs that they use to stop them from looking at themselves and perhaps feeling less than you. If you haven't already, then you're gonna hear things like 'Get outta here man, you ain't gonna be no lawyer' or 'Man, stop mind-fucking yourself, you ain't never gonna see no ten million dollars' or 'Hey, man, she don't want you ('cause she damn sure don't want me). You ain't never gonna get nobody like her.' Please, Claude, don't take this with a grain of salt, young man, because this is important. In other words, they're saying 'How dare you dream about being something I don't believe I myself can ever be?'

"Never let anyone place a ceiling on your dreams. Try to let no one poke holes in or try to stymie your commitment to anything positive, especially if you have a plan in motion. Absolutely, no negative T.A.N. words, no ankle weight girlfriend, no best buddy whose familiarity has bred contempt—absolutely no one. Your definition of yourself should keep changing and evolving according to how far or how high you choose to go, young man. You create your own dictionary definition of who you are. Never forget that. I say thank you, Questlove, see what your words have inspired!"

"Okay, thanks for that, Mr. Bernard. Thanks a bunch. Time to roll. Remember, Mr. Bernard, if you need anything, call me. Peace out."

"See ya soon, kid," replied Mr. Bernard.

# CHAPTER 5

Mr. Bernard Saint was just a year shy of becoming an octogenarian. As a matter of fact the Late Contralto and first African American opera star Ms. Marian Anderson performed at the Lincoln memorial on Mr. Bernard's second Birthday in the late 1930's. He had lived through the 1940s—or the war years, as they were sometimes referred to (in reference to World War II). The 1930s and 1940s were a time when a young Mr. Bernard watched truly great, talented African American actors and actresses (Willie Best, Stepin Fetchit, Butterfly McQueen, and Hattie McDaniel). Mr. Ira "Buck" Woods and Ruby Dandridge had to sublimate their talent, deign, and act/behave like dimwitted, shuffle 'n' buck, docile, meek American Negroes just to continually get work at their chosen professions so that they could eat.

Ms. McDaniel, who had recently become the first African American to win an academy award in 1939 for her role in the classic film *Gone with the Wind* still had to settle for subservient roles. Later, she had a TV role as Beulah, who was (you guessed it) a maid. Although the lighter-complexioned Ms. Fredi Washington and Ms. Lena Horne were probably still underappreciated and most likely underpaid for being black but because of their ultralight complexions, they would receive less unsavory roles more often. As the educator Mr. Stanley Crouch said, "When you are light-skinned, white Americans can see some semblance of themselves in you, but when you are dark, they tend to see an aboriginal savage."

This again is referred to in the Willie Lynch letter: "You must use the dark skin slave verses the light skin slave." This letter was written over three hundred years ago, and you could still see how effective its philosophy was to this day. Blacks were no longer physical slaves, but the mentality was as effective today as it was when blacks were slaves. It was what pisses Mr. Bernard off so very badly—that his and Claude's feelings toward T.A.N.s was actually exactly what the gist of the letter wanted to create. It wanted to create an atmosphere where all we wanted to do was be at one another's throats. It was the core reason why he knew that T.A.N. behavior was learned, that a T.A.N. actually had to make up his or her mind that they were going to live and behave this way.

Mr. Bernard felt that was what (T.A.N. behavior) actor Adolph Caesar was trying to say in the classic movie *A Soldier's Story* when he said (and I quote verbatim), "The black race can't afford you no more."

There had been (and still are) many Caucasian Americans and other ethnicities in American society that treated blacks like this (subservience) was their permanent station in life during this time. To be at one another throats, to crab in a barrel with one another, and to find a reason to be jealous of one another and deplore one another's accomplishments—this was what was expected of blacks in the 1930s–1940s and the years that preceded that era. It was a kind of control over the black race by pitting them against one another, hence the term *throwback American Negro*.

During his youth, Mr. Bernard saw many a black adult behave like a condescending society wanted them to behave, and they did this in order to assimilate, to live up to someone else's expectations, and then maybe, possibly they could prosper. Then they could rise and be better than the other black folk that they helped tear down or, at the very least, have more tangibles than a lot of their own people. That is the true spirit of a T.A.N. today.

In those years, in order to get and maintain employment at that time, if you were black, you had to keep your mouth shut. Don't show *any* racial pride. Just go to work and remain in a robotic state, like an automaton, for the eight hours or so. Doing your job by rote. Mr. Bernard and the folks he knew were taught to never expose their true opinion about anything, to try to never exhibit a strong sense of self. Remember that black strength mixed with fortitude and initiative—any sign of strong love of self—will render some Caucasians uncomfortable. They tended to think the blacks were militant. Or, as they used to say in the 1940s, *uppity*. (A lot of African American's say it's still that way at the workplace today!)

Mr. Bernard saw this put forth to one of the greatest boxers of the twentieth century, Mr. Joe Louis, "the Brown Bomber." When he became champion in 1937, he was the first African American to win the heavyweight title since the great Jack Johnson (the first African American heavyweight champion and one of the greatest champions ever, 1908–1915). Mr. Bernard heard and saw on films (films he wasn't able or allowed to obtain in his youth) that Jack Johnson beat all the white heavyweight contenders of his time convincingly. He would loom over them menacingly and taunt them verbally throughout the fight. Jack also dated and married Caucasian women, was gregarious and outspoken, and from what Mr. Bernard remembered being told, he was way over the top to white America. So bold was he that all of his clothes were tailor-made, even his shoes and underwear. Jack Johnson owned cars when most *Americans* didn't own and couldn't afford to own cars. He had patents on three tools that he designed (wrenches) to work on and repair his own cars.

(Mr. Bernard suggest to all readers to purchase and read what he thinks is the best biography written about Jack Johnson, *Unforgivable Blackness*. If you're a corner cutter, then view the story of the same name in the PBS documentary.)

This, of course, sickened a great deal of Caucasian Americans. As a result, Joe Louis was told to never be photographed with white women, to never gloat after defeating a white opponent, to never loom over a white opponent after knocking him down or out. He was to *always* remain composed and appear humble. When Joe Louis won a round or a fight, especially against a white opponent, he *had* to nonchalantly return to his corner. Absolutely no theatrics were allowed. For years, Mr. Bernard thought he was cool. He had no idea until he was a man that Joe behaved this way because he was tethered to an agreement to not show any emotion or celebratory adulation in the ring after a victory so as not to aggravate or incense white America.

Then Mr. Sugar Ray Robinson, one of Joe's contemporaries, a welterweight and soon to be middleweight, after suffering his first loss at the hands of Jake la Motta, would start a streak of ninety-one wins before losing another fight. At one point in his illustrious career, Mr. Robinson had a record of 120 wins and 1 loss. *Wow!* Yeah, the 1940s was when the Tuskegee Airmen said, "Move over Caucasian American bombers, let us join this war. If you do move over just a tad, we will serve as your escorts during your bombing missions."

Yeah, in the 1940s, Richard Wright wrote two very socially poignant and critically acclaimed novels: *Black Boy* in 1940 and *Native Son* in 1945. Yes, this was the decade that would resonate in American society and sports forever. In the year 1947, the sport that became America's pastime was none other than baseball. The man Mr. Jackie Roosevelt Robinson was the African American who said, "A life is not important except for the impact it has on other lives." And then he lived his prophetic words and endured the most heinous physical, emotional, spiritual, and mental torture. The resilient Mr. Robinson had an unparalleled pressure to endure while still being productive from a most racist league and society and his own hero-seeking people, who needed him to be successful. He worked at an extraordinary high level to ingratiate himself in a most difficult sport—baseball. By doing so, Mr. Robinson provided *everyone* else (Latinos, Asians, and African Americans) an opportunity to compete.

It was in the 1940s when Miles Davis, Charley "Yardbird" Parker, Max Roach, Lionel Hampton, Charley Mingus, Lester Young, Duke Ellington, Ella Fitzgerald, Cab Calloway and his band, and the awesome Billie Holiday and the man who made *"unforgettable"* music – especially when he popularized Mr Mel Torme's Christmas song. Claude could still hear it now (chestnuts roasting on an open fire, Jack Frost nipping at your nose) Mr. Nat King Cole. Yeah, the 1940s was when Sarah Vaughn, Dinah Washington, Billy Eckstein, and Nina Simone were just getting started. These talented folks all confounded and baffled the world with their exquisite talent by further exposing the world to Jazz, which was seemingly so difficult for most to play on the instruments used by these musical giants. Oh, how effortlessly these most talented artists made sounding good look so damn simple! In the 1940s, Mr. Louis "Satchmo" Armstrong, jump-started in the 1930s, was still going strong. Mr. Louis Jourdan, the multitalented musician and singer, mixed swing with bebop and created a hybrid, something new and unique, kind of like the hip-hop of that era. With his sound, Mr. Jourdan entertained millions. And sadly, in 1946, the first African American Heavyweight Boxing Champ, Mr. Jack Johnson died.

Mr. Bernard lived through the 1950s. With his music contemporaries, Little Richard was the one whom many gave credit to as being the first Rock-and-Roll star. Of course, this was the decade when the phenomenal pianist Thelonious Monk made his mark. Howling Wolf and Muddy Waters both drove the ladies wild with their very relevant Blues music. None could forget the strong, sweet voice of Ms. Etta James or forget Mr. Chuck Berry, the duck-walking and very talented guitar player and rock-and-roll singer who didn't use drugs or alcohol.

During a time referred to as the McCarthy era and America's Red Scare (fear of communism). It was a time when many actors and entertainers and celebrated individuals of all races were ostracized, blackballed, blacklisted. Many African Americans were blackballed and shut out of American society's mainstream at this time: the actors Mr. Canada Lee, Mr. Ossie Davis, Ms. Ruby Dee, Ms. Fredi Washington, and Ms. Lena Horne; the writers Mr. Richard Wright and Mr. Langston Hughes; and the pianist and musician Ms. Hazel Scott. Most notably, the brilliant scholar, athlete, singer, and actor, the former lawyer, a true renaissance man in every sense of the word, the great Mr. Paul Robeson was blacklisted as well. Though he and many others were able to resume their careers, Mr. Bernard remembered that Mr. Robeson never again regained the superstar status once bestowed upon him. If any further validation was necessary, then one could read in its entirety *I Never Had It Made* by Jackie Robinson.

It was in the 1950s when an accomplished African American attorney named Mr. Thurgood Marshall won the *Brown vs. the*

*Board of Education* case and helped desegregate schools, making it possible for every African American child to get a better-quality education. Yes, the 1950s was the decade when the country witnessed the birth of one of the most successful African American businesses in American history—Detroit's own Motown Records, headed by Mr. Berry Gordy. When the country weaved the dynamic African American rhythm and blues into the musical experience of our country's arts fabric, this company had contributed (and was still contributing) heavily to the American and to the world's soundtrack for the next sixty-plus years and counting.

Yeah, it was in the 1950s when Mr. Ralph Ellison penned the most poignant, race-relevant novel that Mr. Bernard has ever read, *The Invisible Man* (no, not the science fiction book written by H. G. Wells several decades earlier). *The Invisible Man* was a brilliantly composed work of art written by an African American, an exposé about the plight of the black man in America and his search for identity and acceptance. The same year Dr. Charles Drew (the African American Physician who revolutionized blood transfusion and saved many American lives during World War II) died. The year 1955 – the date, January 7th the day Ms. Marian Anderson became the first African American opera singer to sing at New York's World Renown Metropolitan Opera House. It was the fifties, all right, and Ark Blakey, drummer and front man, started his Jazz Messenger genre with interchangeable musicians to expose the world to his talented musical finds. There were musicians like Lee Morgan, Freddie Hubbard, Benny Golson, and Robert Watson, just to name a few. It was a practice he would continue for close to the next thirty years.

The year 1953 was the year the great African American writer James Baldwin wrote a novel, *Go Tell It on the Mountain.* And Ray Charles, now a superstar, told everybody, "Hey, ya'll, I'm so happy because 'I got a woman,' and I love her so much that to avoid trouble, you better 'leave my woman alone.'" These were two of a string of hits he started making for the next sixty-plus years. He really took off in the 1950s in more ways than one. To this day, Mr. Bernard still enjoyed his Ray Charles music.

Oh yes, it was in the 1950s when America's first most celebrated African American filmmaker Oscar Micheaux died. Mr. Bernard also remembered during the fifties the meteoric rise and then the death of the great trumpeter Mr. Clifford Brown. (What a talent he was!) He died tragically at the age of twenty-five in a car accident. Then Mr. Dizzy Gillespie made his mark. When he played the trumpet, his cheeks would balloon with air—like a squirrel with a mouth full of acorns. Man, oh man, could he play the trumpet! Then here came the empress of jazz and soul music again—none other than the great Ms. Nina Simone. She created a unique sound that resonated around the world and would never be forgotten.

In the fifties, the smooth, silky, warm voice of Johnny Hartmann came on to the jazz set and when Ms. Ruby Dee teamed with Mr. Sidney Poitier in two of the decade's finest racially themed movies. Ms. Dee costarred with Sidney Poitier in 1950 in the racially charged movie *No Way Out*, and the duo again teamed up in 1957 in the movie *Edge of the City*. So it was now the 1950s, and tennis was a sport dominated by Caucasians throughout the world. Well, this lovely African American woman named Ms. Althea Gibson said, "Hold on a minute, and allow me to introduce my game," and Ms. Gibson went on to become the first person of color to win a grand slam title (the French Open). In 1957 and1958, Ms. Gibson won both Wimbledon and the precursor to the US Open, the US nationals.

Mr. Bernard remembered the year the talented Oscar Brown Jr. ushered in the 1960s when he mimicked an actual slave-trading auction in his song "Bid 'Em In" and told every listener what it was like. On the same album, the thought of being sold into slavery disgusted him so much that he wrote the song "Somebody Pour Me a Drink." Rock would take its place in the music industry during this new decade. Of course, there were African Americans right at the door of this new rock genre sweeping the globe. There was the new heavyset lightning-quick drummer that all the races adored. They all adored him even though his mind was going through changes which he expressed in his song. It was none other than the great Buddy Miles.

Then a family of rockers decided to make their mark and stamp their brand on the rock set. Then they made their move with their song"Time". They believed and were right that time was on their side. It was, of course the Chambers Brothers. It was also at this time that perhaps the greatest rock-and-roll guitarist of all time shot through the music scene like a bolt of lightning, Mr. Jimi Hendrix himself with "Purple Haze," "Hey, Joe," "All along the Watchtower," and the classic song (performed and recorded live) "Who Knows?"

So you'd think we were not diverse, huh? Well, the sixties gave us Mr. Rufus Harley on bagpipes. That's right, bagpipes in the jazz genre—how cool is that! Then Mr. Jimmy Smith on organ made some sweet music for all jazz lovers to hear. At this same time, Mr. Wes Montgomery, perhaps Mr. Bernard's favorite guitar player (ahead of only Mr. George Benson, who is a close second) in jazz, entertained us all.

This was also the decade when the O'Jays with their songs "I dig your act" and "I'm gonna be sweeter tomorrow than I was yesterday." Then the very wicked (wicked Wilson Pickett, his nickname) Mr. Wilson Pickett acknowledged that everyone needed a sugar to kiss and a sweetheart to miss with his song "everyone needs someone to love."

Motown, now well established and really taking off, employed a Ms. Diana Ross and the Supremes who popularized the songs "when the love lights starts shining through his eyes." "baby love" "nothing but heartaches" and "Where did our love go?" At the time, the lovely, lanky Martha Reeves, whom Mr. Bernard had a crush on, and the Vandellas popularized the songs "Heat Wave", "Dancing in the Streets." "Love makes me do foolish things," "in my lonely room," "forget me not" "I'm ready for love."

In the year 1962, this blind twelve-year-old African American genius named Stevie Wonder exposed the entire world to his explosive, tremendous talent, and he did so with his song "Fingertips." The novel "The fire next time" was published in 1963 was the year James Baldwin had his inspirational talk with God, when he had an epiphany about God's conversation with Noah. He dreamed that God told Noah, "No more water—'the fire next time.'" The same year the fantastic Afro-American educator, activist, and orator W.E.B. Dubois died. The year 1968 was the year Mr. Bernard remembered when a black woman ran for the presidential nomination. Ms. Charlene Alexander Mitchell of the Communist party, became the first African American woman to run for the presidential nomination as a third party candidate. The 1960's – Yes It was the decade when everyone at least heard of Wilt Chamberlin scoring a hundred points in a professional basketball game, a record that had never been broken or even matched.

Mr. Bernard was still a young man in the service during the 1960s when Mr. Muhammad Ali became the first celebrated African American to change his inherited slave name. The African American that told America and the whole world, "I don't have to be who *you* want me to be." The same man that refused to be drafted into the service. He said, "Ain't no Vietnamese ever call me nigger." When asked if his superior boxing skills were original, he replied, "Originality is the ability of concealing one's sources."

Good Lord, did Mr. Bernard admire Muhammad Ali! He held Mr. Ali in the same esteem he held Mr. Jack Johnson. Courageous, trendsetting, bold—they were true African American warriors.

He also maintained the ultimate respect for Mr. Medgar Evers, Dr. Martin Luther King Jr., Mr. Malcolm X, Mr. Stokely Carmichael, Mr. Elijah Muhammad, Mr. Huey P. Newton, Mr. Bobby Seale, Dr. Ralph Abernathy, Mr. Andrew Young, Ms. Elaine Brown, Ms. Kathleen Cleaver, and the absolutely phenomenal Ms. Angela Davis. They were all in vogue at this historical time, letting the world know that they were mad as hell and were not going to take it anymore. To this day, Mr. Bernard didn't understand why the three civil rights activist—Goodman, Chaney, and Schwerner—were not lionized or, at the very least, had the congressional medal of honor bestowed upon them posthumously for giving their lives to secure the right to vote to all blacks in Mississippi.

He remembered when Mr. James Brown sang his song "say it loud: 'I'm black, and I'm proud.'" Mr. Bernard remembered thinking at that time that he never thought he would hear a strong, uplifting message to black people as a song on the radio. James also came out with the songs 'superbad' 'please, please, please,' 'get it together' 'think' 'the big payback.' 'this is a man's world' and 'hot pants.' just to name a few of the Great songs he would offer to the world. The same decade, Mr. Bernard saw a stand-up soul singing R & B group the Parliaments and its leader, George Clinton, came out with their songs "I wanna testify" and "I bet you" they hinted that they were really going to expand into two groups, change and intensify their style, and become Funkadelic in the process.

It was the decade when the late great Mr. Julian Bond helped organize a very poignant civil rights group made up of students and youngsters, the SNCC (Student Nonviolent Coordinating Committee). The year 1967 was when the accomplished attorney Mr. Thurgood Marshall (whom Mr. Bernard said he adored, admired, and had the ultimate respect for) became the first African American appointed to the US Supreme Court. First, years earlier, he argued forty-two (42) cases in front of the Supreme Court and won thirty-nine (39) of them. Then, years later, he got *appointed* to the Supreme Court.

Oh, good Lord, the things African Americans had accomplished! Yeah, this was in the tumultuous 1960s, the decade Mr. Bernard's most famous, favorite jazz song was made by Mr. John Coltrane, the aptly named "Dear Lord." He also enjoyed John Coltranes song "My favorite things" and Mr. Coltranes collaboration along with the Great Duke Ellington of the song "in a sentimental mood."

Oh, man, in the 1960s, Marvin Gaye (also of Motown) popularized the songs "Ain't that peculiar?" he said. He also wanted to know "Can I get a witness?" and "I wouldn't be doggone, I'd be long gone." This was also the decade when Mr. Berry Gordy and his company employed a stand-up group of five talented, handsome male singers who all had lead-singer ability, a group that had changed its original name from the Primes to the Temptations. They made a joyful noise with the songs "Say you" 'the way you do the things you do.' 'my girl' 'Ain't too proud to beg,' 'get ready' 'my baby' 'cloud nine.' and of course the great song 'dream come true.'"

This was the same decade when the renowned sociologist Mr. Harry Edwards created the OPHR (Olympic Project for Human

Rights). In the 1968 Olympics, after the two-hundred-meter race, which was won by USA's Mr. Tommie Smith, African American Mr. John Carlos placed third and won the bronze medal. At the awards ceremony, Mr. Smith wore a black scarf to represent black pride. Mr. Carlos had his track suit unzipped to show solidarity with all of America's blue-collar workers. Mr. Carlos also wore a necklace of beads, which he wore for American blacks who were lynched, tarred, and feathered and for the many thousands who were tossed off to slave ships during the middle passage. The gentleman who placed second, a Caucasian Australian national named Mr. Peter Norman, also wore an OPHR badge to show emphatic solidarity support.

When the "Star-Spangled Banner" was played (the national anthem of the country whose athlete places first in an event is always played), Mr. Smith and Mr. Carlos raised their black-gloved fists and bowed their heads. What was virtually unnoticed and has gone unmentioned for nearly fifty years was that the Aussie Mr. Norman provided Mr. Carlos (who had forgotten his own black glove that he left at the US Olympic compound) with the black glove he wore. What a day and time! Wow, what a powerful social statement! Such a profound moment in African American and American history.

In the 1960s, another group, also employed by the Motown machine, known as the Four Tops had been "standing in the shadows of love" for a long time. They got tired of that, so lead singer, Levi Stubbs, told his girlfriend, "Bernadette," "'Baby, I need your loving' right now because 'since you been gone,' I find it hard to carry on. If you don't believe that this is difficult, then 'just ask the lonely.'"

Also employed by Motown was the supertalented Gladys Knight and her backup group (maybe the best backup group ever), the Pips, said to all that would listen that "everybody needs love." Gladys said, "You know how I know? 'I heard it through the grapevine.'"

This was the decade when perhaps the greatest rhythm-and-blues songwriter of all time, Mr. William "Smokey" Robinson, penned some of the greatest ballads and love songs ever "Can you love a poor boy?" 'I second that emotion.'" "going to a go-go." "shop around" "the tracks of my tears" "girl has gone" "the love I saw in you was just a mirage." "Would I love you?" "choosey beggar" "more love." "a fork in the road," "the agony and the ecstasy." (This song was done as a Solo Artist) and "you can depend on me". Just to scratch the surface, the tip of the Iceberg of the great work Mr. Robinson gave to the world. Mr. Robinson was so talented that not only did he write these powerful songs for himself and his group that was full of miracles, he also wrote a plethora of hits for many of the other groups employed by the Motown machine. God, what a talented, supersensitive man! Oh, the talent that was recorded in their music in that building once known as Hitsville USA!

Yes, the 1960s was the same decade the awesome Curtis Mayfield and the Impressions gave us "keep on pushing" "amen" and "I'm so proud". The sixties was when the multifaceted, extraordinary talent and educator Maya Angelou wrote the classic *I Know Why the Caged Bird Sings*. Yeah, the sixties was when the phenomenal Quincy Jones, talented musician, was not only making great music for us to enjoy but was also musically scoring movies.

Yes, the year 1968—that was very much a historical year for African Americans. That year, Martin Luther King was assassinated. Carl Burton Stokes became the first African American mayor of a major American city (Cleveland, Ohio). That same year, Ms. Shirley Chisholm became the first African American woman elected to Congress. Mr. Bernard started a positive joke that year. He said, "I always knew a woman's place was in the house and the senate!" Mr. Bernard remembered the sense of pride all these folks gave him not only about himself but his race as well. Through these people (at the time), he now felt he had a voice—an *international* voice. These folks, with their "give us human and civil rights" activist behavior, were awakening the world to the plight of blacks in America.

Oh yeah, the year 1969 was when the ten-year-old Michael Jackson and four of his older brothers came on the scene with their number one hit "the love you save" This was the decade when the "Queen of Soul," Ms. Aretha Franklin, ascended to her throne. She did so with her hits "'I never loved a man the way I love you.' 'respect', "'Baby, baby, baby, I love you' and 'do right woman, do right man.'"

He survived the 1970s when the brash Last Poets rose to fame with their songs "E Pluribus Unum" "jazzoetry" "black soldier" 'white man's got a God complex'. This group initially sold over a million records without any air play (Radio exposure).

Yes, the year 1970 was when Mr. Charles Gordone became the first African American to win the Pulitzer Prize for drama award for his classic play "No Place to Be Somebody," a play that took Mr. Gordone seven years to write. A primarily jazz-themed group named Kool & the Gang got started in the 1960s, led by a supremely talented bass guitar–playing man named Robert "Kool" Bell, their songs "light of the worlds" "jungle boogie" and "summer madness."

Yes, in the 1970s, "The Sound of Philadelphia (TSOP)" exploded across the airwaves. Creating their own music and backing up groups like Blue Magic, Mr. Billy Paul, Ms. Natalie Cole, and even the O'Jays came to Philadelphia and joined the TSOP party. Then Marvin Gaye came back with his songs 'to keep you satisfied,' and 'come get to this.'" And eventually one of his biggest hits "sexual healing". That same decade, Earth, Wind & Fire made one of his favorite songs that made Mr. Bernard think of his mother every time he heard it—the sweet song simply titled "Mom." Then the group also recorded the spiritually based "Open Our Eyes," a message for black people that is still applicable to this day.

Then a few years after, Mr. Eric Burdon of the English group the Animals introduced everyone to the group War. This group came out with a powerful style (that included a harmonica) that was manifested in songs "'Where was you at' 'the Cisco kid'? 'in Mazatlan,' 'city, country, city' 'low riders.'" "smile happy" and "baby, it's cold outside." Then a factory worker (Bill Withers) came on the set with his guitar and gave the world two songs that remain relevant to this day. The songs 'lean on me' and there 'ain't no sunshine' when she's gone."

The 1970s decade saw Ms. Shirley Chisholm continue to rise to political prominence. She, elected a congresswoman in 1968, had become in 1972 the first African American woman to become a Democratic presidential candidate. Although she didn't win, she still received 152 first-place ballot votes at the Democratic National Convention. Sweet Lord, talk about courage and political aspirations!

Mr. Bernard also remembered this as the decade when the blaxploitation (black exploitation) films were popular in Hollywood. Yes, a lot of these movies were poorly funded and with pedestrian scripts (that was why the moniker *blaxploitation* was coined). But what a lot of folks seemed to forget was that a lot of struggling African American actors and actresses now had steady, plentiful work at this time, a practice that was unprecedented in mainstream Hollywood.

That was the same decade when Sly and the family Stone, after their debut in the late 1960s when they released "dance to the music." This group stayed on the set and gave us truly great music that included the songs "stand" "everyday people." "Don't call me nigger, whitey" "in time" "caught you smiling again" "running away" "family affair." (Their songs carried a great message to all people especially black people).

At this time George Clinton and his Parliaments –Now were also represented by their off-shoot group – The Funkadelics (Wow to have two groups recording and releasing albums simultaneously – How cool). They gave us "mothership connection" "better by the pound," "Chocolate City" "good to your earhole" "side effects" "together" and one of Mr. Bernard's all time favorites "cosmic slop".

The 1970s were the decade that the Marsalis family, natives of New Orleans, rose to prominence and the world got a taste of pure jazz, revitalized by the Marsalis brothers Wynton (trumpet) and Branford (saxophone), and their dad, Ellis (keyboard). His already established following grew exponentially when his sons joined him in exposing to the world the Marsalis family's gift of music. Yes, jazz was an African American creation and a donation to the American arts experience.

Also stamping his deep, base voice and full orchestra style on to the public consciousness was the guy who gave the world "I got so much to give." and a whole collection of sweet music that was made up of Ballad and Love songs (Romantic mood music) of course it was none other than Mr. Barry White.

It was also in the 1970s when the multitalented Prince came on the set and exploded successfully. In the 1970's, the first syndicated television show hosted and created by an African American was in vogue. That show was *Soul Train*. The host was the trendsetting Mr. Don Cornelius. On *Soul Train*, Mr. Bernard got his first look at both Chaka Khan and her group, Rufus. Man, oh man, what a beauty and an awesome talent Ms. Khan was. She, her good looks, and great talent floored Mr. Bernard.

That same decade, the Sugar Hill Gang ushered in hip-hop with "Rapper's Delight." Yeah, it was the 1970s all right. It was when one of Mr. Bernard's favorite actresses, Ms. Cicely Tyson, made two of Mr. Bernard's favorite movies, the critically acclaimed *Sounder* and *The River Niger*. To this day, that extraordinary woman is still making great movies.

Oh, it was also in the 1970s when Hank Aaron decided that baseball's home run and RBI (runs batted in) records would now belong to him. It was when the supremely confident and productive Reggie Jackson, whom Mr. Bernard called the greatest clutch baseball player ever (the man who said, "I'm the straw that stirs the drink") hit three consecutive first-pitch home runs off three different pitchers in a World Series game. It was a feat that to this day still hadn't been matched.

Yes, and of course, Stevie Wonder now on his own is still making classic music. He now gave us great songs like "Smile" "ain't no reason" "Think of me as your soldier" (The song Mr. Bernard calls one helluva poem) "Sunshine in their eyes" and "super woman". Yeah, this was the decade when a talented young actor named Laurence Fishburne started a long productive and illustrious acting career with the movie *Cornbread, Earl and Me*.

Mr. Bernard was in his late forties to early fifties during the 1980s when, in 1983, Mr. Kenneth Burke of the very talented Burke family (and little brother Cubie), who were popular in the sixties as the Five Stairsteps, made a very positive and inspiring song entitled "Keep on Rising to the Top"—great motivational words for a race that needed motivation.

Mr. Bernard was hip enough to appreciate some of the hip-hop artists (now referred to as old school), especially the ones whose songs in the 1980s and 1990s bore a strong social, racial, and political message (Public Enemy's "Cant Truss It," KRS-One's "Black Cop,"

Nonchalant's "5 o'Clock in the Morning," Gangstarr's "Just to Get a Rep") and Ahmad's "Back in the Day."

Yes, in the 1980s, the teenage talent LL Cool J shared with the world his songs "I'm bad" "Mama Said Knock You Out" "The Boom System" and "I need love"!

The 1980s were also the decade when the silky smooth songwriting talent of Mr. Luther Vandross became famous. So pleased was Mr. Bernard with his people's moviemaking ability that he became a big fan of Mr. Spike Lee, a filmmaker, who was now his favorite all-time writer, producer, and director of films and documentaries.

Yeah, in the 1980s, the phenomenal Mr. Guion Stewart Bluford Jr., in the year 1983, became the first African American astronaut to fly his first of four space shuttle missions between 1983 and 1992. God, the man received a PhD in aerospace engineering (damn, aerospace engineering, how cool is that?) and was accepted to become an astronaut in 1979 and went to space. *Congratulations, sir!* Mr. Bernard thought. *What an achievement!*

The 1980s decade was when Oprah Winfrey stamped her brand on to public consciousness, making her mark in journalism, television (initially as a talk show host), and cinema. To Mr. Bernard, she was still the greatest interviewer ever. How disarming she could be during the most intense interviews. He sincerely loved her strength and the fact that so many students get scholarships from her and every other philanthropical endeavor she embarks upon. She is truly one of his favorite people ever!

In the 1980s, Alice Walker (1982) published *The Color Purple* and won the National Book Award and the Pulitzer Prize for fiction. Mr. Bernard observed an immensely talented, baby-voiced Iron Mike Tyson do his impersonation of the Tasmanian devil (a whirling dervish) and ran through boxing's heavyweight division like a hot knife through butter. In the process, he became the youngest heavyweight boxing champ ever as he unified the heavyweight title by defeating all reigning champions.

This was also the decade (1988) when Ms. Toni Morrison won the Pulitzer Prize and American Book Award for her powerful novel *Beloved*. And Stevie Wonder still made classic music as, this time, he collaborated with Spike Lee for some of his songs like "jungle fever," "queen in the black" and "Miss, I 'got to have you' for me."

Yeah, in the eighties, Mr. Rick James became known as the King of funk with his songs "You and I" "Give it to me, baby." "Big Time" and "fire and desire" (which he collaborated) on with the talented Teena Marie).

In the year 1989, a group of rappers (KRS-One, Kool Moe Dee, Ms. Melody, MC Delight, MC Lyte, D-Nice, Daddy-O, Doug E. Fresh, Chuck D, Flav-Flav, Heavy D, and Justice) decided to unite and make the song "Self-Destruction" and try to tell all black youths to please stop killing one another. Well, close to thirty years later, with the help of ignorant T.A.N.s, black youths (and black adults) are still killing one another.

Mr. Bernard was really moved by the home computer age (the PC) of the 1990s. John Singleton, very much the talented filmmaker, through his new movie *Boyz n the Hood*, spoke clearly to the girls and boys. Mr. Bernard remembered that Mr. Singleton then gave a history lesson to all and taught about a small Florida town through his Film *Rosewood*, where blacks were slaughtered like sheep over a false rape accusation. In the movie, the actress Ms. Ester Rolle played one of its leading characters, who forewarned, "You ain't seen nasty until you've seen those white folks get nasty." For that time and place and many times hence—even today—how true!

Then came the musical group the Roots with some purely lovable hot, hot music. With their hit "the next movement" and see for yourself what "hot, hot music" really was! In that decade, the Hughes brothers showed America and the world about social injustice and inequalities and lack of employment opportunities seasoned with a tad of self-hate and a pinch of ignorance in their film *Menace II Society*.

Mr. Bernard loved how television evolved in his lifetime to cable and satellite TV during the 1990s as well. In particular, he loved the music videos and how high tech, elaborate, and expensive they were. His eclectic taste in music allowed him to appreciate everything in video form now, from country to hip-hop to rock, R & B, jazz, and everything in between. The elderly Mr. Bernard really appreciated the Hip hop genre. He once told Claude "These kids have created a genre – a movement that is steeped in creativity, style, and talent. A genre with a rapid rhythmic pulse (that works just as powerfully when its slowed down). He also said "In Earth, Wind and Fires song "I Write the Song" rappers proved and brought to life the lyric "Songs they never dissipate – they only recreate in another place in time." – Is it Iron Butterfly 'In a Godda Divida, or Nas "A Thiefs Theme" Is it Notorious B.I.G.'s "One More Chance" or DeBarge's "Stay with Me". It is the Isley Brothers "Who's that Lady" or Kendrick Lamar's "I" (I love Myself). To be able to take beats, hooks, and songs that were successful years ago – and bring them back years later and make them successful again. That takes skill, insight and foresight. It also takes a knowledge of marketing and a business savvy. That's really a leap – a hop that's really hip. None can deny that", said Mr. Bernard. The rappers' use of alliteration and of metaphors and similes and also their extraordinary ability to paint a vivid picture with their storytelling and carefully chosen rhythmic words and rhymes.

That's one of the reasons Mr. Bernard really appreciated Eric B. & Rakim's 'move the crowd' which told all that in this genre there "were no mistakes allowed". Wow, was Mr. Bernard impressed because now he could see the sexy, talented, melodious-voiced Mary J. Blige, who chose to sing and act out her music through "Reminisce." And Busta Rhymes (formerly of the fantastic group Leaders of the New School) who came out with his song 'put your hands where my eyes can see.'"

Mr. Bernard wasn't about to let the media make up his mind *not* to listen to this African American creation. When he heard other contemporary African Americans say dumbass stuff like "All those rappers talk about is bitches and hos." How stupid, grossly uninformed, and short-sighted. That was what happened when you let your opinion be formed and given to you by others—in particular, the media.

Yeah, the close of 1989 and the beginning of the 1990s were when the African American a cappella group Take 6 implored the world with their song "Spread Love."

Right after, Public Enemy encouraged everyone with their song "fight the power" which was used in the Spike Lee movie "do the right thing." Mr. Kenneth "Babyface" Edmonds came in vogue in this decade as a brilliant writer, singer, and producer of some of the finest music of the decade. Yes, this man's music was truly great. If one wanted to experience just a taste of his greatness, then one could listen to the soundtrack to the movie *Waiting to Exhale*. Then a duo told all who chose to listen that their being naughty wasn't a put-on, that they were actually Naughty by Nature. They proved with their songs "OPP," "Uptown Anthem." and "Hip-hop hooray."

At this time, Little Kim and Foxy Brown said, "Hold up, everyone, we ladies can represent hip-hop also. Then Foxy Brown collaborated with Jay-Z and the two released the song 'paper chase.' and Little Kim (with Notorious B.I.G. in the background) released "No Time. Then Mr. Christopher Wallace (a.k.a. the Notorious B. I. G.) and Mr. Tupac Shakur exposed the world to how talented they were before the world lost them forever. Then Mr. Nasir "Nas" Jones claimed his spot in hip-hop hierarchy. Was Nas an excellent poet and rapper, a truly extraordinary talent? Well, after all, he did release great songs like "I made you look" "halftime" "it ain't hard to tell" "Nas is like," "represent" "life's a bitch" and 'God's son.'

This was also the decade when Floyd "Money" Mayweather Jr. (TBE) became the richest fighter ever in any weight division. He started his run of forty-nine victories without a defeat. Now think of that for a moment. The richest athlete in the world was all of 5 feet 8 inches and 150 pounds. That was how extraordinary Floyd Mayweather was. That was why he called himself the best ever (TBE).

Oh, how Mr. Bernard remembered the 1990s. It was when O. J. Simpson, hall of fame running back football player, pitchman, and actor was found innocent of double murder even though most of the evidence that the prosecutors couldn't use (because of piss-poor police work and illegal tampering of police evidence) had pointed to his alleged guilt, a verdict that racially polarized the entire country. Mr. Bernard didn't know one black person who was unhappy with the verdict. Nor did he know *any* white person who was pleased with it.

Now one shouldn't jump to ill-informed conclusions. No black person was happy that the duo was murdered. But all who were joyous were ecstatic that white America *finally* knew what it was like to have one of their own brutally murdered, have all the evidence point to guilt, and have the courts set the accused free. It was something Mr. Bernard had seen and read about happening to black Americans thousands of times. Now white America could feel what American justice was truly like. This same thing had repeatedly happened to blacks (and was still happening) and minorities since before reconstruction. Could you imagine what slavery was like? Being raped wasn't illegal. Legally, it wasn't rape since these women (and men) were someone's property.

Then Mr. Bernard said a lot of them just fucked and fucked over whomever they wanted to and whenever they got ready. Just ask the Native Americans; they murdered, lynched, whipped, and gave their oppressed victims bullshit to eat for hundreds of years! Anyone who couldn't accept the truth could simply watch the film *12 Years a Slave.*)

"Shit, where's my forty acres and my mule?" asked Mr. Bernard (or at least the equivalent in today's dollars). Yes, it was in the 1990s when Sister Souljah published both *No Disrespect* and *The Coldest Winter Ever.*

The decade was when perhaps the most comedic, talented African American family in the country made a lot of noise in Hollywood and showed the world how belly shaking funny they were after a couple of really funny hit movies that they made in the late 1980s. They started doing it on TV *in living color* with one of the funniest skits Mr. Bernard had ever seen. One portrayed how well-to-do T.A.N.s thought about other African Americans when brothers Keenen and Damon brought to life the characters Tom and Tom. Yeah, they're known as the Wayans. They were known for their roles in the movies (Eldest Brother Keenan wrote both movie screenplays). A ""Low-down dirty shame" and 'I'm gonna get you, sucka,'"

That same decade, Mr. Bernard remembered hearing Slick Rick sing his lullaby in the day and night: "Children's Story." Then M. C. Lyte made it quite clear that she didn't only want a man but that she had to get a "Roughneck". And T-Boz, Left Eye, and Chilli (professionally known as TLC) Rose to fame with their hits 'I aint too proud to beg.' 'scrub,' 'Waterfalls.'

Many members of the group Wu-Tang Clan became as successful individually as they were collectively. They got started with their hit "Protect Ya Neck". This first offering from this group of nine talented African American rappers (the song was devoid of a "hook," which was unheard of in the Hip-Hop genre at this time) was so successful that five of the group's nine members signed lucrative solo contracts after only one album and while still remaining as a group. Their talent was living proof of what happened when talented blacks worked together instead of fought one another.

Now Ms. Terry McMillen was on the set with her talented self. She made a joyful noise when she published *Waiting to Exhale* in 1992, and "How Stella got her groove back" in 1996. Both books were well received and spawned very good movies with great soundtracks. Then De La Soul sang "Say No Go" and "stakes is high" to all who still tried to smoke crack and kill one another.

Yes, this was the same decade when Mr. Daymond John read *Think and Grow Rich*. Then started FUBU, a multibillion-dollar clothing business. It was during this time (the late 1980s–1990s) that Mr. Bernard witnessed the rise of a plethora of African American music moguls and entrepreneurs, like Sean "P. Diddy" Combs, Dr. Dre, Ronald "Slim" Williams and Birdman, Master P, Russell Simmons, and of course, the supertalent who would continue to withstand the test of time, Mr. Sean "Jay-Z" Carter, whom Mr. Bernard called the consummate entrepreneur, showman, writer, and rapper. He was pleased to see the evolution of the African American musical artist from just vocal talents to owners of their own music and as music producers.

At the turn of the twenty-first century, what really got Mr. Bernard's goat, as he put it, he being a career serviceman and quite the patriot, was September 11, 2001, and the attack on US soil on the twin towers of the World Trade Center in New York City and also on the Pentagon in Washington, DC. It was something he thought he'd never see.

Notwithstanding, Mr. Bernard, who had to be the hippest elderly man alive, was so happy he lived long enough to see African American actors again win the most coveted Academy Awards or Oscars for best actor and best actress, a feat that hadn't been accomplished by African Americans in fifty years, not since Mr. Bernard's favorite actor of all time, Mr. Sidney Poitier, received the first Oscar for best actor by an African American for his work in the movie *Lilies of the Field*.

The newest winners were Denzel Washington for *Training Day*, Forrest Whitaker for *The Last King of Scotland*, Jamie Foxx for *Ray*, and Halle Berry for *The Monster's Ball* in the beginning of the new (twenty-first) century. It was in the turn of the century when a gorgeous singer-musician named Ms. Alicia Keys came on the set and took the music world hook, line, and sinker with her drop-dead looks and sweet unique sound. Then two very talented women with avant-garde style and avant-garde names gave us a new sound: Ms Indie Arie and Ms. Erykah Badu, of course!

Yes, it was in the early 2000s when perhaps the most unsung hero of the new century, state representative Ms. Barbara Lee (D-Oakland, California, Ninth District) spoke and told all Americans live on C-SPAN that America's involvement in the Iraqi war was based on lies and that they should never have been there. God, what cojones, the chutzpah that woman had to take that kind of unpopular stand and go public with it! That African American woman's heart was bigger than her head!

At the turn of the century, the Williams sisters Venus and Serena made their marks in professional tennis and became the winningest sisters ever in the sport. Then Ludacris released the song "Rollout." Then came Juvenile with his hits "Back That Azz Up" '400 degrees" 'Gone Ride with Me' 'flossing season,' and 'soldier rag.' Yes Mr. Bernard love it all.

# Chapter 6

Mr. Bernard was so proud of the continual progress of his talented people. Really ecstatic was his appreciation of the rich history of his people, African Americans, and the contributions the descendants of slaves had made and were continuing to make to America's culture.

He was actually, literally, rendered breathless when America elected Mr. Barak Obama, its first African American president, in 2008.

*Wow*, he thought, *what a coup! What an accomplishment!*

It was purely the harvested fruit of hope. He was enthralled to see hip-hop artists—like Ice Cube, YoYo, Queen Latifa, Sticky Fingers, Busta Rhymes, RZA, Will Smith, Tone Loc, Method Man, Common, Eve, Ice-T, DMX, both members of the group OutKast, Redman, Ludacris, 50 Cent, MC Eiht, and the supremely talented LL Cool J—transform from musical artist to talented actors. It was a practice that, years before in this country, was reserved for the likes of Dean Martin, Burl Ives, Tony Bennett, Frank Sinatra, Doris Day.

Mr. Bernard was so pleased that, in the post-2010 era, national news programs, which were once dominated by Caucasian males (Walter Cronkite, Eric Sevareid, Chet Huntley, David Brinkley, and Sam Donaldson) had truly been infiltrated by capable, upwardly mobile, extremely talented African American journalists and legal analysts: Mr. Joey Jackson and Ms. Asuncion "Sunny" Hostin, a former federal prosecutor (*Damn, you go, girl!* thought Mr. Bernard), the very competent Mr. Don Lemon, the cute-ish Ms. Fredericka Whitfield, Mr. Ryan Young (whom Mr. Bernard called the Rover because he covered news events on the ground all over the country), the extremely impressive Mr. Marc Lamont Hill (professor at Morehouse College and the host of The Huffington Post Live). Mr. Bernard loved Mr. Hill's quick-witted, intellectual responses to the most difficult and loaded questions. *Keep doing it, Mr. Hill, with your intellectually badass self.*

Then there's also the caramel-complexioned, extremely articulate Mr. Joe Johns, who, much like Mr. Ryan Young, covered news all over the globe. And there's Mr. Victor Blackwell, who served as the weekend man on CNN. The aviation and government regulation correspondent was the very pretty Ms. Rene Marsh, and the political analyst with perhaps the best smile of any journalist on television, a smile that would light up a dark cave, was Ms. Athena Jones (all of CNN).

Mr. Bernard's absolute favorite journalist was the sexy Ms. Tamron Hall. Ms. Hall's comeliness brought to mind the classic poem "Karintha" by Jean Toomer (Toomer), the accomplished African American writer of the Harlem Renaissance period during the 1920s–1940s and author of the classic novel *Cane*. In particular, he recalled the line "Karintha carrying beauty, perfect as dusk when the sun goes down"! Ms. Hall, whom Mr. Bernard had seen on OWN (the Oprah Winfrey Network) and the ID (Investigation Discovery) network, was employed primarily by MSNBC. The lovely lady had a strong on-screen presence and clear, concise delivery. She comported herself with the confidence of Floyd "Money" Mayweather Jr. (TBE). The young lady was most articulate and extremely professional in the discharge of her duties and oh so naturally gorgeous.

*You go, girl!* Mr. Bernard thought. *Wow, what a turn-on you are—mentally and physically!*

Yeah, the 2010s were the same decade (2014) when thirteen-year-old Mo'ne Davis became the first African American—and American female, period—to pitch in and *win* a Little League Baseball World Series game. That pretty-eyed young lady's got bukoo talent and much skills! And though not an African American, a thumbs-up and serious kudos had to be given to black English director Mr. Steve McQueen for his excellent work on the gut-wrenching slavery exposé movie *12 Years a Slave*.

Yes, today's talented African American hip-hop and pop musicians deserved a mention as well: Wiz Khalifa, Little Wayne, Two Chains, Drake, Chris Brown, Raphael Saadiq, Rich Homie Quan, Future, Beyoncé (she's another multifaceted, absolutely beautiful, well-rounded, unparelled supertalent), Bruno Mars, Rihanna, and the drop-dead-gorgeous, body-cut-to-kill vixen Nicky Minaj. Also blowing up in the hip-hop genre is the Flatbush Zombies and the talented Mr. Kevin Gates with an extremely powerful presentation!

*Oh my goodness,* Mr. Bernard thought, *the talent, just to mention a few!*

Finally, Mr. Bernard had developed an immense respect for rapper, poet, author Mr. Kendrick Lamar. The lyrics this young brother is spitting are some of the most motivating he had heard in years. The song "Alright" which states that if "God got this, then it's going to be alright." Also there was the song "I," which had a hook that continually repeats the phrase "I love myself."

*Wow, how poignant and how timely!* thought Mr. Bernard. *If our people need to repeat anything, it's the phrase "I love myself."*

Mr. Lamar also has a song entitled "King Kunta." In reference to Kunta Kinte, a character from the book and miniseries *Roots* written by Mr. Alex Haley.

*Thank you, Mr. Lamar*, thought Mr. Bernard. *Please keep up the great work.*

Still, again, what sickened Mr. Bernard, as it did Claude, was the existence of T.A.N.s and the draining way they sucked the blood out of the veins of progress through which the strength of their people's forward momentum flowed. He wanted to caution young Claude to be very careful not to hate T.A.N.s. He knew that would be falling in line with what Willie Lynch wanted blacks to do. T.A.N.s were an ignorant backsliding lot. But they were still your people. He wanted to refer Claude to one of Booker T. Washington's quotes: "I will let no man drag me so low as to make me hate him." One could just replace the word *man* with *T.A.N.*.

No, Mr. Bernard didn't agree with much of Booker T. Washington's philosophy for his people, but he certainly agreed with that. One could pity them, dislike them, try to help them no matter how futile the endeavor might seem, keep some space from them when it was necessary, but one should never ever hate them. If you did, you'd deign, and in the process, you'd become just like them! As Mr. Bernard's pastor once said, "Hate the sin, not the sinner!" If one would only remember the core, the source of their foolhardy ways, then not hating them would be easier to do! He sincerely hoped his young buddy, Claude, found his niche in life, for as with all his people, he sincerely wanted the best for this young man.

After Claude left his home that night, Mr. Bernard felt empty, filled with uncertainty and consternation—somewhat hopeless.

"That kid is a minority amongst minorities," Mr. Bernard said aloud to himself. "He's an anomaly. I don't see very many African American kids his age who are interested in what he's interested in, save for the extraordinary youths—who are multiracial—that started the organization Black Lives Matter, which had twenty-five chapters throughout the country. Man, oh man, am I proud of them for doing something, anything to let the country and the world know that we really do matter! Most of the kids today don't aspire to anything positive or productive. What they really want is bling, a nice car, and to look and sound good. Most don't read *anything*.

"To them, reading is a boring, colossal waste of time. Many have very little interest in respecting elderly African Americans, let alone listening to an elderly African American or heeding any advice the elderly have to offer. Nothing they desire is of any true substance. They behave as if they have no heritage. There's not an inkling of self-worth. Yes, many—though not all—of today's black youth are a truly frightening, highly disrespectful, and ignorant lot. These are the black youths who are T.A.N.s in the making. Please, Father, forgive them, for they know not what they do." He unwittingly quoted Jesus Christ aloud.

Like the comedian Mr. Redd Foxx once said, "If you follow an ugly kid home, you can bet your bottom dollar an ugly parent will come to the door."

It was the same thing with young T.A.N.s. They wouldn't get there by themselves! Most of the time, they got to that stage of bellicosity, foolishness, and ignorance with poor parenting or a complete lack of it. The black people had donated so much to the country and to the world, in medicine, sports, agriculture, and literature as with all the arts—politically, scientifically, and architecturally. The youngsters had no idea how much they had to be proud of: the afore-mentioned innumerable examples left behind by their own people to aspire to.

*My Lord, what can be done to set these youngsters on the right path? What the hell will it take for us to start reinventing ourselves all together!* He then made himself a spot of herbal tea (Tension Tamer, his favor-ite) and retired to his bedroom to call it a night.

"Good luck, Claude," he whispered to himself, still thinking of the youngster as he climbed into his bed and grabbed one of his favorite all-time novels, *Things Fall Apart* by Chinua Achebe.

*How appropriate*, he thought to himself. He read until the can-dy-colored clown called the Sandman arrived and slumber took its course.

# CHAPTER 7

Claude grew up in what eventually became a single-parent (father only) household. His siblings included two older brothers and a younger sister. His parents, still married, had been separated for a little over fifteen years. Claude had been an average (C-plus) student throughout middle and high school. He was never really interested in athletics even though he did like tennis and international soccer which is called futbol in Europe and Asia. Claude had for all his life loved working with his hands; he had been fixing things around the house ever since he was in third grade. Being mechanically inclined, post high school, he enrolled into trade school to sharpen up his carpentry skills, learn about plumbing, and then get licensed and bonded for both.

His parents were extremely pleased at his initiative and desire to assist them with things around the home. He wasn't a child who had to be chided for not completing his chores. Say not so. When left with a list of things to do, Claude always did it all and then some.

His mother, a pianist and organist, played both instruments at church on Sundays and sporadically taught Claude his way around the keyboards (less over the last fifteen years because of her separation from his father) over the years, in between his learning amateur carpentry from his father. Prior to receiving his carpentry and plumbing diplomas and licenses, he did small jobs around the neighborhood for friends and neighbors to keep spending money in his pocket while he was still a matriculating student. His work requests increased exponentially from word-of-mouth advertising.

He always remembered the lessons about integrity his mother drilled in him before he set out on his entrepreneurial pursuits. It was understandable why Claude was vigorously sought. His father, who had been contracting on the side most of his life, expressed to Claude ad nauseam the importance of being on time, especially for business purposes. "When you respect your clients and customers' time, that in and of itself is some of the greatest advertising you can offer," he'd say.

By the time he completed school, Claude had procured a very satisfied and loyal client base. However, in need of medical and life insurance and the other benefits he would receive, he chose to contract on the side. He really liked the job he had and looked forward to staying on for a while.

Though he was miffed that his parents couldn't work out their personal problems, he was oh so pleased at the direction and focus he received from both parents. Even though separated, both of his parents always had time for him. What he could actually feel from both was how much they wanted him to do well, to prosper. He felt that many of his friends were enduring a hellacious experience as they went through life with the people who were their so-called parents.

One of his female friends, Diana Maximum, was sent to a boarding school from the age of eight until she graduated from high school the same year as Claude. Diane's mother, Ms. Denise Maximum, was actually the polar opposite of what her surname implied. She spent very little time with Diane and her other daughter named Sister. Her goal for Diane, or what she tried to sell to Diane, was that once she graduated from high school, she would receive a completely accessorized, brand-new computer. If she chose to enroll in college all of her tuition would be paid by the boarding school if she maintained at least a B average. Notwithstanding, the whole experience traumatized the young lady, and she lived in a perpetual state of infuriation. She felt her mom just didn't want her around, especially once she found out what her father meant by always telling her mom she had a white liver. She never spent any time around other African American kids and was really uncomfortable when circumstances placed her in their company. Also, she could sense that she was somewhat of a novelty in the all Caucasian settings she continually found herself in.

Claude's buddy from the neighborhood, Benton, had a horrific story of his own. He too, like Claude, came from a single-family home (his mom only). Benton had spent the bulk of his life in and out of foster care as his mom struggled with drug and alcohol addiction. Neither Benton nor Diane could accept the lives their parents chose to live. They felt like it was they themselves who were nothing but a burden to their parents. Diane's mom, Denise, a staunch verbal supporter of Jesus Christ (and that was all she was—a *verbal* supporter of Jesus Christ), year after year would always miss at least two of the four special-occasion dinners put on by the school, leaving her lonely daughter's face drenched in egg.

Then she would come with the same sorry excuse every year. "Oh, Diane, I would've come, but I was so busy."

*Busy, huh. President Obama had time to read about the NCAA March madness basketball tournament every year. He knows the who's who in the final four, and then he has time to run a country,* Diane remembered thinking. *Now that's busy. Geez, Mom, you ain't busy. I just ain't a priority in your life.*

Claude would always count as one of his blessings that these parents to his friends were not his parents. To this very day, when someone—anyone—would tell Diane, "Girl, I was so busy," she'd feel like the person was insulting her intelligence. It perturbed her. Busy was no excuse for being rude, inconsiderate, or self-centered. Rude was definitely no excuse to ignore someone because there was nothing tangible they could give me. "I can't even manipulate nothing out of them," they'd subconsciously reason. "I'll get to them when I have nothing else to do or when it benefits me." If that same person contacted them and said, "I have five hundred dollars dollars for you," they'd quickly become un-busy.

At one time, Claude was under the impression that all T.A.N.s came from impoverished or troubled backgrounds. Well, as he grew older, finished school, and entered the working world, he realized that T.A.N.s, just like African Americans, came in all shades, weight, height. Nothing was different. What made a T.A.N. was her or his spirit—or lack thereof. From what Claude and Mr. Bernard had discussed, affluent or well-educated T.A.N.s firmly believed that part of being successful was to not live around their own people. This was a condition among high-and-mighty T.A.N.s that made them see people of color (their own people) and instantly assume that other ghetto-dwelling black people weren't as capable or as competent as them—an implicit inner racial bias. Some actually were disgusted that other races looked at them as being the same as other African Americans.

Two of the friends of his brother Carter were both from affluent families, yet they set up Carter to be robbed and shot, leaving him paralyzed. Charles Fakirr was called Chuck the Fuck because he was always trying to fuck his friends' girlfriends. And his cohort, Willis Gate, was affectionately known as Poco Diablo Blanco, or Willis Diablo for short, because of his sneaky, devilish ways and his white skin (even though he was a black man!). They could act as if they were holier than thou, a manifestation of their House Nigger heritage. That was what Clyde Paine called the worst kind of black man there was. Success afforded them the ability to get away from their own people, and they did so as quickly as possible.

*Geez*, he thought, *one day, I wonder how many Caucasians or Latinos or Native Americans or blacks from other countries—Africans, Haitians, or Jamaicans—felt like that.* He could think of none—at least none that he ever met. *My Lord, he thought, what a ridiculous, race-divisive, pitiful mind-set.*

Chuck Fakirr and Willis Diablo were the quintessential House Negroes (niggers). Claude's dad said their behavior was a culture passed down through the years. They felt they were definitely better than other blacks because they had Caucasian grandparents or relatives. It was kind of like they were another race altogether. Clyde stated that folks like Chuck Fakirr and Willis Diablo were the absolute worst kind of T.A.N.s because their behavior and better-than-you attitude were so deeply ingrained that it was possible but not so probable that they would ever change their belief system of hating their own race, which was nurtured every day in their homes, their upbringings. They possessed a spirit or attitude of entitlement.

ANYTHING a Ghetto dwelling Blackman had (especially if he was poorer than them) they were entitled to. Their positions in society (not as good as Caucasian. But definitely better than a Darkie) Afforded them the right of first refusal to any attractive woman, any job, any real-property, especially any money that the Ghetto dweller had. Neither of those two house – Niggers had any remorse or contrition for what they did to Carter or any other Ghetto dweller. Clyde also stated that when a slave revolt was in the making, the first folks whom the slaves had to kill were those of the House Negroes, like Chuck the Fuck and Willis, if they expected their revolt to succeed.

Claude remembered the old saying, "It's not your word that matters. It's who you give it to." As he grew older, Claude realized that nothing was as wrong as that or any further from the truth. Your word mattered all the time and every time you opened your mouth. If you were intentionally dishonest sometimes, it was easier to get your wires crossed and be dishonest all the time.

A lot of communication went on between Claude and his parents but *never* any lying, not since he was caught in a few lies while in elementary school. Whatever Claude did, however poor a decision he might have made, when his parents got the truth from him, neither of them rarely overreacted, yelled, screamed, tried to embarrass him in public, or got violent with him—not if what he said was the truth.

"No one can or wants to help you, son, if you lie to them."

# CHAPTER 8

En route to work the next day and while stuck in traffic, Claude decided to cut off his radio for a second so he could concentrate and gather everything he needed for work during this lull in traffic movement so he could avoid rushing at the last minute. His mind drifted a bit as he mentally went back to his elementary school days. He was reminiscing for some reason about how cruel he was to fat, overweight, and short people. He had teased them every chance he got, embarrassed them without any consideration about how bad he was making them feel. But today he was about forty to forty-five pounds overweight according to all observers' standards. How difficult it had been for him to lose weight, and he'd had health problems due to his excessive weight.

Just then, he quickly thought of his conversation with Mr. Bernard, and he blurted out, "Laws of reciprocity, huh!" *If being overweight is one of God's lessons, then it's a cruel one that I surely brought on my own self,* he thought. That teasing-other-folks-for-a-laugh stuff was being mean spirited and extremely harmful. *Geez, yeah I was young, but no excuses. That's T.A.N. shit. Was I a T.A.N. in the making?* he asked himself.

Quickly, he came out of his little daydream after several long horn toots from the motorist who wanted him to inch along a little more steadier. "Close the gap, man." He let his foot off the brake too quickly, and he just missed rear-ending the SUV in front of him by mere inches. While he was still rooting around the interior of his car frantically, looking for his daily planner, which he wanted to find before traffic started rolling again, he noticed a police car coming up next to him in the service lane. The officer stopped right next to him and shined a flashlight in his car even though it was morning.

When Claude looked up and saw the cop, he gave a sigh of exasperation. *What could he possibly want with me being stuck in rush-hour traffic?*

The officer, his face pimpled, overtly racist, hideously ugly, contorted, and scowling, said, "Is there something wrong, buddy? Are you hiding something?"

"Oh no, sir, just trying to grab all I need before I exit the car for work. I'm only ten minutes away," said Claude.

"Where do you work?" queried the officer.

"Johnson & Johnson in Metuchen," replied Claude.

"Oh," said the officer. "Are you some kind of scientist or what?"

"No, sir, I'm a carpenter and a plumber. A laborer," replied Claude.

"Well, keep your eyes on the road. That's how accidents happen," barked the officer, the inflection in his voice raising some three to four octaves.

"Sure, I sure will," said Claude.

"Sure, huh, you smartass. Pull over and shut off your engine!" barked the officer.

"Why?" said Claude. "For what?"

"Because I said so—that's why," said the suddenly irate officer.

Claude complied immediately.

The officer called for backup before exiting his car and making his way to Claude. After thoroughly searching Claude's car, he asked Claude to pop the trunk. He tossed everything onto the highway ground and told Claude to come to the rear, retrieve everything from the ground, and put it back in the trunk. After checking his computer for the validity of Claude's license, insurance, and registration (and moving at a snail's pace as he did it), the officer handed Claude a citation for texting while driving—a seventy-five-dollar offense.

Claude immediately said, "Sir, I was not texting. You know that."

"Well, tell that to the judge, mister smart-ass carpenter, and don't tell me what the fuck I know, got it?" said the officer.

Claude was fuming, but he remained silent. He could feel it was now time to curtail any further conversation. He had heard of and seen predicaments like this get so out of hand that someone ended up dead. *So mum is the word until the surly "RoboCop" is gone*, he thought.

Claude thought about all the times he was stopped by the police while he was driving; 95 percent of the time, it was for *nothing*—absolutely *nothing*. Almost every time, it was a clear case of racial profiling, like the police (it was always the Caucasian ones who would stop and harass him) was lying in wait for him or anyone who resembled him racially. It made him wonder what the reason for this was. Was it an indoctrination? An African American's passage into driving adulthood?

Claude began thinking. *We're stopped, agitated, really debased, and annoyed and then purposely sent back to live among one another, loaded with venom that we eventually spew onto one another. After that, they can leave us alone for a little while and watch us vent most of the time at one another. Yeah, all they really have to do is watch us implode.*

Like the historically renowned French conqueror, Napoleon Bonaparte once said, "Never interrupt your enemy when they are destroying themselves."

They'd become a source of entertainment for their detractors, pundits, and agitators. They eventually actually do their jobs for them by doing in one another (like that self-hating aforementioned man proud that his gang killed a great deal of black men, that flaming butt wipe Connie Limb).

Claude knew that Mr. Bernard didn't drive and hadn't driven in years. After work that day, he went past Mr. Bernard's house to bring him some Black & Mild cigars. He really wanted to pick the elderly man's brain about bullshit traffic stops by racist police. He rang the bell and waited for what seemed to be an inordinate amount of time—definitely longer than usual.

Mr. Bernard yelled out, "One minute! I'll be right there."

When the door opened, Mr. Bernard apologetically explained that he was in the bathroom, and he asked Claude, "Please forgive me, young man. When you get to my age, you don't move so quickly anymore."

Claude handed him the cigars, and as Mr. Bernard reached out to take them from him, Claude got a faint whiff of doo-doo (feces) from Mr. Bernard's freshly-used-to-wipe-his-butt, partially soiled left hand. "Hey Mr. Bernard, you didn't forget to wash your hands, did you?

"Ooh, wow, I'm sorry, young man. No, you're right. That ain't no piece of chocolate under my fingernails. Excuse me for a moment." He made his way back to the bathroom to finish washing his crap-smelling hand.

"Okay," said Claude sarcastically, "you're excused."

"Okay, son, don't be a smart-ass."

And both men laughed heartily.

"Thanks for the stogies, son. Where are you headed? Have you been home from work yet? Did you eat dinner yet? Are you hungry."

"No, sir, I did have a question or two for you, if you have time," said Claude.

"Sure, I definitely have more time than money. What's the problem?" replied Mr. Bernard.

"Well, I know you don't drive. As a matter of fact, I've never seen you drive. Why is that?" asked Claude.

"Well, why, young buddy, cops been pulling you over lately?"

"Yeah. Wow, how did you know that?" asked Claude.

"Young man, I haven't driven in almost thirty years. I stopped just before my fiftieth birthday. I got tired of those damn cops pulling me over like it was SOP for them. Always I was paying fines for nothing. They would pull me over with a baiting 'I dare you to get smart' look on their faces. I got so tired of that shit. Hey, Claude, have you ever heard of policing for profit?"

"Huh?" said Claude. "What's that?"

"Well, that's how a lot of police departments in this country generate hundreds of thousands of dollars by citing poor African Americans for the most minor horse shit. Then, if you don't come to court, they issue a warrant for your arrest. Now you're in the system when you've done nothing to get there, nothing but driving while black. 'Grass needs to be trimmed. Here's a citation.' 'Neighbors said your music is too loud. Here's a citation.' 'Driving twenty-seven miles per hour in a twenty-five miles per hour zone in a traffic-less thorough fare at midnight. Here's your ticket.' No one on the road but you. 'Just bought that car? Is it registered, insured?' 'No, sir, I just left the auction where I purchased it. Here's the bill of sales, the receipt. I'm on my way to register it now, sir.' 'Well, here's your tickets—a hundred fifty dollars' worth. Take that to court and explain that to the judge.' Failure to signal as you're changing lanes. The three cars in front of you, who all did the same thing, don't matter. They weren't black. 'Your rear left tire is under inflated. You're about to get a flat. Here, take this to the judge. You can pay the fifty-dollar fine or fight it—it's up to you!' I've heard every bullshit reason/excuse there is."

"I'll bet you have," said Claude.

"The last ticket I got was at a parking meter. I returned with about twelve minutes on the meter, and the parking authority cop was just finishing writing out the ticket. When I approached the car, I knew there was more time on the meter, so I looked at it carefully. It had snowed that morning, and the meter was partially obscured by a small buildup of snow. I wiped off the snow and beckoned to the officer to look that there were almost twelve minutes left on it. 'Well, well, you're right, mister. Well, once we start a ticket, it *has* to be posted on the vehicle or handed to you—the driver. I'm sorry, but you're going to have to go to court and explain that to the judge.' 'Oh I have to go to court for your incompetent mistake, huh!' 'Look, talk to me like that one more time, and I'll have you arrested. Good day, sir,' said the officer."

"Wow, so after that, you just quit driving?" said the surprised Claude.

"Yeah, son, I refused to take any more. You see, young buddy, the last ticket-giving crap eater was a T.A.N., and I could see in his eyes how anxious he was to ticket someone—*anyone*—who was black. He knew he was more likely to be supported by his superiors if the alleged law breaker was black. I cannot live in peace with that kind of aggravation from my own people. Dealing with racism is bad enough. Shit, if I gotta take that from my own, I'll be damned! If I had said one more thing to him, I guarantee you, I would've spent the night in jail for sure—or worse. I'll be eighty soon, son, *eighty*, and I didn't get here by allowing my blood pressure to rise off the charts!" said Mr. Bernard.

"But to stop driving altogether, how could you do that? Isn't that a bit extreme?" said Claude.

"Well, son, you're asking the computer to give you information that it hasn't been programmed for," replied Mr. Bernard.

"Huh?" said Claude.

"Well, live fifty more years, and in the interim, go through what I've been through, then you can answer that question yourself," quipped Mr. Bernard. "What a lot of today's youngster's seem to forget is that there is a god."

"Well, I guess you're right, sir," said Claude reluctantly. "But God can't take you to run errands, sir."

"No, he can't, I agree. But he did send you now, didn't he?"

# CHAPTER 9

After almost fifteen months at his new position at Johnson & Johnson, Claude's attendance record had only one blemish on it. That came on the day he was pulled over a year ago by the police.

When he arrived late that day (some thirty-five minutes), he was summoned into the Human Resources office by the human resources manager, a T.A.N. named Mr. Deltoid.

*What an appropriate name*, he thought. *That bastard T.A.N. is always flexing.*

When Claude explained to Mr. Deltoid what happened to him en route to work, he didn't believe him, and he said so in no uncertain terms, "Listen, brother, that's a bit of a stretch, don't you think?"

*What brother you talking about?* thought Claude.

"Are you sure you didn't have a rough morning due to partying all night? I've heard you like New York clubbing."

"No, sir," he replied. *Who the fuck told him that?* Claude thought. He successfully hid his disgust at this person calling him a liar no matter what his position. Claude felt this reaction was way off base. "Listen, sir," said Claude. "I have the ticket he gave me, it's in my car. Do you want me to get it for you?"

"Sir, huh?" quipped Mr. Deltoid. "No, that's not necessary. I know what can be created with computers. Anyway, I'm still going to give you a disciplinary written warning for being late during your probationary period." He was still in his initial six months.

Claude chose not to take this issue any further because work-wise Claude landed on his feet running. Every assignment he was given was completed thoroughly and in a timely manner. He hadn't seen Garry Foreman in over five months as the two now worked on alternate shifts. That was fine with him because he didn't think very much of Garry.

*Could it have been Garry, that Lackey dipped in chocolate, who told Mr. Deltoid that I-like-clubbing crap?* he thought.

It had been quite some time since Claude had seen his mother, Estelle, or his sister, Carmen. She, soon to be a senior in high school, had moved in to live with their mother in Baltimore at the end of her sophomore year to attend Baltimore's high school of perform-ing arts due to her artistic and acting abilities. His oldest brother, Clarence, still had approximately three years minimum left on a possession-with-intent-to-deliver conviction, and he was serving his five- to ten-year sentence in Rahway State Prison in Rahway, New Jersey.

Claude's father, Clyde, was a retired bus driver from Paterson, New Jersey, who now devoted all his time to his contracting business. He now lived in Somerset, New Jersey, with his son Carter, Claude's brother, who was paralyzed below the waist (from his midthigh down) from a botched armed robbery (that his friends and cohorts tried to commit on him) and shooting when he was seventeen years old.

Claude made his home in Somerville, New Jersey, the next town over, some seven miles away. Claude liked living less than twenty-eight miles from New York City. He was able to hang out and party in New York without living there, and that was fine with him. What he deplored was the traffic on the George Washington Bridge. It was the only way he wanted to travel into the city. He was claustrophobic, and he dreaded the thought of being stuck in either the Lincoln or the Hudson Tunnels. So it was either the Verrazano Bridge when he wanted to party in Brooklyn because that bridge fed right into the Brooklyn-Queens expressway (Route 278) or the George Washington Bridge when his party destination borough was the Bronx or upper Manhattan.

Claude, settled in at the job and the neighborhood, decided to start running daily as a beginning to addressing his weight issue. He drove around and made a route to run for himself. He had already put five straight days together. The lush green tree-lined roads that encircled his neighborhood were perfect for his running. *This is also a great time to pray*, he thought.

He ran four miles every weekday morning before work. It felt absolutely great. It released endorphins and was an actual high in many ways. Any feelings of disgust he harbored most days were left on the road during his run. Good Lord, what a spiritual experience! He'd run just before sun-up and see the deer grazing and looking up at the slightest of sounds, especially Claude's pounding footsteps. The red foxes darted by like crimson streaks of light. Oh what beautiful coats they had!

The fat, rotund ground hogs waddled by, so uncomfortable to leave the security of their moist, dank burrowed-out hole of safety to look for food before the roads became congested with traffic. The mouse-like little chipmunks scurried around with their multicolored, streaked, furry little coats, they too looking for food before the throngs of humans interrupted their search or the schoolkids tried chasing and catching them for sport or to cage them and make pets out of them. The hawks soared around, trying to zero in on rodents and other small animals for their breakfast and to feed their young. The frightened white bushy-tailed rabbits hopped around, trying to grab some sustenance for themselves and their young before all the predators that put the fear of God in them grabbed one of them to make fine cuisine out of them. Oh, good Lord, the bucolic sights!

*God's wonderful creations and the beautiful picturesque masterpiece of the morning. I'm not giving-up this running routine for anyone. What a way to maintain good health and prepare myself for the day. Oh my Lord, thank you!*

On several mornings as he started out, most of the time around 5:30 a.m., he would run past the local high school's football field and witness the thick, foggy dew hovering over the field, like a cloud had decided to vacate the heavens, descend, and then float just above the grass, like a drone hovering above sand dunes in a desert.

*This is a photographer's dream*, he thought. Then as he returned, the dew had lifted and dissipated, and then he could see the beautiful birds, the stunningly gorgeous birds. There were the bluest blue birds, the rouge-red cardinals, the red-breasted robins, the voluminous little brown sparrows. Once in a while, he'd focus in the buzzing, whirring sound and pick up a floating humming bird. Once, he had witnessed these jet-black ravens gathering and then loudly caw-cawing while, one by one, they'd dart out from the pack to attack and chase off an owl that was three times their size from the top of a nearby pine tree when it had gotten a little too close to a raven's nest.

Immediately, he thought, *See what blacks can do? What strength they have when they work together!*

# CHAPTER 10

Claude was due after eighteen months for a promotion and a raise. When he went to Human Resources two weeks after he had been there for eighteen months to meet with the arrogant, obnoxious Mr. Deltoid, he was greeted with a disgusting oratory about his progress. Yes, his work had been superb. Yes, he had never called in sick, and yes, he took the two week's pay instead of his vacation because he was in the middle of a job and didn't want to leave it for someone else or have it waiting for him when he returned. Notwithstanding, there was this issue that Mr. Deltoid was really annoyed with. That was Claude's veracity.

As Mr. Deltoid continued, Claude's blood had started to boil, and his head began to pound incessantly.

"That day you came in here, brother"—*There's that brother bull-shit again*, Claude thought—"and told me that bullshit about a cop stopping you and putting all your belongings on the ground and making you put everything back yourself . . . well, Claude, I checked the story out. I contacted the police and verified the whole thing," he continued. "Yes, you were stopped for texting while driving and the time of the ticket didn't jibe with the time you arrived at work. As I see it, Claude, you should have arrived at work much quicker. You know, Claude, I have a problem with these damn cell phones and people like you on the road placing everyone else in imminent danger with that texting crap. Secondly, what did you do once the officer let you go? Did you smoke a joint to calm down, go somewhere for a quick drink, or what? Neither of these things—or whatever the heck you did—represent good decision-making, and at this time, I don't think you possess the character to be promoted to shift supervisor or to receive a 5 percent raise. Now what you need to know, Claude, is that I come from where you come from. Yes, I'm an alumnus of Patterson's East Side High, in the hood, and I know our people and how most believe everything should be handed to them. Such is not the case with me, brother. No, the buck stops here. I suggest you pull yourself up by your bootstraps, get your act together, continue your good labor, stay in line, try to be a tad more honest, and in six months, we can meet again and discuss some forward progress for yourself as an employee of this company."

Claude was flabbergasted, livid, and he could no longer contain his disgust. Raising his voice, he retorted, "Hey, Mr. Deltoid, that's some straight-up bullshit. First of all, nigger, I wasn't texting."

"Nigger?" Mr. Deltoid rudely interjected and queried.

"Yeah, you ball-less, nigger lackey motherfucker. I wasn't texting, and fuck what you think about my goddamn veracity. Ain't that some shit! There has never been a custodial worker here as good as me. My record proves that. My work speaks for itself, and my attendance is also immaculate, impeccable—save for that racist fucking cop's assertion that I was texting while driving."

"Assertion." Mr. Deltoid chuckled with a derisive smile on his face as Claude was still in the midst of his righteous rant.

Claude stopped immediately, hauled off, and bashed the smirking Mr. Deltoid in his wide ethnic nose with a straight right hand, breaking it, and, drawing blood. "You motherfucking bastard!" Claude yelled as he jumped over the neatly arranged desk and began pummeling T.A.N. who had his face bashed and was now petrified, scared for his life, cowering, now balled up in a shell, and screaming for dear life. After delivering between eight to ten vicious successive blows to Mr. Deltoid's bloody, swelling face and ribs (Mr. Deltoid had gotten into his protective shell by he turning on to his side to protect his neck and face, thus exposing his ribcage), Claude then grabbed Mr. Deltoid's neck and began to squeeze unmercifully. The gagging Mr. Deltoid, trying desperately to gasp for air, began to see spots and was losing consciousness quickly.

Just then, two workers—a Mr. Juan Salvador, a recently hired coworker of Claude's and whom Claude was actually training, and a Mr. Tom Retter, also from the Human Resources office—grabbed Claude from behind and wrestled him off Mr. Deltoid. They actually prevented him from killing the just-got-what-was-coming-to-him, wheezing, whining, crying, happy-to-be-alive Mr. Deltoid. Claude was subdued as three more males, all security, came to Mr. Deltoid's rescue.

Screaming and now sweating profusely, Claude yelled extremely loudly, "Get the fuck off me, motherfuckers, *now!*"

They all complied, and they quickly called 911 and tried to assist the gagging, coughing, disoriented, severely beaten-up Mr. Deltoid.

Claude, not a scuff or scrape on his person, then gathered himself, straightened out his bunched-up and disheveled shirt and slacks, went to his locker, grabbed all his belongings, and left the building in a huff. Claude, realizing he had just allowed his temper to get the best of him, wanted to drive, so he headed straight to Baltimore, Maryland, to talk to his mother, whom he hadn't seen in months. This drive that was almost three to four hours would give him time to clear his head. He knew he was in legal trouble and that he might be locked up. Still, he had a genuine feeling of relief, a contentment for some reason. It made him think about the time his father told him that most black men were angry. When a society had a foot in your neck, that developing and festering anger was natural.

"Believe me, son, *most* black men in America [whom his dad said were really pseudo-white men] are angry either consciously or unconsciously."

It was a fact the TV journalist Anthony Bourdain allowed to go right over his head. While in Mozambique, Africa, Mr. Bourdain asked a native Mozambican why he didn't appear as angry as the young black men in America. It was a very insulting, dumb-ass question. The Mozambican man's heritage and history were still intact. He even spoke his own native tongue (and it's not French!). That was something African Americans didn't have and couldn't do. Most only knew English, the tongue of their former enslavers, and most didn't know diddly about their ancestors or heritage. African Americans didn't know which African country they came from either.

*So, Mr. Bourdain, up to that point, I liked your show, and I still admire your work. But in the future, when it comes to black history, please look before you leap. Then do your damn homework before you ask stupid-ass vacuous questions. Please!*

"Damn," Claude unknowingly said out loud. "I should've handled that much better." That T.A.N. Mr. Deltoid had exposed his arrogance and disdain for not only Claude but also all his people. Claude thought, *Possibly, when that asshole was younger, the brothers in the hood probably took his lunch money from him. Maybe they stole his girlfriend or practiced their boxing skills on him. Whatever had happened to him, he's one screwed-up colored man—or T.A.N., which is the same thing.*

Claude remembered his father telling him, "People like that fuck with a whole lot of people. When they screw with you, try to remember that you don't have to fight every battle. Eventually, they're going to fuck with the wrong person and get what's coming to them."

*Well,* thought Claude, *today I was the wrong person because that ignorant, condescending T.A.N. got exactly what was coming to him. Geez, now I got legal troubles.*

# CHAPTER 11

When he arrived in Baltimore, he stopped at a Days Inn motel to clean himself up, grab a bite to eat, and rest for a couple of hours. After his meal, he dozed off for what seemed like twenty to thirty minutes. So exhausted and emotionally drained was he that he had no idea he slept through the night, some nine and a half to ten hours. So deep was his slumber that he had drooled, and the spit streak had dried and encrusted on his face.

"Boy, oh boy," he said out loud, "I didn't realize how tired I was." He showered again, dressed, and did a beeline to his mother's house in East Baltimore. When his mom came to the door, he saw in her eyes a look of resignation. He could tell from her posture that she knew something about the events of the day before.

"Hey, Mom." He approached and hugged his mom. He could feel her trembling. "Mom, look, I know you know something," said Claude.

"Son, stop right there. I have to tell you that the police are looking for you, and I'm sure here is one of the places they'll be soon. If you want to tell me what happened, fine, but money is the issue right now. If you're gonna be arrested, bail is what we need to think about now. Have you been saving money?"

"Mom," said Claude with a smile on his face that can only be derived after receiving statements of reassurance from someone who loved him unconditionally, "do you really think you have to ask me that?"

"Good," said his mom, and she began to cry harder as each moment passed. "Son, I don't know what that guy did, but I am your mother, and in your entire life, the only other time you lost it like that, you were damn sure driven to that point. I only know he's still alive, and there can't be a murder charge. So I know losing you forever is not probable. He must have really dug deep, huh, son."

"Oh, Ma, if only you could've heard the things he said to me," said Claude.

"I'm sure." said his mom. "Look, Claude, that's not your nature, son. You never in your life been the aggressor, the initiator of some crap like that. I know it was bad, baby. Did he initiate the violence, or was it you who threw the first punch?"

Claude hung his head, drew an elongated and deeply inhaled breath, which he exhaled so slowly his sigh became entangled with his answer. "I'm the one who flipped, Mom."

"Well, you gonna turn yourself in. Please don't try to talk me out of it either. I'm definitely coming with you!"

"Oh, come on, Ma, that can be kind of embarrassing," Claude replied.

"I don't want to hear that crap, I'm coming. I have one son doing time, one son who can't stand up or walk, and now you! I'll be damned if I let you hang in the wind. Anything can happen with the cops in Jersey. You know the old saying. 'The two states that no one wants to get arrested in are Texas and New Jersey.' So I'm coming, and video-recording everything leading up to walking in that building," said Estelle.

"Hey, Ma, did they mention charges?" said Claude.

"Well, your dad, whom I think you should call first chance you get, said that you were being charged with aggravated assault and other toss-against-the-wall-and-hope-they-stick charges. The aggravated assault might be upgraded to attempted murder once they've heard your side of the story and the preliminary hearing takes place. Your Human Resources manager—geez! Who the heck beats their Human Resources manager to a pulp? It's almost comical. Look, son, you don't have a record. We talked to the lawyer, Ms. Evans, and she said that depending on what they finally charge you with, you might get out ROR [released on your own recognizance). No bail money might not even be necessary. Mr. Delray is saying that you tried to kill him," said Estelle.

"Mr. Deltoid, Mom," Claude interjected.

"Okay," said his mom. "But the cops told your dad that the witnesses said it looked like a fistfight to them, so they really need to talk to you."

*Wow*, thought Claude to himself. *Those guys pulled me off that jackass. They knew I was strangling him. Their involvement, their words, the things I thought would sink me, might be the very things that will keep me from getting hung—figuratively.*

Just then, his mom said, "What, son? What's on your mind? I know you, young man. As soon as I mentioned witnesses, you went twilight zone on me. What's that about? What ya thinking?" said his mom inquisitively—a mother's keen intuition at work.

"Oh, okay, I'll just go on up and see what's what," said Claude, avoiding the question.

"Okay," said Mom. "I know you'll tell me when you're ready. But anyhow, Claude, how much you got saved?" asked his mom.

"Close to 5k, Mom, not counting my last-resort stash," said Claude.

"And I got some money stashed myself, son," said Estelle.

"Well, Mom, don't you always?" said Claude, and he and his mom both got a good laugh.

After speaking with his father about his intentions to return immediately and face the music, Claude wasn't surprised that his dad wasn't so cordial (like his mom) in his telephone interaction with his son. He chided Claude something fierce about allowing anyone to get him to a point of reacting that way. He stated how easy it was to throw his life away, to kill any hope of his future being productive because of one second of losing his composure.

"You spend all your time berating ignorant black-folk behavior, you even got a name for them—T.A.N.s, right? Then you can't even compose your damn self! What the hell do you call yourself when you get down in the mud and behave like them, huh, when *you* behave like a throwback jackass, huh? All because you were mad! Is there a cute word for that! For your sake, son, I pray that this thing works itself out with minimal consequence. Lord knows I do."

Mr. Dale Deltoid, Human Resources manager of Johnson & Johnson, Metuchen, New Jersey, spent two nights and three afternoons in the hospital under concussion vigil. Besides an obvious concussion, he also had a broken nose, two cracked ribs, a lacerated bottom lip that required sixteen stitches (eight interior and eight exterior), and his right eyetooth was knocked out whole (lucky for Mr. Deltoid). It was recovered during office cleanup and sewn back in, albeit somewhat askew.

His official police report story was, "In the middle of him giving employee [Claude] Paine his mandatory eighteen-month evaluation and pay raise meeting, Claude become visibly agitated, started hyperventilating, and for the life of me, I didn't know why. I was all set to give him his promotion and a 7 percent raise then have my secretary write it up. But before I had a chance to do so, he just lost it. He starting flailing away at me, yelling, cursing, and screaming obscenities. Then that bastard tried to strangle me to death. His ranting didn't make any sense to me, Detective Cleverly. It was like he was on something—some drug or chemical. If the two workers didn't arrive when they did, I'm sure I would've been killed."

"Well, Mr. Deltoid, neither Mr. Salvador nor your coworker Mr. Retter concur with your version of the facts, sir. "Excuse me, sir. What do they say happened? You can see the bruises on my neck!" stated a quickly becoming frantic Mr. Deltoid.

"Well, Mr. Deltoid, both men said that you two were wrestling about and that neither of them could tell who the aggressor or instigator was," said Detective Cleverly. "I guess it will all come out as this thing moves forward. Okay, sure, we'll definitely get to the bottom of this."

"We definitely will," said Mr. Deltoid.

Claude turned himself in—with his mom, sister, and father in tow—that evening. This was by design as he wanted to assure his family that he would see the bail judge first thing in the morning. He met briefly with Detective Cleverly and chose to exercise his right to remain silent with regard to this case—per the instruction of his attorney until he met with her. His attorney, Ms. Elaine Evans, was currently finishing up a night court case, and she was due to visit him by eight thirty that evening. Claude was charged with aggravated assault, destruction of property, and disorderly conduct. Due to his lack of a criminal record and the absence of a weapon, Claude's bail was ten thousand dollars—cash or bond.

# CHAPTER 12

When Ms. Evans ESQ arrived, she appeared to have just prepared for a fashion model shoot. Every hair was in place, as if she had just left the hairdresser. Her five-thousand-dollar Armani business suit had not one wrinkle or cat faces on it, as if she had just gotten dressed. Upon arrival, she was made aware that Claude's bail would be nominal and that she could meet with him briefly and then again in the morning once he had been released.

Ms. Evans was one of the most experienced, popular, capable, and expensive attorneys in Northern New Jersey. Very much the intellectual, she had a BA and a master's degree in English from Howard University and a doctorate in education that she received from Rutgers University. Ms. Evans didn't decide to become a lawyer until she was thirty-six years old. She attended and graduated law school at Pennsylvania's Villanova University.

After just under fourteen years of practicing law, she had accumulated a 97 percent exoneration rate. Of the one hundred cases, she took, she lost only five, and two of those were won on appeal. Only one of her one hundred former clients went to jail, and nothing annoyed her more than the thought of that client. (It was really the thought of losing that case that stuck in her craw!) The other two lost case clients received only probation. She only took cases she could feel and truly believed in, according to her.

Being a friend of the family (she grew up with Estelle, Claude's mother) and knowing Claude since he was an infant, she was more than happy to take the case for less than the fee she usually charged. The very next morning, after less than fifteen hours in lockup. Claude was released after his father posted a thousand dollars, a 10 percent bond of the ten-thousand-dollar bail. The first thing Claude did once his cell was unlocked and the officer began the escorted walk to the desk for Claude to recoup his valuables and sign his release paperwork was pray.

That night, the things that crossed Claude's mind were filled with gratitude. How fortunate he was to have Ms. Evans, Esquire in his life, a family friend. How truly blessed he was to have a mother and father who had the money and were willing to support him and bail him out. He was aware that most African Americans he knew did not have the wherewithal to do as he and his family did. Most would still have been in lockup at the very least until the preliminary hearing.

Oh, how happy he was that the T.A.N. lackey, colored man . . . eerrr . . . person, Mr. Deltoid, didn't die because God knows he sure enough had tried to kill him.

"Good Lord, thank you for everything I have to be thankful for. God, I love you," he whispered as he walked out of the police station. The minute he opened the door, there stood his mom; his dad; his sister, Carmen; and his wheelchair-bound brother, Carter.

"A round of hugs for everyone is in order, my dear son," said Estelle. With a big cheese-eating grin, Claude, of course, complied.

"To the diner for some breakfast, everyone," said Dad.

"Yeah, I'm so hungry," said Carmen. "All this unexpected drama. Damn you, Claude! You scared me to death." Carmen sniffled as she wiped away her tears. "I didn't sleep a wink all night!"

Carter grabbed Claude's arm and wouldn't let go. He pulled Claude close and whispered in his ear, "Damn, Claude, you really fucked that dude up. Go ahead with your bad self, little brother." Then he and Claude engaged in an prolonged guffaw.

"What's so damn funny?" said Estelle. "Let me in on it. I wanna laugh too!"

"Mom, I gotta meet with Ms. Evans at eleven thirty this morning," said Claude.

"Okay," said Estelle. "I stopped by your apartment and picked up all your mail. It's in my car."

"After we eat, you can stop by my house to shower and dress for your meeting with Ms. Evans," said his dad.

The Paine family then boarded their two cars and then went directly to the Red Bull Inn and Diner on Route 22 in Somerset, New Jersey. Claude loved their pancakes and thick turkey sausage links. These were his favorites since he was a child. This was the very reason his mom chose the Red Bull Inn for breakfast.

*Good God!* thought Claude. *The way my mother treats me!*

It brought to mind the lyrics of one his dad's favorite singing groups when his dad was a child in the 1960s. The song was "I Want a Girl" by the Tennessee Mad Lads. The lyrics were "I want a girl, just like the one that married my dad"! Wow, what a mother! From the stories Claude heard from his friends and acquaintances, he needed to thank God every day for her. The only women that he became romantically involved with that came close to treating him like his mom were from other ethnicities. The only African American women who treated him with respect and admiration and exuded love for self and their own people every time they opened their mouths were the women he had a plutonic relationship with. Those were his true female friends.

The black American women he took up with and became romantically involved with eventually all exposed themselves to be T.A.N.s—avaricious, manipulative, cunning colored cunts. They all had an agenda. They wanted to know how much they could get out of him. Money, dates in high-cost venues, paying their bills for them, buying them some jewelry or Victoria's Secret undergarments, or letting them borrow his car. The two times he did lend his car out, both times the women drove directly to another man's place. Both cads lived at home with Mommy and Daddy and allowed these other men to drive his car—without Claude's knowledge or permission.

One of their favorite request was always "Ooh, do you have fifty dollars or one hundred dollars or two hundred dollars I can hold?" Most of these request were made _before_ he even had sex with these cretins. The more attractive these women were, the more they requested, and the more problems came with them. Once Claude had sex with them, they felt like he owed them his life and/or he shouldn't dare say no to anything they requested. Claude trusted absolutely none of the women he had sex with. Yes, sadly, suffice it to say, the only women he had sex with that never exposed an underhanded ulterior motive were either Caucasian, Latino, or Asian. If they were black and decent, of African descent, they usually hailed from Jamaica or Haiti or the Virgin Islands or Canada or Africa itself.

The T.A.N. women's agenda was to get all they could get while giving up as little as possible. *These* (T.A.N.) colored women were never loyal. *Loyalty* to them was synonymous with *gullible*. The minute Claude told T.A.N. women no to any of their obnoxious requests, they became vindictively diabolical. He knew they would get him sooner or later if he kept them in his company. Claude accepted that he had to take ownership for bringing these women into his life; he blamed himself for the vicious cycle of self-indulged pain he had involved himself in. It would be unlikely that he'd find himself involved with women like these again.

His African American female friends from school, the neighborhood, or church were, in comparison, the crème de la crème. They wanted nothing but to give a helping hand or to expose Claude to good advice or helpful direction. Their goal was to spread goodwill. When they were mean or nasty attitude-wise, they were apologetic and contrite as soon as humanly possible.

One day after church, as Claude made his way to his car, his friend Kevin had a forlorn, dejected look on his face, like he had just lost his best friend or a high-paying job. When Claude approached him to inquire what was wrong, Kevin replied, "Hey, man, I took my wife to the hospital this morning for what she and I thought was a minor procedure. After sitting in the waiting room for an hour, she came out and told me they were keeping her overnight for observation and to run some test. Now, Claude, I have to go home without my wife! Do you know how horrible even the thought of getting in bed without my wife is? Geez, I won't see her until tomorrow. My God, Claude, that's a depressing thought," said Kevin.

*Wow, what a sentiment*, thought Claude. He was rendered speechless. It had been years since he heard a man talk about his wife in such glowing terms. It astounded him. It filled Claude with a tremendous sense of hope that if he himself didn't compromise his own principles, the same was possible for him. And man, oh man, did he respect Kevin for that. *What a real man!* he thought. But being flabbergasted with joy, he was rendered speechless. All he could get out of his mouth was "Hey, brother, I will keep you and your wife in my prayers. God bless you and her, Kevin."

There was still a couple of hours to burn before he met with Ms. Evans, Esquire, so Claude went to pay a visit to Mr. Bernard, whom he hadn't seen since his lockup.

# CHAPTER 13

When he arrived, he again as usual was greeted very warmly. That old-timer loved Claude's company. Mr. Bernard made himself and Claude some tension tamer tea. Claude before you tell me about this fight you had have there been any ugly dreams. No not recently. said Claude "Hey Mr. Bernard why you ask me about those dreams?" "Well", said Mr. Bernard. "It sounds like PTSD"- Post Traumatic Stress. I lot of guys I was in "Nam" with (referring to the time he spent in Vietnam) they have dreams like that. You have a psychologist friend – Why don't you talk to her about it? Oh, okay, said Claude – Maybe I will. He then wasted no time apprising Mr. Bernard of the entire story of his fight with Mr. Deltoid and the charges he now faced.

"You know, young man, in your conversation and consciousness, I hear a lot of confliction," said Mr. Bernard. "You really have developed a deep-seeded disdain for your own people, which is beginning to fester into hate. I warned you about that. That flaming jackass you beat up and almost killed didn't deserve the serious attention you paid him. He was to be ignored. You played right into his hands. You just gave him more than he expected. He ain't worth your anger or you spending that much spiritual energy. You gave him the rise he was seeking. You almost destroyed your own life in the process. You are talented and supported by a phenomenally close-knit family. You don't have to listen to that bullshit or be around it unless you choose to. Anyone would hire you. Every African American can't say that. You have to endure bullshit, sure, but so does every other black person in America—T.A.N.s and African Americans alike.

"Imagine not having a family like yours or not being as talented or as skilled as you are—plus, no money, savings, or credit. Then how understanding would you be? How many people would you annoy? You get an excellent employment opportunity, and you blow it by getting so angry that you got violent with someone who *lived up* to your expectations, a sorry ass excuse for a man whose attributes were already made manifest to you. What's the old saying 'foretold is forewarned'? Those mean-spirited, self-hating T.A.N.s you talk about—most aren't as talented or as employable as you. Many of them are violent because a lot of them have no hope. Like Dr. Ben Carson, former presidential candidate and the brilliant retired neurosurgeon who separated Siamese twins said, 'Chronic hopelessness exists in the black community." He also said with his brilliant brain surgeon self, "Far too many families are torn and tattered by self-inflicted wounds." He too knows how we try to destroy one another, but instead of browbeating his people, he's trying to quantify the sources of their socially interactive maladies.

"That's what you have to do. Yes, young buddy, I agree with you that T.A.N.s are ignorant, self-hating, devious and that they behave poorly, embarrassingly and that asshole, that Mr. Deltoid, that condescending colored man, needed a wake-up call. But not from you, and definitely not with violence. 'Violence often walks alongside people who have given up hope,' which is another Dr. Ben Carson quote. A whole lot of T.A.N.s are uneducated or undereducated, unemployed or underemployed, and abusive because many of them have been abused, ignored, and like all black folks, always fired first and most of the time for things Caucasians and other immigrant employees only receive reprimands for. So they're filled with rage! Yes, they are so ignorant that they adversely affect the forward movement of our people. When a person has no guidance, no expertise, little talent, no skills, and no hope, they get violent, and they get violent quickly. Since none of the aforementioned describes you, young man, what's *your* fucking excuse for being violent, huh!"

Both Mr. Bernard and Claude now stared at each other, wordless for close to fifteen to twenty seconds in the midst of a pregnant pause.

"At this point, young man, you have to become contrite, apologetic. Like I said before, that's the difference in remaining a T.A.N. or continuing to develop as a real African American adult, like a real man should. The heck with apologizing to Mr. Deltoid, that sorry ass Negro. Keep as much distance as you possibly can between yourself and everyone who talks and behaves like him. You have to apologize formally—and with class—to your employers. Leave that business and that job, then apologize to yourself. Young man, the only reason you didn't kill that sorry son of a bitch was because you pray every day. I'm absolutely sure of that. If you don't apologize, then you will behave like and remain a full-fledged T.A.N., the very thing you despise. Yeah, I agree. "Let's not be satisfied and be patted on the head and kept like a pet." Still, another Dr. Ben Carson quote. Let them know we are discontent, but make sure your message is received and that you all are clearly heard in the process. Protest, vote, and gather in organizational political strength—but *never* violently.

"Claude, my whole family, save for my mom, are veterans. Hundreds of thousands of our people have fought in every war involving Americans. This country's, and other countries', soil is drenched with black blood and our sacrifices. Our people have being hung, tarred, feathered, whipped, and massacred because of that. Like the great singer, writer, and musician Curtis Mayfield said, "This is my country" too. So please, young man, make it work for all of us T.A.N.s and African Americans alike. But do it within the confines of the law and definitely without violence against anyone, *especially* within our own community or against our own people. Violence should only be used in self-defense or to protect your family and loved ones. Despise T.A.N. behavior, but just try to understand it. Again, I say, never ever hate them," said Mr. Bernard.

"Mr. Bernard," said Claude, "you act like those T.A.N.s don't bother you."

"Damn if they don't bother me, young man. I can't stand them or the shit they do. But when the American medical society starts saying things like heart disease or sickle cell anemia are the number-one killers of African Americans, well, I think that's *bullshit!* From my eighty years of life experiences in this country and in the world, I believe racism is the number-one killer of our people and has been for over four hundred years. Now, my friend, it's only my opinion, and you know what they say about opinions, but I also believe racism is also the reason T.A.N.s are so fucked up. All those rich athletes and entertainers who are adored by white America, they are rich and enjoy more freedom than most African Americans, just like the Manuscript Manumission Doctrine allowed talented slaves to earn their freedom. What did W. E. B. Dubois call talented folks in his classic book *The Souls of Black Folk*? The talented tenth, which means one-tenth of the world's people are extraordinarily talented. But what I don't think you realize is that a lot of those celebrated individuals have clay feet," said Mr. Bernard.

"Huh?" said Claude. "Clay feet? What the heck does that mean?"

"Clay feet—it means a lot of them are seriously flawed. Just check the police blotters in any city or any given night. Many of them might be the T.A.N.s you and I talk about. We don't know. They are just easily readily accepted because their talent makes everybody associated with them richer. So be careful not to lionize them because they're so talented. They too can and will do fucked-up shit. Okay, youngster," said Mr. Bernard.

"Okay, Mr. Bernard, I gotta get going."

"Okay, I guess you had enough truth for one day."

"Yeah, and I'm hungry again for some reason," said Claude. "One more thing, Mr. Bernard. It still don't make no sense to me that you don't drive."

"Hey, Claude, wait one minute before you go." Mr. Bernard then made his way to the kitchen while Claude waited in the living room. Claude could hear the spigot running full blast in the kitchen. Mr. Bernard then came to the living room, moving quickly especially for him.

He said, "Claude, think fast!" He busted Claude in the head with a filled-to-the-brim water balloon. "I should drive, huh," said Mr. Bernard, laughing so hard that he fell to the floor, urinated on himself (just a couple of droplets), and blew a short-burst, old-man, popcorn fart. "Like they used to say when I was younger, Claude,

'Now you're all wet!'" He laughed so hard he could barely get the words out.

Claude, now soaked from head to toe, didn't know what to make of what just happened, nor had he ever heard the expression "You're all wet!" However, Mr. Bernard was still laughing so hard that not only did he wet his old-man pants but his eyes started tearing something fierce. Claude found humor only in the fact that Mr. Bernard found this whole thing so funny even if he was a bit disgusted at being soaked and the butt of Mr. Bernard's joke.

# CHAPTER 14

Claude rushed to his dad's house, which was closer to Mr. Bernard's home than his, did a quick change, and left for Ms. Evans's law office in Manhattan. He arrived at exactly 11:30 a.m. As usual, Ms. Evans greeted him warmly. Surprisingly, she had done her homework. When she had time to do it, Claude could not fathom.

"Well, we got an assault of your Human Resources manager. Tell me what you want me to know," she said, baffled that he did not hear. "Tell me what happened."

Claude was a bit dumbfounded at the candid request. He told Ms. Evans everything he could fit into twenty minutes, and it was much more than what Ms. Evans expected to hear.

She took a deep breath and said to Claude, "If I were you, young man, I would continue to maintain my silence. I have to interview your coworkers, Mr. Salvador and Mr. Retter. I'm also going to attempt to interview Mr. Deltoid's secretary, Ms. Taggart. Keep in mind, young man, that none of them have to talk to me unless they want to, unless there's a trial and we subpoena them."

"Yes, I know," replied Claude.

"You know, both Mr. Salvador and Mr. Retter told Detective Cleverly, whom I've embarrassed in court several times, that they weren't sure who started the fight. Mr. Deltoid said you tried to strangle him. Is that true?"

Claude hung his head and very somberly replied, "Yeah, I did, Ms. Evans."

In an instant, like she had sat in a thumbtack or a hot seat and was somehow electrically shocked, Ms. Evans jumped out of her seat and adamantly shrieked, "Mr. Paine! I'm going to tell you something you better never forget, understand?"

Surprised and a little annoyed at the inflection in Ms. Evans's voice, Claude said, "Sure, Ms. Evans, what is it? What did I say?"

"Well, from this point on in your life, never ever volunteer information in any legal proceeding that will indict you. Okay, my friend?" Ms. Evans barked.

"Sure, I just thought you didn't want me to lie to you, Miss Evans," Claude replied.

"Lie, what lie?" Ms. Evans queried. "If no one saw you do it, then it didn't happen. Do you understand me, young man?"

"Yes, ma'am," Claude retorted.

"Good, and we never had this conversation—got it?" she continued. "Look, after I interview the three of them this week, I'll know how to plan our strategy. Okay?"

"Sure," said Claude, "when do you want to see me again?"

"Well, young man, I'll probably call you Thursday, so plan to see me Friday afternoon or Saturday morning, if those days are okay with you," said Ms. Evans.

"Either day is fine with me," said Claude. "And I really thank you for your time. Oh, one more thing. Are my chances of getting off altogether good or bad?"

"Well," replied Ms. Evans, "at this point, I'd say your chances are fifty-fifty, and that's damn good at any time. But I'll know more, have a better feel, post interview of your coworkers and Mr. Deltoid's secretary. Just hold your horses, and if I were you, I'd start upgrading my resume."

"Okay, Ms. Evans, thank you for your time, and I'll await your call," said Claude, extending his hand.

"Oh, hey, look, young man, I don't shake hands—I think it's a disgusting habit. Here, let's do this," said Ms. Evans as she extended her fist for a knuckle bump.

Claude responded in kind and then left Ms. Evans's office. *Wow*, he thought, *what a strange lady. Well, lawyers are strange anyway.*

Claude, now unemployed and possibly getting ready to go to jail, thought about his conversation with Mr. Bernard about being contrite and apologizing. Therefore, en route to his apartment, while stuck in traffic on the George Washington Bridge, he decided to call Mr. Carlson, his immediate shift supervisor at Johnson & Johnson for an exit interview.

"Hey, Claude, how goes it?" said Mr. Carlson.

"Oh, hey there, Mr. Carlson. Look, sir, I called to apologize for my behavior last week, and I really want to express to you how grief-stricken I am that our professional relationship has to end this way. I'd like to schedule my exit interview with you, if you currently have the time."

"Well, hold on a minute while I grab my book. How is Wednesday morning 11 a.m.? Is that okay with you, Claude?" said Mr. Carlson.

"It sure is. I'll be there at the ready at 11 a.m.," said Claude.

"No, you won't," said Mr. Carlson. "If I know anything about you, buddy, you will arrive at 10:30 a.m., and you'll be sitting in my office at 10:45 a.m., am I right?" Mr. Carlson chuckled faintly.

"Oh, sure," said Claude. "Hey, Mr. Carlson, thanks for everything, and I'll look forward to seeing you Wednesday."

"Okay, buddy, before you go, do you want to give me a synopsis as to what happened? Short version."

"Well, Mr. Carlson. I'm caught in traffic on the GW, so now is not a good time. I promise you the entire story in depth when we talk on Wednesday, okay, sir?" said Claude.

"Sure thing," said Mr. Carlson. "See you then, and take care of yourself."

Carter Paine, Claude's older brother by three years, was wheelchair-bound ever since he was seventeen years old. Initially, he had no feeling from his waist down. However, over the last four years, a bit of sensation had been crawling down the upper part of his legs gradually. Oh so overwhelmingly pleased was he one day when he tuned in a pornographic movie on his cable television and experienced an erection for the first time in over ten years. He had continued to get more sensation further down his legs incrementally until today; he had feeling midway between his knee and his hip on up.

Notwithstanding, he still needed help with washing, being fed at times, and keeping his portion of the house clean. The agency his dad used for him had sent some very good assistants and/or nurses. Some were licensed practical nurses, some nurse's assistants, and once a week, an RN came to make sure he was receiving the home care and medical attention he required.

His last attendant, a Ms. Maria Vasquez, a Dominican national living in the USA on a work visa, had to leave two days ago due to the expiration of her visa. The agency sent in Maria's stead a black woman named Ms. Barbara Steel. Ms. Steel hadn't worked before for this agency; however, her resume spoke volumes about her experience and education. Barbara turned out to be an attendant from hell.

# CHAPTER 15

During her initial visit, the first thing that sow did was to rummage through the refrigerator for all she could stuff in her face the minute Carter went to his bedroom to use his computer. This, according to Carter, was what she did best the entire day. Seemingly, Barbara made it a point to evade Carter at every turn so that she could do only what she wanted to do when she wanted to do it. She always had some pressing business in one of the other rooms in the house. Carter tried to be patient and allowed her that first day to get settled in.

The next day, she came in quickly, saying, "Excuse me, Mr. Carter, I got to run to the bathroom." After staying in the upstairs bathroom for close to twenty-five minutes, she came out and came downstairs with a basket of dirty clothes. "Oh, excuse me, I got a load of clothes to wash, Mr. Carter. I'll be in the basement. If you need me, just holler," said Barbara.

"Hey, Barbara, I've had more than ten attendants for almost the last eleven years, and I never had to holler for anyone," said Carter.

"Oh, okay, I'll only be a minute," Barbara replied.

"Well, said Carter, what clothes you gotta wash? All of mine are clean or in the dryer, waiting to be put in my dresser drawers."

"Oh, really," said Barbara, "well, there was a hamper full of clothes outside the upstairs bathroom."

"Those are my dad's clothes, and you ain't being paid to take care of him. So please, dear, your job is to wait on me," said Carter.

"Okay," said Barbara as she ran down the basement steps with the basket full of clothes she had extracted from the hamper, ignoring

Carter, and being wheelchair-bound, there was nothing he could do. She made him feel helpless, useless in the process.

Carter was angry, so he used his stair-lift and went to his bedroom. He certainly didn't want anyone in his home running around, doing as they pleased. When Barbara came up from the basement, Carter called for her to come to his bedroom.

"Okay, Mr. Carter, I'll be right up after I get done in the basement," Barbara replied.

She then came up from the basement and did a beeline to the kitchen and made a cold-cut-and-cheese sandwich before she went to see what Carter needed. First, she wolfed down the hastily made sandwich in three and a half bites. When she reached his room, he asked her to bring up some typing paper from the computer table in the living room.

"Couldn't you have told me that while I was downstairs?" said the irritated Barbara.

"I told you lady that I'm not in the habit of yelling. Please do as I ask, dear. I really don't need a difficult time," said Carter.

"Sure, honey, is there anything else you want before I come back upstairs?" said Barbara.

"No, please, just bring me some paper," Carter replied.

"Okay," said the slovenly, wide-assed Barbara as she made her way downstairs, walked right past the living room computer table where the typing paper was, sat her fat butt in one of the dining room chairs, and made a phone call to her supposed fiancée.

After between eight to ten minutes, Carter was calling Barbara again, wondering where she had disappeared to this time.

"Hey, Miss, where is my damn paper?" Carter yelled.

"Wait a minute, buddy," said the ignorant, insolent Barbara, "watch your language. I ain't one of those damn foreigners that don't understand English, okay?"

"What the fuck are you talking about? What the hell did you come here for? This ain't no damn clubhouse for you to eat and lounge around in," Carter replied.

"Well anyway, what is it I can do for you?" said the irritating Barbara in a tone inferring Carter's requests were really annoying her.

"You can get the fuck outta my motherfucking house, you lazy-ass bitch," said Carter.

"Well, I ain't going nowhere until my day is done. Shit, I'm going to get paid for the day. I ain't leaving here just because you don't know how to talk to people. It ain't my fault you paralyzed," replied the coldhearted, ornery Barbara.

"Okay, we'll see about that," said Carter.

Carter looked all over, but he could not find his cell phone, which Barbara had shoved under the living room couch with her foot, so he wheeled himself into his father's room to use the landline. His first call was to the agency, and he complained about Barbara and implored the agency to replace her. Knowing Claude was home due to his legal troubles, he then called Claude, apprised him of the situation, and asked Claude to come to their dad's house immediately.

In the interim, he asked Barbara, the surly sow, to leave his home again. She just sat on the couch, placed her tree-trunk-like legs and her thick stubby feet on the coffee table, started whistling, and turned on the downstairs television.

Carter said, "Okay, you fucking cow, have it your way. Someone will be here soon enough."

Barbara sighed, continued to ignore Carter, and started whistling again. In twenty to twenty-five minutes, Claude let himself in. The tension was so thick in his father's house it was stifling, as if someone had turned up the heat in the house full blast in the middle of July.

"What's going on here, miss?" said Claude.

"Hey, man, tell this fucking ho to get the fuck outta this house right now!" said Carter. "This fucking cunt is whack, man."

Claude looked at Barbara, who had a look on her face of pure disgust, like how dare these niggers disrupt her day. Claude then said to her. "Well, what the hell are you waiting for? You heard my brother, Miss. It's time to leave."

"Okay," said Barbara, "but you niggers are going to see to it that I get paid for the whole day."

"Hey, Claude," said Carter, "you see what I mean? I been putting up with this greedy ho's shit for two days. Please, Claude, get this fucking monkey the hell out of here."

"Or what?" said the irate, contentious, fattish, slovenly Barbara.

"Look, Miss, either you get out of here, or I'm going to throw you out on your fucking big-ass, jack-o'-lantern head," said Claude, reaching the limits of his endurance.

"You put your hands on me, nigger, and we'll see who gets thrown outta here after I call the cops on your ass. You know how quickly they shoot niggers like you. So go ahead, toss me out now, you tough-ass black motherfucker," said the suddenly brave Barbara.

She then sauntered ever so slowly around the living room, creeping along, like she had slippers on her feet that kept slipping off. Oh, how badly Claude wanted to kick her up her four-butt-cheek ass. But realizing he was already cased up (involved legally with a court case), he then reluctantly allowed Barbara all the time she needed to grab her belongings and leave. He then called the agency and told them whom they had sent to their home. He implored them, of course, to never send this jackal again.

Carter could not believe what he just experienced. He was so upset that he started crying. Never in all his years as a paraplegic had he ever felt so emasculated, so helpless. He told Claude everything the fat-cunt monster (as Carter put it) had done in his father's house the last two days.

Checking the refrigerator, Claude found the cold cuts unpackaged and loosely thrown about. The mustard and mayonnaise lids were no longer screwed on tight. The loaf of bread was opened and sitting on the kitchen table. The butter knives had remnants of margarine, mustard, and mayonnaise on them with a swipe mark like they all had been licked.

Carter said, "Please, Claude, pour me a drink, and call Harry the Hebrew." That was Carter's Jewish friend who doubled as his weed connection.

Claude complied while consoling his brother in the interim. Claude neither smoked nor drank—at least not in his father's home to date. So the minute Harry arrived, Claude immediately left. He went directly to the trolley car diner, and much to his chagrin, sitting there and talking to one of the short-order cooks was none other than Barbara Steel, the attendant from hell whom he had thrown out of his father's home over an hour ago.

Not wanting to engage in conversation with the arrogant, ignorant, unprofessional Ms. Steele, Claude immediately exited the diner. On his way home, he stopped and bought a hero sandwich. Claude had not given his current employment predicament much thought. He didn't know which of his problems to devote the lion's share of his concern to—being unemployed or possibly going to jail.

# CHAPTER 16

Some of the many things he learned from his parents were saving his money (his mother) and the necessity of budgeting his money according to his bills and income (his father). Claude had planned to purchase a house and pay the mortgage with his continual earnings from Johnson & Johnson. However, that plan, of course, had to be shelved until he procured another job. This was a time when Claude could really thank God for giving him the ability to be self-employed. Having plumbing and carpentry skills at a time like this was invaluable.

He was always getting calls from relatives and friends of previous customers. The original customers always returned from time to time also. Being totally out of work was something that Claude never experienced and thought he probably never would. His car was entirely paid for. He had enough money saved to theoretically pay his bills for another year at least. He was a bit lonely, but given his track record of taking up with women who didn't have his best interest at heart, he was okay to stay to himself for the near future.

Notwithstanding, he did have several sex ships going on. He wanted to entertain tonight, so he looked forward to contacting a friend or two or three, whichever it took for him to hit pay dirt. He remembered that Mr. Bernard was short on his Black & Mild cigar stash, so he stopped at the quick stop and purchased a couple of boxes for his elderly buddy. He still didn't know how to take Mr. Bernard's water balloon joke. Did he annoy the old fellow with his "I still think you should be driving" statement? Or was Mr. Bernard just in a jovial mood?

He went home, showered, and attempted to watch an old movie. Claude loved nostalgia. One of his favorites was *Things to Do in Denver when You're Dead*, a twenty-plus-year-old movie starring Andy Garcia, Treat Williams, Bill Nunn, and William Forsythe. He really wanted to nap for a couple of hours before he contacted his prospective sex partner for the night, and he had to deliver the cigars to Mr. Bernard. He just wanted the movie to lullaby him. However, midway through the movie, he heard actor Treat Williams utter dialogue that really intrigued him.

Treat (Critical Bill in the movie) was in the midst of having terse words with Bill Nunn (Easy Winn in the movie) when he said, "That's the trouble with you mudflats [derisively referring to black folks], that's why ya'll are falling apart, y'all don't stand up for one another." Having not followed the movie because of exhaustion, he really wasn't sure what the two actors were arguing about. But those words resonated with Claude because of how true they were and still are.

It was a problem with his people that, to Claude, just wouldn't seem to go away. Nor could Claude see a solution for the inner racial problem he saw and experienced every day. His latest issue with the tyrant nurse Barbara was the kind of thing that just made Claude shake his head and suck through his teeth. Where the heck did she come from? Who the hell would hire a slob like that? He'd bet his life that aberration of a female would never have behaved like that if Carter were white.

The things she said to him and Carter: "I'll call the cops on you. You know how quick they are to shoot niggers." Why would anyone harbor such ill will toward strangers who were black like her? Where did it come from? Why would anyone say to a paraplegic, "It ain't my fault you're paralyzed"? Geez, how callous! He could hear the hateful venom in the inflection of her voice.

*Why?* thought Claude. *Why is there such anger between us? Geez, we are all victims of the same social degradation, the same hypocritical social order. Why do we hate one another like that?*

It brought to mind a song by the talented Mr. John Legend. The song was titled "Who Did that to You" from the Quentin Tarantino movie *Django*. He sighed out loud, thought about what Mr. Bernard said about the importance of peace of mind, and before he knew it, he had dozed off again into an unintentional deep sleep.

After two and a half hours of deep slumber, Claude was awakened by the ring of his landline phone. He jumped out of bed and answered his phone. It was Ms. Evans, the family friend and barrister.

"Hello," said the freshly awakened Claude.

"Hey, Mr. Paine. It's Ms. Evans. How are you?"

"Oh, I'm fine, Ms. Evans. How are you?"

"Well, young man, if I'm alive and awake, I'm always fine," said Ms. Evans. "Mr. Paine, I have extraordinary good news for you. Can you be in my office by 11 a.m. tomorrow?"

"Sure. So it's good news, huh?" said Claude. "Can you wet my whistle a little by just giving me a hint?"

"No can do," said Ms. Evans. "I will not spoil the suspenseful surprise that awaits you. Just be here on time tomorrow, young man, okay?" replied Ms. Evans.

"Will do," said Claude. "Hey, Ms. Evans, just one more thing before you go."

"Okay, young man, what is it?" replied Ms. Evans.

"Well, it's not that I don't appreciate it, but you've been a friend of my family all my life," said Claude, "so why do you call me Mr. Paine?"

"Well, Mr. Paine, you've never given me permission to address you as Claude or anything else during our business-related meetings. To do that without permission, well, that's rude," she continued. "It contradicts the way I was raised. That's akin to popping over your home without an invitation or removing a hat from someone's head on my own volition. I never do either. Okay, young man?"

"Okay, well, you can call me Claude, Ms. Evans," said Claude.

"Okay, fine, Claude," said Ms. Evans. "Just don't ever call me Elaine, and you and I will be fine. Cool?"

Claude chuckled and said, "Yeah, Ms. Evans, that's cool. See you in the morning, and thanks for everything. I really appreciate all that you're doing, so thanks again, and I'll see you in the a.m."

Claude remembered that he was going to contact one of his sex partners before he fell asleep. He was pleased with Ms. Evans for calling and inadvertently awakening him to give him some good news to look forward to—and keep him from sleeping all night. He was thinking about whom to call for tonight's sexual tryst.

While at the market some two to three weeks ago, he had bumped into an old sex partner friend of his from high school, a former classmate named Parris Simmons, whom he used to bunn when they were in high school. Since he hadn't seen her in over a year, he wasn't so sure he wanted to spend that kind of time with her. The last time he dated her, almost a year ago, she had converted into a born-again Christian, which to him was cool. He admired anyone who was seeking God through religion. It didn't matter which religion.

However, Parris was quite the sickening sort. Every other word was "Praise the Lord" or "Thank you, Jesus," which was also cool, but she behaved in a way that it was like she was, as his mother used to say, "Holier than thou." She never owned up to anything negative she did or apologized for anything. She had grown so self-righteous that she behaved like she truly believed she was never wrong, like the Pope had nothing on her. She gossiped like an old maid, talked about anyone who wasn't a Christian contemptuously, like they were lower than her.

If she insulted anyone, she immediately blamed them for provoking the insulting words *she* used so that anytime she said anything that annoyed anyone, it was ultimately their fault. She would then say as an affront, "I'll pray for you, brother [or sister]." It was as though she believed everyone was always wrong and in need of prayer but her. If she was caught in a lie (like the time Claude gave her a manuscript his mother had written that she swore she read but she couldn't tell him anything about it) or told that if she was really a Christian, she would wait until she was married before having sex again, she would act as if you hadn't said anything to her. It was like everyone else should live according to her morals but her and that since she was so close to God, only she was able to do anything she wanted and still remain in God's grace.

She used to swear that she didn't hold on to anything negative and that she never lied. But Claude remembered telling her that he didn't appreciate the condescending way she had begun to talk to him, like he was a little boy or her son. He remembered not seeing or talking to her for four months after that.

When he did call her to wish her season's greeting that Thanksgiving, the first words out of her holy, sacred, sanctified mouth were "Hey, Claude, I been praying for you every night for what you said to me last time."

Not remembering what their last exchange was about, Claude remembered saying, "Hey, Parris, you lost me. Please refresh my memory. What the heck were we talking about the last time we talked? I'm sorry, dear, but I don't remember."

"Oh, you know," said Parris, "when you said you don't like the way I talk to you. It annoyed me. It was unpleasant, so I decided to pray for you."

"Oh," said Claude. "That shit. Geez, woman, I didn't even remember that! Okay, miss—I don't hold on to things, so keep praying for me. I can use all the prayer I can get. But try to remember to pray for yourself that one day you'll be able to look at your own faults and that you'll grow up enough to say the words 'I, Parris Simmons, was wrong' or 'I'm sorry for what I, Parris Simmons, said or did.' Try praying for that, okay?"

Man, oh man, she got so hot she looked like her head was going to pop. Like the old saying goes, "The truth will set you free, but first it will piss you off."

*Geez*, he thought. What a fucking, full-of-shit, I-got-Jesus-so-I'm-better-than-you shrew of a female she had become. For even considering contacting her, Claude was unhappy with himself for wasting his own time. He then unknowingly said out loud, "That woman is a true Bible-thumping, sacred-soul, hypercritic pain-in-the-ass. I might be horny tonight, but I'll never be so desperate to put up with an annoying woman like her for five minutes again. I'll masturbate all night first."

"People who can make you believe in absurdities—can make you commit atrocities!"

—Francois-Marie ("Voltaire") Arouet,
French philosopher


Most of my Niggahs are CucKoo, easy to gas to shoot you.

—Mr. Trevor George "Busta Rhymes" Smith Jr.,
rapper, actor, entertainer

# CHAPTER 17

Claude then considered a night with Meechie, a woman he met one afternoon while grocery shopping. He had never spent any carnal time with her. He and Meechie had a breakfast date a few weeks ago. They also talked several times for hours on the phone. To date, he had never been romantic with her and decided he would invite her to his apartment and prepare dinner for her. Meechie accepted his invitation, but she also informed Claude that she was not available until tomorrow night. Claude was pleased because Meechie Hernandez (who was half–Puerto Rican and half-Dominican) was extremely attractive. Her only obvious physical flaw was her stomach, which looked like she swallowed a small watermelon whole.

Meechie, a so-called recovering drug addict, had recently reunited with her only child, who had been in foster care since she was five years old, a ten-year-old daughter whose father was African American. Although he was horny tonight, he decided to wait until tomorrow. He had a deep sleep, which for some reason Claude seemed to be experiencing more now than ever. He took a shower, got dressed, and since he had over two hours to kill before his appointment with the family barrister, Ms. Evans, he decided to stop on Route 22 and have breakfast at the Trolley Car diner.

When he arrived, he noticed that one of the short-order cooks was the same guy he saw talking to the wretched Barbara Steele, his brother's former attendant from hell. Claude believed he was addicted to the turkey sausages at the Red Bull Inn, but he liked the cheese omelets at the Trolley Car even more, so he ordered a bowl of oatmeal, a cheese omelet, an order of turkey sausages, and French fries instead of his usual home fries.

When the cook (Harvey), who was apparently a friend of Barbara's, received Claude's breakfast order slip, a heinous, evil, vindictive countenance engulfed his entire being. In the midst of preparing Claude's omelet, Harvey cleared his throat, hawked up a glob of mucus-filled sputum, and lathered the interior of Claude's omelet with the vile, thick, yellowish, viscous, bogey-mixed fluid. Harvey then picked his nose clean and took the moist bogey out and mixed that into Claude's order of oatmeal.

Claude received his breakfast platter, prayed, and commenced eating. After his first fork full of the most foul-tasting omelet he ever put in his mouth, he heard someone call his name. The restaurant was less than a quarter full, so the cook (Harvey) was taking a break and decided to introduce himself to Claude.

"You're Mr. Claude Paine, right?"

"Yes, and you are?" said Claude.

"Never mind my name," said Harvey. "Do you know a Ms. Barbara Steele?"

"Sure, she was an attendant for my wheelchair-bound brother for a couple of days," replied Claude.

"Yeah, well, she told me that you and your brother treated her like shit and threatened to beat her up," said Harvey.

"Well, she is a liar and the absolute worst attendant that my brother ever had. A real slob she is. Why, is she a friend of yours?" said Claude.

"No, she not a friend, *brother*. She's my wife," said Harvey.

Claude, who had stopped eating the omelet and was now putting sugar and a pat of butter in his bogey-laden oatmeal, looked Harvey in the eye and said, "Well, my brother, you ain't bragging about that, are you?" said Claude.

"No, smartass." Harvey was now laughing heartily. "I gotta get back to work. Enjoy the rest of your breakfast," said Harvey between his sadistic calculated chuckles.

It then hit Claude why his omelet was so foul tasting. Claude was now livid. It took everything in him not to jump over the counter and beat Harvey about his face and head to within an inch of his life or at least stuff his head into the deep fryer. Harvey, still chuckling, looked at Claude with one of the most sinister gazes Claude had ever beheld. The moment seemed to last for a half hour (even though it was only a matter of seconds).

Claude pushed the contaminated breakfast away from himself, grabbed his bill, and commenced to leave the establishment, but not before summoning the manager. The manager, a Mr. Dibble, who was familiar with Claude and his family, listened to Claude's story of disgust at length. He then asked one of his waiters to bring him Claude's plate. Mr. Dibble opened the omelet, which, save for the one fork full Claude ate, was almost whole and still intact. He was unable to discern if anything foul had been added to it. He smelled it and again came up with nothing to raise his eyebrows.

Mr. Dibble then tasted a fork full and, without chewing it, was able to taste Harvey's sputum, so he immediately spit it out into a napkin and discarded it. He was beyond disgusted. He told Claude that he didn't have to pay his bill. He then told Claude how sorry he was, and he implored Claude to return and that Claude's next two visits to the restaurant would be on the house.

"Let me handle this, Mr. Paine," said Mr. Dibble, "and please try to enjoy your day."

Claude left the restaurant so angry that he considered going back and shooting Harvey. Wow, what a fucking, ignorant bitch T.A.N. that Barbara was.

What Harvey and Barbara had actually done was live up to Claude's negative expectations about some of his own people. This slob of a woman had disrupted his and his brother's daily routines with her bullshit and created a rift with her dumb-ass, vile husband that Claude didn't know and whom, until the preparation of his contaminated breakfast, had never interacted with. En route to one of Ms. Evans's offices in Manhattan (she had recently passed the New York bar exam, and she was setting up shop there also), Claude could think of nothing else.

This was not the only time a T.A.N. woman had recently created a rift between Claude and a T.A.N. stranger. There was that one morning, a few weeks past, when Claude was in the middle of his morning run. As always, when a car rode past him, he waved or gave a thumbs-up to the passing motorist. Well, on this morning, one of the cars he had just given a thumbs-up to did a U-turn and came speeding back towards Claude.

When the car reached him, the driver lowered his window and said, "Yo, nigger, you got a fucking problem?"

"No," said Claude. "Why are you asking me that?"

"Well," said the irate, incensed driver, "my woman said that when we rode past you, you gave us the finger, and I wanted to know what the fuck I did to you to deserve that."

"Listen, sir, your woman is grossly mistaken. Whenever a car approaches me when I'm jogging"—since Claude always jogged into approaching traffic to avoid being hit from behind—"I always give a wave or a thumbs-up. She probably mistook my thumbs-up gesture as a middle finger." Claude continued, "I would never give a fuck-you finger to a complete stranger for nothing."

"Well," said irate driver, "just make sure you don't get shit twisted." Brandishing an automatic pistol, he delivered his unveiled threat.

Claude gave a long, exasperated sigh as he looked at the woman sitting in the passenger seat of the irate driver's car with an evil smirk on her face.

*This is what T.A.N.s do*, he thought.

# CHAPTER 18

*Good Lord, what the fuck is wrong with these damn ignorant T.A.N.s? How much more of this crap do I have to take?* What had dawned on Claude was the statistics of black-on-black crime. The more he interacted with his people, the more disgusted many of them made him. He now understood the words of the song by the old-school rap group Cypress Hill: "Here is something you can't understand—how I can just kill a man." At this very moment, that was exactly what he wanted to do with Harvey, the fat Negress Barbara, and the ignorant T.A.N. cunt who tried to prod her stupid-ass boyfriend into shooting him.

Claude was so disgusted he pulled over and purged his stomach in a futile attempt to regurgitate the disgusting piece of egg he swallowed. As he continued on, his mind was inundated with thoughts of retribution. He wanted to torture and beat to a pulp both Harvey and that ignorant bitch T.A.N. Barbara.

*I just can't let anyone get away with doing something like that to me! I'll never forget it*, he thought.

So engrossed was he in his vitriolic thoughts of vengeance that he arrived at Ms. Evans's office in Manhattan in what seemed like seconds.

Prior to getting on the elevator, he went to the sweetshop in the lobby and purchased some mints and seltzer water to remove the vomit taste out of his palate from his recently purged abdomen. He arrived at Ms. Evans's office almost half an hour earlier and was told by her secretary to have a seat while she summoned her boss.

Ms. Evans appeared a few minutes later, again dressed to kill, and of course, every hair immaculately in place. "Wow, Claude, look at the look on your face! Geez, what the hell happened to you?"

"Long story," said Claude. "How about that good news, Ms. Evans? What do you have in store for me?"

"Well, young man, you don't have to return to Johnson & Johnson anymore. I took care of your exit interview. Here is your severance pay." Ms. Evans then handed Claude a check for eight weeks' pay. "Also, I have three letters of recommendation."

"Wow, thank you, Ms. Evans! How the heck did you get all that?" Claude queried.

"It seems your Mr. Deltoid had already been charged with sexual harassment before the melee, so he was terminated after your fracas in his office."

"Huh," said Claude.

"He had plenty of enemies there. Mr. Salvador despised him something fierce for the condescending way he treated him along with the piss-poor references he made about Latinos. His secretary told Mr. Retter that Mr. Deltoid continually referred to him as the resident Nazi, so Mr. Retter wasn't a fan of Mr. Deltoid's either. With that information and my reputation, Johnson & Johnson was scared to death that another lawsuit would add insult to injury, so we cut a deal to save your professional reputation and to save their business reputation from public scrutiny for hiring such a dickhead as Mr. Deltoid and keeping him employed in the midst of an ongoing sexual harassment lawsuit. The police couldn't get anyone to confirm his attempted-murder accusations, so at the request of Johnson & Johnson, the charges were dropped. Now, my dear Claude, you're free to go with a fat check to boot. Dig me, young man."

"Sweet Jesus, Ms. Evans, you are the schiznick. My God, is there anything I owe you?" said Claude.

"Nah, this was really a piece of cake, young man. Just be sure to tell everyone you know how really good I am. Just drum me up some more business, and all will be well between you and I, okay?"

"Sure thing," said Claude. "Wow, eight weeks' severance pay! I never would've dreamed of it." Claude was suddenly ecstatic.

"Oh, two more things," said Ms. Evans. "Call your mother before she passes out from happiness. I already gave her the good news. And I'll contact you in about three weeks to go to court and to apply to have your police record expunged. Now, young man, keep your butt out of trouble, and stop letting the small percentage of ignorant black folk rile you up. They are not worth your freedom, okay?"

"Sure thing," said Claude.

He then grabbed Ms. Evans and hugged her like he was her lover. So tight was his hug that the ambient aroma of the expensive perfume that emanated from her neck began to sexually arouse him.

*What a motherfucking-class act!* he thought as he made his way to his car. Claude, having just received some extraordinarily good news, now looked forward to his dinner date with Meechie. He went directly to the bank and deposited his eight weeks' severance paycheck. He felt exactly like what Wiz Khalifa and 2-Chainz, the rappers, said in their song that was used in the soundtrack of the *Fast and Furious 6* movie: "This moment, we own it." So ecstatic was he that he had forgotten about what the disgusting idiot T.A.N. Harvey had done to his food. He now entertained no thoughts of vengeance.

# CHAPTER 19

He now was thinking about what he would prepare for the gorgeous Meechie. When he got to the market, still floating on clouds nine, ten, and eleven, he decided on seafood. He purchased two pounds of raw shrimps (twenty-one to twenty-five counts per pound), two pounds of sea scallops, and two and a half pounds of russet potatoes—perfect, he thought, for some really good homemade French fries. He also purchased a pound of fresh asparagus. Meechie was due at his house at 5:00 p.m., so he had over three hours to straighten up his apartment and prepare dinner. When his cleanup work had culminated and his attempt at becoming a world-class chef began. He had planned to fry the shrimp and grill the large sea scallops with some fresh mushrooms and green peppers he already had in his refrigerator. The asparagus he decided to steam with a tad of margarine a couple of sprinkles of Romano and Parmesan cheese. For desert, he had bought some fresh strawberries that he planned to serve with whipped cream.

He set up his table with class. His muslin-silk combination tablecloth that he only used during the Christmas and Thanksgiving holidays was first. His elegant 100 percent silver candleholders and sweet-scented candles followed. The dinner was all ready, save for the frying of the shrimp and French fries, which had to wait until Meechie arrived so that they were hot when dinner was served.

At 5:50 p.m. his doorbell rang, and although he was slightly perturbed at Meechie arriving late (Claude was raised to be a stickler for time), he was still extremely excited to greet her and let her in. When he opened the door after the obligatory "Who is it?" he was quite surprised and a tad annoyed. There stood Meechie and her ten-year-old daughter.

"Geez, Meechie, why didn't you tell me you were bringing your daughter? I would have prepared more food," said a clearly irritated Claude. This was a game Claude had been through before with some other woman on their first date to his apartment. It was a game he abhorred. It seemingly was what some women did as a way of saying, "There'll be no sex tonight, mister."

"Oh, well, I didn't know she would be coming. At the last minute, the babysitter cancelled," lied Meechie.

"Mommy, that ain't true. You told me last night we'd be going to dinner over your friend's house. You didn't tell me nothing about no babysitter," said her daughter, Marissa.

"Hmm," said Claude, "babysitter, huh?" He now wanted to ask Meechie to leave, but he was already too far out on the limb. "Okay, ladies, dinner is almost ready. You two can wash up as I put the finishing touches on our sumptuous repast."

"Huh," said Meechie, "what's that?"

"Just another way of saying 'our delicious meal,'" said Claude.

The two made their way to the bathroom to wash, and Claude, who used a mixture of safflower oil and olive oil to fry (he had been told by his mother that these oils were much healthier than using animal fat, canola oil, or even vegetable oil), retrieved both oils from his cabinet and made his way to the kitchen.

The two females were really hungry, and since Claude had anticipated that only he and Meechie would be the only ones dining, he had only prepared enough for two.

"Mommy, these candles smell really good, don't they?" said the young Marissa.

Meechie, still embarrassed and a tad angry at Marissa for exposing her babysitter lie, mumbled something to her daughter in Spanish, which was indiscernible to Claude. He set the table, and both women started in immediately with the salt and pepper. Then Marissa, smacking her lips at what she was about to eat, reached for the ketchup.

"Whoa," said Claude. "Ladies, let us not touch our food until we've said grace, please."

Meechie sighed in disgust and said, "Oh, okay."

Marissa then said, "Mr. Claude, we never say grace at home." It drew an angry glare from her mom.

"Oh yes, we do sometimes, young lady. Stop being so fresh, please, and pass me the ketchup," barked Meechie sternly. After Claude blessed the table, the two females went at it. Both were eating like this was their first meal in a week. Claude wanted to start some dinnertime conversation, but he chose not to dare interrupt the two of them while they were in the midst of wolfing down their meal.

"Mommy, these shrimps and scallops are so good, ain't they?" said Marissa.

"Yeah, they are," replied Meechie between the poorly masticated clumps of food she anxiously continued to place in her mouth nonstop.

"Wow, Mister Claude, you can really cook," said Marissa.

"Yeah, this is good," said Meechie.

When the two were done, they immediately got up from the table, leaving the two cleaned-of-every-morsel plates behind. Marissa went to the bathroom, and Meechie sat on Claude's recliner, kicked back, let out an obnoxious belch (without saying 'Excuse me'), and said, "Wow, Claude, that was a meal fit for queens."

"Thank you. Now, let me clean the dishes," he said aloud, expecting/hoping Meechie would say, "Let me help you." But he waited in vain as the offer never came.

Meechie said, "Well, while you're doing the dishes, I'm going to have me a smoke. Is it okay?"

"Well, sure," said Claude, "but you're going to have to step outside. I don't allow smoking in my home."

"Oh," said Meechie, "you're one of them, huh, okay? I'll go outside. Let me out, please."

"Oh, you can go out on the terrace. The sliding door is open," said Claude, growing more disgusted with this classless woman with each passing moment.

"When Marissa comes out of the bathroom, let her know I'm having a smoke," said Meechie.

"Sure thing," replied Claude. He now, while washing the dishes, wished anyone would call so that he could feign an emergency and ask the two to leave. When Marissa came out of the bathroom, he informed her where her mommy was and asked her if she wanted to watch some TV or play some video games.

"No, thank you, Mr. Claude. But I would like to get on your computer."

"Oh, okay," Claude reluctantly agreed. Her mom, in the midst of lighting a second cigarette, was not close to coming in and joining them. "Well, young lady, what grade are you in?" asked Claude inquisitively.

"I'm in fifth grade," Marissa replied. "That dinner was really good, Mr. Claude. Most of the time, Mom don't cook. We eat food from the Chinese takeout—you know, fried wings, shrimp fried rice, and stuff like that. Or we eat sandwiches and potato chips all the time," said Marissa.

"Oh, is that right?" said Claude. "Well, I'll talk to Mom and see if I can get her to start cooking once in a while, okay?"

"Thanks, Mr. Claude," Marissa continued. "Actually, the last time I had a really good cooked meal like this was about three months ago, when I spent the night at my friend's house."

*Geez, that's terrible*, Claude thought, but he dared not express those sentiments out loud.

Just then Meechie came in, reeking of tobacco smoke. She made her way back to the recliner, sat down, and let out a deep belly belch. It was so loud this time that she had no choice but to excuse her manner-lacking self.

Claude was impressed at Marissa's request to use the computer. They didn't have one at home, according to Marissa, and she had recently discovered that she was the only student in her class bereft of a computer.

"Well," said Claude, "let's cut a deal, little lady. If you still don't have one at first report card time, if you show me a report card with no Cs, Ds, or Fs on it, I will buy you a computer if it's okay with

Mommy." He thought it was terrible this woman didn't cook for her daughter and didn't provide her with all that she needed for school. "Also," said Claude, "since school is beginning next week, do you have all your school supplies?"

"No, not at all. Mommy said we were going to go school shopping last week, but we never went," said Marissa.

"Oh no," said Claude, pleased that the young lady had grown comfortable with him enough to be candid and sincere.

"Well, Meechie, bring her back tomorrow, and let's go get her stuff for school, okay?" said Claude.

"Bet I ain't got no money, brother, so if you gonna pay for all of it, then what time you want us to be here?" said Meechie.

"Is any time after twelve noon cool?" asked Claude.

Claude then put on some Miles Davis (the song was "Freedom Jazz Dance," one of his favorites). He chose smooth jazz so as not to disturb Marissa on the computer and to allow Meechie to continue her post-meal rest, and he went back in the kitchen to prepare the strawberries and whipped-cream dessert and finish the dinner dishes alone. After about three or four minutes, he peeked in the living room and caught Meechie dozing off and Marissa hard at work on the computer.

He gingerly walked past the slumbering, coarse, wouldn't-help-him-wash-dishes Meechie and placed Marissa's dessert next to her on the computer table. Walking back to the kitchen as he past Meechie, he gingerly placed her dessert on the end table next to the recliner so as not to awaken her.

While washing the dishes, Claude heard Marissa ask Meechie aloud, "Mommy, how do you spell the word *consume*?" There was no answer, so he told Marissa how to spell it. He heard Mom snoring and decided to let her catch a few winks while he finished his post-dinner cleanup. Just as he finished washing and drying the last dish, he heard Meechie let out a disgusting loud rat-a-tat fart between snores. Claude just negatively shook his head.

"Ooh, Mommy," said Marissa out loud, awakening her mother from her post-dinner nap.

"What, who, *que pasa*?" said Meechie, unaware that she had dozed. "Did somebody say something to me."

"Yeah, Mommy, you just let out a big stink while you were sleeping," said Marissa.

"Who, me?" said the still-not-fully-awake Meechie. "Oh my, I'm sorry, Claude. Forgive me." She and Marissa both laughed heartily. Claude found nothing at all funny.

When the dishes were done after about twenty minutes, Claude, who sat on the sofa alone, said after a feigned yawn, "Hey, I've had a busy day, and I'm going to catch a few winks. Please come tomorrow, and we can all get Marissa her school supplies, cool?"

"So you throwing us out now, huh?" said Meechie.

"No," said Claude, "don't say that."

"Oh, I'm just kidding," said Meechie. "Thanks for the dinner. We'll see you tomorrow."

Claude got their coats, shook Marissa's hand, gave Meechie a light, titular hug. Then he lied through his teeth when he said, "Thank you both for a lovely evening. See y'all tomorrow." When the two left and boarded the cab Claude had called for them, he was so relieved.

# CHAPTER 20

"Thank God that's over," he said out loud. "Just another class-less female. Seems I'm doomed to take up with women like that. God, please help save me from myself!" Claude, now despondent, was thinking of his past, about when he started dating, and how most of his life he spent very little time familiarizing himself with his prospective girlfriends before having sex with them. For some reason, his nostalgic thoughts of previous lovers quickly jumped from old girlfriends to his eldest brother, Clarence, who was currently serving time in Rahway State Prison for possession with intent to deliver.

Clarence, according to Claude, took no tea for the fever. He was absolutely the toughest guy on the east side of Paterson, New Jersey. Clarence's reputation was not without merit. Claude never had to fight when he was young because other guys in the neighborhood would say, "That's Clay's (Clarence's nickname) little brother, yo."

He avoided most fights until he turned twelve and got into a scuffle with Terrence. Terrence was fifteen at the time and a sophomore in high school. Anyway, during a pickup basketball game, Claude, usually too young to play ball with Terrence and his contemporaries, was asked into the game because there were only nine guys and they needed one more to choose up a game. Well, midway through the game, Claude, who wasn't very athletic, missed an easy layup, and Terrence started yelling at and berating him something fierce.

When Claude said, "Fuck you, pussy. I ain't no punk," Terrence grabbed the ball and busted Claude in his head. A fight then broke out, and Terrence really put it to Claude, rattling off a four- or five-punch combination of unanswered blows. Claude, now afraid of the older Terrence, then stopped fighting and ran home to get his brother Carter to fight Terrence for him.

Claude came through the door crying, and he wasn't sure if the only one home was Clarence, who Claude felt was a little too old to come and beat up Terrence. Sniffling when he opened the door, Claude, in a whining voice, asked Clarence if Carter was home. Clarence, seeing his little brother that upset, inquired, "Why do you need Carter, Claude?"

"Why? Because that fucking Terrence has been bullying me and he needs his ass kicked," said Claude.

Clarence was now livid. He yelled at Claude for running home from a fight and vociferously said, "No, Claude, Carter ain't here." Carter was in his bedroom, playing video games with his pal Mike Burwell. Clarence then started getting dressed and prompted Claude to accompany him back to the playground. Claude was even happier that big brother Clay was going to do the job. Much to Claude's surprise and chagrin, when the two arrived at the playground, Clarence angrily prompted Claude, "Go head and kick Terrence's ass. I'll be right here."

Claude was petrified, but he now had no choice. He then squared off with Terrence and got in two quick blows, slightly busting Terrence's bottom lip. Terrence then let loose with another four- or five-punch combination, knocking Claude squarely on his ass. A crowd had now gathered and let out a collective "Whoa!" when Terrence landed the blow that knocked the younger Claude on the fleshy part of his buttocks. He immediately got off the ground and heard a loud "That's enough!" come from Clarence.

Clarence then cautioned Terrence, "Back up off my brother, motherfucker."

And Terrence, who was well aware of Clarence and his reputation, complied with Clarence's demand immediately.

"Come on, Claude."

Then he and Clarence walked home from the playground. When they came in the door, there stood Carter and Mike Burwell, wondering what happened. Clay then asked the two to leave for a moment, that he needed a few minutes to talk to the young Claude.

After the two went outside, Clarence started in on Claude. "Listen, little brother, don't ever run from a fight again—ever! Always put up the best fight you can. Fuck it if you win, and fuck it if you lose. Just put up the best fight you can. Swing and keep on swinging until it's broken up or all is over. If you getting your ass kicked, then bite the motherfucker, or get close enough to him and try to gouge one of his eyes out. Just don't ever turn tail and run—*ever*! If you do, you gonna have me to deal with, and I'll kick your ass worse than anybody else. You dig?"

Claude was silent for a moment. He then murmured, "Sure, Clarence, sure."

Clarence then went back to watching TV as if nothing had happened.

# CHAPTER 21

When Claude came out of his deep thoughts about Clarence, he promised himself that he would visit his oldest brother this weekend. About 9:00 p.m. that night, it dawned on Claude that he had purchased two boxes of Black & Mild cigars for Mr. Bernard that he never brought to him, so before it got too late, he wanted to bring them to his elderly buddy. He made his way down the road to Mr. Bernard's house with the intention of just dropping off the cigars. When he arrived and rang the doorbell, one of the most stunningly beautiful, body-built-for-speed woman he had ever seen in his life answered the door.

Claude stood there with his mouth agape. "Can I help you?" said Lady Lovely.

"Aaah . . . sure," stammered Claude. "Eerrr, I'm here to see Mr. Bernard." Claude, having never met Ms. Lovely, then said, "Miss, who are you?"

Lady Lovely immediately countered Claude's obviously ridiculous question with a quick "Who are *you*?"

"Oh, miss, please forgive me, I'm Claude Paine." He extended his hand in the process.

"Okay, I'm Ms. Betty Willis. Mr. Bernard, as you call him, is my father."

"Wow, I knew he had children, but he and I never discussed you before," said Claude.

"Well, is that some kind of slight?" Betty replied.

"Oh no," said Claude. "Please forgive my less-than-savory intro-duction. I must admit, Ms. Willis, I'm quite taken by your beauty. It caught me off guard."

"Well, young man, my father is not heating the street. Young brother, please come in."

"Oh, okay," said Claude as he made his way to the living room and had a seat.

"One minute," said Betty as she went upstairs to alert her father that he had company.

"Hey, Claude! What's up, good buddy? I'll be right down," said Mr. Bernard from the upstairs bedroom. He then slowly came down the steps. Claude could see by his countenance that he was a bit forlorn.

"Hey, Mr. Bernard, here're your stogies that I forgot to bring the other day," said Claude.

"Oh, thanks, young buddy. I was just going to send my daugh-ter to buy me a couple of packs. These, as usual, are right on time. Hey I meant to ask you last time I saw you. Have you had any of those horrible dreams lately?" said Mr. Bernard.

"No Sir. No dreams lately. There is a God. So, Mr. Bernard, that's your daughter, huh?"

"Yeah, why? You in my house, lusting, you little pig!" replied Mr. Bernard in jest.

"No, no, you know I would never disrespect you like that," said Claude.

"Yeah, sure, you know, Claude, I was once twenty-five or twen-ty-six—however the hell old you are. And I got a dick too, so tell that crap to someone else, okay?" said Mr. Bernard, and the two good buddies broke out in laughter.

"Like you're always saying to me, Mr. Bernard, what's been troubling you? As you came down the steps, your face was long and devoid of its normal joviality," said Claude.

"Joviality, huh? Ain't that some cute shit?" said Mr. Bernard. "Well, son, it's an astute observation. I've had a really difficult day today. That's why my daughter is here."

"Are you going to share it with me?" said Claude.

"Sure," said Mr. Bernard. "First, young buddy, tell me about your case. Any new news?"

"Sure is, sir. You are a very intuitive person, Mr. Bernard," said Claude.

"Well, junior, I call it wisdom. Once you've been on this earth for a while, if you have any sense, you'll develop that kind of wisdom also," said Mr. Bernard.

Claude then updated his elderly friend about all the goings-on of the last few days, beginning with the sullen sow nursing attendant, Barbara, and right up to the dinner he had just prepared for the coarse Meechie and her young daughter, Marissa.

"Fantastic," said Mr. Bernard. "Severance pay and letters of recommendation to boot, huh? Wow, Claude, you must've been kissed by angels the day you were born! Your family is bosom buddies with the best criminal attorney in northern New Jersey. Geez, can you be any more blessed than that? Save for that ignorant bastard T.A.N. that served you the foul omelet, everything has been peachy keen, huh? Well, young man, here's what happened to me today."

But just as Mr. Bernard began going over the happenings of his day with Claude, they heard "Dad, do you still need me to go to the store?" His daughter Betty called loudly from upstairs.

"Oh no, honey, I'm cool. Thanks anyway," said Mr. Bernard.

"Okay," replied the gorgeous Betty.

"Anyway, Claude, you know about the illnesses I have. Well, every ninety days, I have to get a full blood test and then pay a visit to the endocrinologist. Well, today, I went to my scheduled appointment with my family doctor to get my blood work form, and I encountered one of the most ignorant young black men I ever interacted with in my life, a man you would call a T.A.N.. He must have been at least fifty-five to sixty years younger than me. First, the butt wipe told me the doctor wasn't coming in today—until I showed him my appointment card. Then he said he would fill out my blood work form himself. Well, the last time this jerk did my blood work form, this idiot put the wrong codes on it, and the insurance company refused to pay until they received the corrected form. So I really didn't want him to fill out squat for me, and I asked him not to do it, that I'd prefer waiting for the doctor to do it. Claude, you should have seen the glare he shot at me. It's what we used to call 'gritting' on someone. I couldn't believe anyone that much younger than me would do something like that, behave in that manner and be disrespectful. Well, you know me, young buddy," Mr. Bernard continued. "I don't take that kind of shit from no one unless you got a blue suit, a badge, and a gun. Anyway, I read that jokester the riot act. Security had to separate us. It got so heated. The stupid ass then said, 'You gotta leave immediately, old man.' Do you believe that shit? Anyway, I told that faggot, 'Shit, *you* leave, Negro. I been coming here for thirty-plus years, and if I have to leave without treatment, I'll sue this fucking place. Then your fucking black ass won't have a job or ever be able to get another job in this field! He then immediately closed his damn pie hole post-haste."

Claude, having never heard the phrase *post-haste*, surmised it meant 'quickly'.

"So you see, young buddy, those T.A.N.s, as you call them, fuck with everybody black once in a while. My daughter who took me there really had a fit, and it was all I could do to calm her down so that security wouldn't ask us to leave," said Mr. Bernard.

"Wow," said Claude.

# CHAPTER 22

"Listen, youngster," said Mr. Bernard, "last week, I was watching CNN, with Don Lemon, and he was interviewing one of my favorite people, Mr. John McWhorter, a linguistics professor at Columbia University and author of the book *The Language Hoax*. Mr. McWhorter made a very salient point, a point that I wholly agree with and one I've yet to hear in the media, and it made me think of you. He said, and I paraphrase, 'The black man being killed by one white cop in a black neighborhood is a problem. But that same black man is in much more danger of being killed by another black man.' Oh, how so much I agree with him. He too is aware that black people's biggest problem is us. Yes, the police do present a problem sometimes—let's not deny or overlook that. However, what the hell are we as a people going to do about us killing one another? Then we behave like it's taboo to even talk about us killing one another. Imagine how the black mother feels to have to bury one, two, or even three of her sons. Most of our inner-racial killers really seem to like killing their own so much that they brag about it. In one of the rapper Nas's songs, "Suspect Witness," there's a guy in the background at the outset of the song, saying, 'I'm gonna get that nigger. Yeah, what?'

"Claude, I'm so tired of how we treat one another. Listen, buddy, I have to say to you, about that story you just told me about that T.A.N. putting something foul in your food—I'm not trying to rile you up, Claude, but if someone had done that to me, I, just like you, would've wanted to kill something too. I really do understand, Claude. Still, I just can't condone that kind of vengeful behavior.

When that jerk disrespected me at the doctor's office, I wanted to set him straight too. That's what made me think of you. Then you come here tonight and tell me a black cook put something disgusting in your food. You see, Claude, from my life's experiences, I know none of those colored men would have done any of that to either one of us if either one of us was white. Damn, I'm going to tell you that if black people like him bother you that bad, then get the hell away from them altogether. Move to a predominately Caucasian neighborhood, then see what's waiting for you. It's possible you'll do what Flavor Flav of the rap group Public Enemy said, that you'll 'jump out of the jelly into a jam.' Or you can do like Ruben "Hurricane" Carter did after this racist system took over twenty years of his life from him for a crime he clearly didn't commit—move to Canada.

"I'm not kidding, young man. You are caught between a rock and a hard place. You are experiencing the irresistible force meeting the immovable object. At this point, I really don't know what to tell you. Our fabric as a people is definitely deteriorating. We as a people continue to take two steps backwards for every one step forward. Now think of how that woman's daughter you invited to dinner is probably going to wind up with a mother like that. Last week, I went to Manhattan to see a doctor about having hip replacement surgery in the near future. I rode the subway. When the train arrived and the doors opened, this ignorant young black woman pushed passed me to get a seat. She was in her late teens or early twenties, and she pushed an eighty-year-old black man, a man old enough to be her great-granddaddy out of the way so that she, not the elderly man, could get a seat.

"When I sat in the seat next to her, a young black man, also early twenty-ish, stood there, looming over me like I had stolen his seat. Obviously, his girlfriend was the one who pushed past me, and there he stood, menacingly looming over me. I looked at him and said, 'Is this your girlfriend?' And with a threatening tone in his voice, he said, 'Yeah, you can see she is, old man.' I then asked him, 'Well, do you want me to get up and give you this seat so you can sit next to her?' Without any hesitation, he said, 'Yeah.' And he gritted on me something horrible. I'm telling you, Claude, if I had had my Desert

Eagle pistol with me, I would've given that jackass two in his belly. Anyway, almost every adult in the train car started saying loudly, almost in unison, 'You better not get up, sir' and 'Hey, mister, fuck him. Don't you dare move.' Just then his ignorant girlfriend said, 'Since we getting off next stop, honey, don't sit down. Fuck this old man.' She then pushed my leg very hard and brushed past me as she got up for emphasis and added insult to injury.

"Yeah, Claude, a lot of us are super fucked-up, like the former drug dealer Frank Lucas, who was portrayed by Denzel Washington in the movie *American Gangster*, once said in an interview, "One thing about my people—they will try you." Claude, what we do to one another is a pitiful reality we have to face. All I can do is tell you that if you hurt or kill one of those disrespectful asshole T.A.N.s and they're not in the process of putting your life in imminent danger, then you're going to fuck up your whole life. Yeah, it's really bad dealing with youngsters whom no one has ever taught manners or respect to. Think of how I felt when those kids treated me that way on the subway and in the doctor's office." Mr. Bernard's eyes were now beginning to tear up. "Yeah, they push you and try you, but you have to think of self-preservation first, young buddy, before anything else. When you see their bullshit coming, then run. I mean that both figuratively and literally. Run because they're coming with some serious provoking bullshit to try you. At that moment, calm reasoning may not be practical. Look, Claude, I once told you that racism is perhaps the root cause of T.A.N. creation. It may truly be how and why they were created. But we *have* to stop making excuses. We *have* to.

"Mr. McWhorter also said, and I paraphrase, that we blame all of our interactive negative behavior on racism. As if we will get better with one another once racism stops. That's like you, who was told by your doctor to lose weight. So you respond by telling him that if they first close all the supermarkets and stop selling food, then you will lose weight. What racist cops and other racists have in their heads is not the main problem we have today. Our main problem is us hurting and killing one another and then believing that we have to. It's tearing us apart and eating us alive. That professor John McWhorter is a true African American. Why? Because he is accepting the truth about his own people and seeking a solution. Like that Black Lives Matters movement, said Mr. McWhorter, we should start a blacks-stop-killing-blacks movement. That is simple and very feasible.

"You know, buddy, you got T.A.N.s wanting to shoot African Americans because they're trying to rob and/or disrespect us. Then you got African Americans wanting to shoot T.A.N.s because they push us, try us to the point of 'I gotta stop this asshole from either disrespecting or trying to hurt me.' Then here come other ethnic groups, watching us interact, saying, 'Geez, look how they treat one another.' Did you ever hear the saying 'Never argue with an idiot because someone walking past won't know the difference'?"

After his oratory, Mr. Bernard broke into a full-fledged cry. Claude was shocked, crushed. He then grabbed Mr. Bernard and hugged him in silence as the old man wept in his arms for about two whole minutes.

Out of the blue, Claude then said, "Wow Mr. Bernard—first, a water balloon and now with tears. You been wetting me up a lot lately."

"Shut up, you smart-ass," replied Mr. Bernard through some chuckles. They both broke out in a hearty laugh. Apparently, levity was exactly what both men needed at that moment.

# CHAPTER 23

When Claude left Mr. Bernard's home that night, he was really exhausted. What a tumultuous day and night! He had received the great news about a court case that was now over. He had prepared dinner that he ate none of because his date chose to be less than honest with him. He had found out who Meechie truly was. Even more importantly, he realized it was he who needed to change his approach when it came to dating women. He had been supportive of his dear friend Mr. Bernard, who truly needed *his* spiritual support this time. With the joy that helping someone close to him gave him, he felt really necessary, useful tonight. Last, but most certainly not least, he had met Mr. Bernard's daughter Ms. Betty Willis.

*What a real peach*, thought Claude. *Yeah, the woman is pretty. No doubt about it.* But what really moved Claude was this woman's body. *Wow*, he thought, *I know this lady is older than me, but so what?*

That was the kind of woman Claude really wanted—the strength of character she exuded and her self-confidence, which was also evident. Claude knew Ms. Betty Willis was about ten to twelve years older than him (Ms. Willis appeared to be in her mid to late thirties). Still, he made up his mind to at least try to make her acquaintance. He was tired of the women he was settling for. He accepted tonight that taking up with insincere, unsteady, coarse women who were loaded with guile was his own fault. Well, tonight might be exactly what he needed.

En route home, Claude stopped at the Sunoco Mini Mart (one stop) to gas up and to buy some snacks since he didn't eat dinner with his guests. When he arrived, he looked for the addict that panhandled and sold curios he made himself for some crack money. Claude looked on the side of the building, and there lay Herbie the hobo, as he was affectionately known in the area. He was sprawled out between the two milk carts that he usually sat on and also used to spread his legs and relax on, waiting for prospective customers.

Claude approached Herbie and noticed Herbie had been beaten up—not severely, but just enough to put the poor crack addict out of commission for a short while. Claude shook him gently, and Herbie, coming to slowly, moaned and then jumped out of his semiconscious condition and immediately went into a shell. He reacted like he thought his previous beating was about to continue.

"Hey," said Claude. "Hey, Herbie, it's me—Thick Guy." It was a nickname Herbie had chosen to bestow upon Claude.

"Oh, owww," Herbie said loudly as he rubbed his knotted-up, recently bashed-in forehead and face.

"Damn, Herbie," said Claude, "what the hell happened to you?"

"Oh, hey, well, Thick Guy, what time is it?"

Claude looked at his Elgin that he wore to impress Meechie and replied, "It's 11:45 p.m."

"Oh, wow," said Herbie, "it was about forty to forty-five minutes ago that I got here to sell the two shingles [wooden artwork] that I made and about four or maybe five young fucking niggers jumped me, beat me up, and took them." Herbie looked around to see if maybe the culprits had tossed his varnished shingles around somewhere. "Oh, damn," said Herbie. "Now I don't even have nothing to sell. Shit!"

Apparently, Herbie was more concerned about his crack money earnings than he was for his bashed-in dome piece or his compromised health. Claude did not really want to ask Herbie if he wanted to be taken to a hospital because, as usual, Herbie smelled like a freshly laid, steamy, heap of sheep dung.

He asked Herbie, "Hey, buddy, do you want me to call 911 for you?"

"No, no," said the foul-smelling addict. "No, I don't want no cops around here or to be sitting up in some hospital for four or five hours. Hey, do you feel like dropping me in front of the Red Bull Inn down the road, huh, Thick?"

"No, Herbie, you know I can't give anyone who smells like you a ride. That odor you carry around would stay in my car three or four days, and I just can't do that to my whip or myself," said Claude.

Herbie then broke out in a chuckle and replied, "Damn, Thick, you always was an honest motherfucker. Well, can you spot a brother some ends?" Money. Claude knew what Herbie was going to do with any money he gave him. He had recently broken Herbie out of the habit of asking him for money or trying to pedal some of his wares to Claude. But tonight, with some good fortune having already come his way, he peeled off a twenty-dollar bill and gave it to Herbie.

He then told Herbie he would get him a gallon bottle of water and some napkins from inside the mini mart so he could wash the encrusted blood, dirt, and sweaty funk off his face at the very least. Before entering the store, Claude, out of curiosity, just wanted to know if the guys who beat Herbie up and stole his artwork where familiar to him.

"Yeah, I've seen one of them here before, a couple of times," said Herbie. "I think the little niggers were college students out for some kicks or maybe even part of a fraternity in the middle of some hazing bullshit."

"Damn," said Claude. *These young stupid-ass T.A.N.s took advantage of a poor slob that bothered no one, a crack addict that was talented enough to try to earn a few bucks to support his deadly habit instead of robbing someone. Damn, these young ignorant idiots will stop at nothing*, he thought. "Hey, Herbie, wait right here. I'll be out with a cup of coffee and some napkins and water for you to at least wash yourself off a little."

"Sure, Thick, I'll wait. Thanks, bro," said Herbie.

Claude then entered the store, ordered forty dollars' worth of gas. Then he purchased a gallon jug of spring water, a small bar of soap, a cup of coffee, and a handful of napkins for Herbie. He then bought some sunflower seeds, a bag of honey-roasted peanuts, and a large bag of chips (that he knew he shouldn't be eating) for himself.

When he paid for all the items and made his way back outside, Herbie and the twenty dollars Claude just gave him were long gone. Claude chuckled and said to himself, "Geez, how stupid am I? Did I really think a crack addict who just got a fresh, crisp twenty-dollar bill was going to hang around? Oh well, time to get home."

# CHAPTER 24

Just as Claude pulled up to his apartment complex, his cell phone rang. The caller ID confirmed that it was his brother Carter.

"Hey, Claude," said Carter.

"Yeah, what's up, Carter?" replied Claude.

"You remember that fat slob Negress Barbara that we had to throw outta here?"

"Yeah, why? Don't remind me of her, please," said Claude.

"Well," said Carter, "some guy called here about an hour ago and said he was going to kill you. He said he was fat Negress's husband and that you got him fired. He said he didn't even know you or do nothing to you and that you lied to his boss and caused him to lose his job. He said he got our address from fat Negress and that he was coming to take care of both of us for what we did to her and him. Hey, man, he said some stupid shit about revenge is food best served like cold cuts. [He was referring to the old adage 'Revenge is a dish best served cold.'] The asshole couldn't even threaten us right! Stupid ass, he really fucked up that saying. Anyway, Claude, please watch your back. I got a nice pearl-handled gat if you wanna borrow it. I know that idiot ain't gonna come here with no shit unless he wants a belly full of buckshot. Dig me, little brother?"

"Hey, Carter, listen, bro, I know his boss, so do you."

"Oh, yeah? Where that nigger used to work?" interjected Carter.

"Never mind that, Carter. Just listen," Claude continued. "We can get his full name and address. I already know a jerk like him called from a traceable number, so all we have to do is contact his boss, get his info, and take it all to the police. In the interim, I'll file a restraining order so that if either one of us sees him, he can be arrested automatically—on sight."

"Oh man, Claude, who you been talking to? Mom, Dad, or your old-timer buddy? You know niggers like him don't give a shit about the law. We need to take care of motherfuckers like him by ourselves, dig me?" said Carter.

"Hey, listen, Carter, don't do anything in no time soon. Just be patient. Thanks for warning me. Let me take care of this, and be careful, okay?" replied Claude.

"Yeah, Claude, whatever. Just watch your back, okay?" said Carter.

"All right, bro. Talk to you in the morning," said Claude.

Claude had a restless sleep that night with thoughts swirling around his dome piece like a whirlwind. He was up at the crack of dawn, and even though he didn't feel up to it, he went out for his four-mile jog. When he returned, it was still early, so he went to the Red Bull Inn on Route 22 for some breakfast. Even though he had two on-the-house breakfasts waiting for him at the Trolley Car Diner, the thought of returning there made him think about what Harvey probably did to his food, and immediately it nauseated him every time he considered it.

After breakfast, Claude went to get a fresh haircut before Meechie and her daughter, Marissa, came over to shop for the young lady's school supplies. He stopped at the Sunoco one-stop market for a *New York Post* newspaper to check up on the Yankees, who once again were in the thick of a pennant race. Although he wasn't really a New York Yankee fan, he always tried to keep up with the Yankees team statistics. It made for good barbershop banter while he waited for his turn at the chair.

When he arrived at the barbershop, his favorite barber had one in the chair and one waiting. He had forgotten his newspaper in the car, so he went out to get it. He opened the car door, reached in, and retrieved the paper.

Upon shutting his car door, a police car screeched to a sudden stop behind him, and he immediately heard, "Hey, you! Turn around slowly, drop what's in your hand, and put your hands in the air!"

*What the fuck?* Claude thought to himself. But still, he immediately complied. "What's wrong, officer?" said Claude.

"Just do what I say—*now!*" said the anxious cop.

Claude now stood there like a statue, his dropped *New York Post* newspaper blowing away with the autumn wind. One of the policemen jumped out of the car, gun drawn, finger on the trigger, at the ready. He frisked Claude intimately, like he was feeling up a prospective sex partner in preparation for intercourse. Humiliated, Claude knew not to utter another word. The patrons in the barbershop were glued to the barbershop's picture window.

Three of the four barbers came outside and started asking from across the street, "Officer, what's wrong? He's in here with us. He just went outside to get his paper."

Just then the other officer jumped out of the passenger side of the car and unbuckled his holster and put his hand on his pistol in a just-in-case gesture. When the initial officer was done frisking Claude, he said out loud, "No problem, guys, We just got a call that there were some nigg—aahh, err, black guys selling drugs on this corner."

No one there bought the cops' bullshit excuse. All the barbers and Claude visibly surveyed the area, and no one was out as it was still just before 8:00 a.m. There were only passing cars. All the other businesses in the strip mall were closed, save for the beauty parlor at the other end of the strip mall. Still, neither Claude nor the barbers or none of the other customers who by now had all come out to see what was up said a word.

The second officer then said aloud, "All is okay, you guys. Go back in and try to enjoy your day."

— CHAPTER 25 —

This was what everyday life was like being a black male in a predominately black neighborhood in this land of the *free* (and home of the brave)—regular goings-on punctuated by the possibility of being shot or, at the very least, arrested for absolutely nothing at the drop of a hat. It immediately brought to mind the lyrics of a song sung by the great jazz musician Trumpeter Louis "Satchmo" Armstrong. The song entitled "Black and Blue" had the lyrics "What did I do to be so Black and Blue?" It was a reality among black folks, *especially* black males.

Every one of the patrons, barbers, and Claude himself had been through something similar several times in their lives. Then you had to deal with self-hating, lying-ass T.A.N.s like the idiot Harvey, who had threatened Claude's and his brother's lives. Thinking of Harvey immediately made Claude think, *What if I had gone to my dad's house and borrowed the gun my brother Carter had offered me? I'd be cased up right now. What if Harvey happens upon me right now? All our lives are lived in continual peril once we leave our front doors we are immediately at Large. We have to deal with the racist cops then everyday racism as a whole. Then we're closely scrutinized all day by everyone, even our own people, because this society treats us like were all potential criminals or need-to-be-in-a-cage animals based not only on the color of our skin but sometimes provoked by provocative, impulsive, antagonistic T.A.N. behavior. Then we have to deal with T.A.N.s themselves, male and female, who are out looking for some other black person to either try, harass, manipulate, or rob.*

*That's not the whole of it*, thought Claude. As black males in America we have neither the right to be angry or to behave angrily. *If you're dark skinned, you have to deal with a great deal of your own people finding an immense amount of humor in being soooo black: "Geez, that nigger is as black as tar. Ha ha ha!" or "Wow, you see how black she is?" or (here's a good one) "She's a sexy, cute female to be such a dark-skinned woman or to be so black."*

Claude perused, in his mind's eye, the entirety of his life. Not one Caucasian, Latino, or Asian ever said anything like that in his company, only ignorant-ass, self-loathing T.A.N.s. Yeah, black was all of the black folks' natural hue (at least the American black man's natural color).

*Prior to coming to this country, were there any light-skinned slaves before "massa" (master) came and got to us and chose at will to infuse/dilute our blood with his own? Oh, how funny it is to be dark. If you're really dark, your own people will treat you like you have some kind of comical disease. Yeah, Mr Satchmo Armstrong, you're so right. What did I do to be so black and blue? The longer we as a people live by the "brown paper bag" standard within our community, the longer we're going to remain fucked by this society*, thought Claude.

It made him realize oh how powerful prayer was. The sweet Lord and prayer were the only solace available to him sometimes. And there was absolutely nothing more powerful than either.

It was time for that most powerful book ever written to provide him with some more *basic information before leaving earth*. There was absolutely nothing, save for prayer and God himself, that continually afforded him more hope than that holy book. Claude, who always became introspective after incidents like the one with those cops outside that barbershop, heavily considered going back to church regularly. Moves like that always started with the initial steps, so he committed to going to church tomorrow—Sunday—and to start back at Bible study on this upcoming Tuesday night.

He, after his fresh-cut and shave, was now home, waiting for Meechie and Marissa. He received a text message from Meechie while in the barber's chair, informing him that the pair would be at his apartment no later than 12:30 p.m.

When he picked up the Bible, he wasn't quite sure what he should read. He decided to call his mom and ask for her advice. Without hesitation, Estelle directed Claude to Philippians, chapter 4, verses 4–9. As he read through it, he thought to himself that this was a perfect suggestion. Once again, Claude recognized how fortunate he was to have his parents make themselves available whenever he needed either one of them. While reading his Bible, he dozed off for what seemed like five minutes. It was actually two and a half hours that he sat in his recliner, snoozing, with his Bible in his lap.

At 1:45 p.m., the doorbell startled him, and he hopped up, unaware of his surroundings, thinking he was still in the barber's chair. The sudden jump out of the chair made him think he might have caused the barber to slice his face up. Oh, so pleased he was that he wasn't.

When the bell rang again, it wouldn't stop. *Ding, dong, ding, dong*, and so on to the point of infuriating him.

*Damn*, he said to himself, *I knew that Meechie woman is coarse, but I didn't think she was a shrew.*

Again, this female was more than an hour late—with no call preceding her tardy arrival. Who the heck would lean on someone's bell like this?

"All right, all right, I'll be right there!" Claude yelled. He made his way to the front door two steps at a time, mumbling curse words as he ran down the steps. The incessant bell ringing never stopped. He didn't buzz the pair in because buzzing folks in on an assumption was a practice he did away with after his brother Clarence unknowingly let the SWAT team into his townhouse, thinking it was his so-called former friend Alvin, the T.A.N. who turned out to be the snitch that set Clarence up.

"Hey, why you keep ringing the bell like that, Ms. Meechie?" said Claude.

With her Latin accent, Meechie replied, "Yo, brother, I only rang it twice. What you being so mean about, man?"

Claude looked at the bell and discovered the bell was stuck and was still ringing. "Oh, geez, Meechie, I was wrong. The damn bell is stuck."

"You see, Claude? You was wrong to be mean, uh-huh, man. You owe a sister an apologize," said Meechie.

"Forgive me for that. It woke me up and the bell kept ringing and I just surmised that because I didn't answer it immediately, you kept ringing it. Again, lovely lady, I'm really sorry."

"Sur who—" said Meechie with a quizzical look on her face. "You sur who—what that *sur* word mean?"

"Oh, I apologize again. *Surmised.* It means I drew a conclusion based on circumstance," explained Claude

"Oh," said Meechie, "I didn't know you can throw a conclusion."

"*Drew, drew*," said Claude, "like the word *draw*. It means to extract or to take something from something else." Claude explained to his friend for whom English was a second language.

"You know some words in English that I don't hear all the time," Meechie continued. "Maybe one day you can teach me more about the English language than I already know."

"Yeah," said Claude. "If you have the time, I will. Well, come on in, and let me wash up a little before we go shopping for Marissa's school stuff. Hi, little lady," Claude said to the now-smiling Marissa.

"Hi, Mr. Claude, how are you today?"

"Oh, me? I'm okay," replied Claude. Once the pair entered his apartment, Claude said, "Can I get y'all anything to drink, or perhaps for you, little lady, how about some fruit?"

"Well, I want a piece of fruit," said the interjecting Meechie.

"Yeah, Mr. Claude," said Marissa. "What kind of fruit you got?"

"Oh, Marissa," said Claude. "It's 'What kind of fruit do you have?' I know a smart young fifth-grade lady like you already knows that."

Now, smiling so broadly she exposed almost every dentist-needing, cavity-laden tooth in her mouth, Marissa replied, "Wow, Mr. Claude, you sound just like my fourth-grade teacher, Ms. Piscopo. She used to say that kinda stuff to all of us every day in class."

"Well," said Claude, "I got some oranges, some strawberries, blueberries, bananas, kiwis, and some."

"Ooh, ooh, Claude," said the again rudely interjecting Meechie, "give me some kiwis. I ain't had no kiwis in years!"

"Mom, it's 'I haven't had any kiwis in years.' May I please have some, Mom?" said Marissa.

Meechie, with a look of utter disdain on her face, immediately replied, "Hey, Iistillo, si tu corrija una vez mas, voy a dar una palmada tu boca me entiendes?" The inflection in Meechie's voice and her taut, rigid posture made Claude aware of how angry Meechie was at that moment. For some reason, the flair in her nostrils and her taut posture exuded passion, and it sexually aroused Claude—just a little.

"Si, Mama, lo siento," replied Marissa.

Then Meechie continued, "Y no olvides que temoscoso. Deja de tratar de avergonzarme."

"Yes, Mom," Marissa replied—this time in English. The young girl then started sobbing uncontrollably.

"Whoa," said Claude, "what was that all about? I hope I didn't say anything insulting."

"No, brother. That didn't had nothing doing with you," Meechie continued. "That's between mother and daughter, okay?" replied Meechie, her nostrils still flaring.

"Oh, sorry, excuse me," said Claude.

After a quick wash, Claude and his female friends jumped in Claude's car, and the trio made their way to the dollar store. It was located in the same strip mall Claude had left a few hours earlier—post cop harassment and fresh haircut.

Marissa said, "Mr. Claude, what should I get?"

"Hey, young lady, get everything you need. Take this shopping cart, and I'll see you when you're all done," said Claude.

Meechie then said, "Wait a minute, Claude. My baby is not used to shopping alone. Let me help her out."

Now, Claude became wary, unsettled. He knew Marissa was ecstatic to finally be getting the things Mom had neglected to purchase for her. Why Meechie hadn't gotten anything for her daughter so close to school beginning was a mystery to him.

# CHAPTER 26

The first thing he did was notice that almost every piece of clothing Meechie was wearing was new. He felt that if any mother had enough money to buy herself new clothing, she should've prioritized and maybe, just maybe, bought herself only half as many clothing items and at least gotten her daughter a portion of what she needed for school, which was just two days away. Still, he had enough experience with other women and their children to know not to espouse anything concerning a mother and her child. No matter how neglectful a mom appeared to be.

After more than an hour of shopping, Marissa brought the cart to Claude and, clearly overjoyed, she said, "Mr. Claude, I'm all done!"

Claude noticed that the young lass had a journal in the cart, and he was pleased that Marissa was interested in writing. He, from his interactive experience with many black women and their children, had noticed that hardly any of the children and mothers he met were interested in reading or writing. Even his so-called friend from high school, Parris Simmons, the woman he nicknamed the carnival barker because she talked so much hypocritical religious horse shit, the same woman who erroneously saw herself as a walking Bible-spouting neighborhood evangelist, even she had an aversion to reading even though she was educated. If it was on a syllabus or a required-reading assignment from class, that was the only time she indulged in a book. He remembered how she lied and said she had read his mother's manuscript when she hadn't read one line of it.

Claude's immediate family and the people he knew personally were the only folks who showed any interest in learning anything by way of research that required reading. It was actually a manifestation of what his dad once told him, "This 'blacks don't like to read stuff' is just another example of the subtle effect of prepared media. The goal is manipulation of concept. Free thought through ideas, reading, and imagination are less controllable!" Not only did most blacks he knew not read *anything*, but they had no interest in the political progress of their own people.

*Many of his people were arrested, and some had even died to give us the right to vote,* he thought. It annoyed him when he would ask his own people if they heard the president's—*their* president's—latest State of the Union address or any other speech that President Obama or the First Lady, Michelle Obama, gave. He would have to speak to his immediate family or Mr. Bernard, who Claude felt knew a whole bunch about just about everything, if he wanted to hold an intelligent conversation about something political or just about anything that required thought. Most of the black people he knew, especially T.A.N.s, were involved in great difficulty when they had to give an informed opinion about most worldly or social subject matters. To Claude, the opinions of most of the black folks he interacted with came from what they heard on the radio or what they heard once removed from someone else's conversation—either live or on television.

Although he abhorred stereotypical jokes, he understood the derisive joke "If you want to hide money from a black person, then stick it in a book"!

*Oh how angry we as a people get when our faults are pointed out to us. Again, the excuse that the reason blacks are so poorly educated is because of racism. Even if that's true, so what?* Claude thought. *The old adage "Each one teach one" is true and very practical.*

When the items were finished being rung up, the total bill came to just under two hundred dollars. This, to Claude, was really no problem. Meechie stood in wonderment as she watched Claude pay for the items with one of his credit cards. As the trio made their way to Claude's car, Meechie began talking to Claude about how long it had been since she had her hair or nails done, how she really wanted a pedicure because catching public transportation required a great deal of walking and her feet were always sore.

Claude, listening to her, felt it was an attempt to manipulate him, and it annoyed him. This, Claude had come to realize from his experience, was a tool usually used by the T.A.N. women he interacted with. Only young Marissa had thanked him and seemed really appreciative of his generous gesture. Her mom, instead of being thankful that this so-called new friend of hers had just saved her close to two hundred dollars of her own money, could only behave like she was thinking that, shoot, if he got two hundred dollars to spend on someone else's child, she should try to get all she could out of him—at least something for herself.

When she began to sigh and say things like "Damn, I ain't going to have any money for at least two weeks when my check comes," it began to really agitate Claude. Though he was trying his best to ignore Meechie, her latest sighing and whining attempt at manipulation prompted him to say, "Hey, look, Meechie, you just saved close to two hundred bucks. Now, you can use that money to get those things you're complaining about. Get your own nails done, pay for your own pedicure. I'm a generous man—not a gullible sucker. Please, woman, stop trying to play me."

"Damn, Claude, Mr. High and Mighty, ain't nobody trying to play you, nigger. I'm just thinking out loud," said Meechie.

"Well, here's a novel thought," Claude continued. "Try to think about saying 'Thank you, Claude for looking out for my daughter.'"

Meechie became very salty that her attempt at manipulation was futile. Marissa, in the back seat, had taken out her journal and began writing in it after opening up one of the three packs of fine-point pens she had. Claude was impressed that this little girl didn't try to sneak any toys in the cart and that, in two trips to his apartment, she seemed only interested in the computer or writing in a journal. It was oh so obvious to him that Marissa was keenly interested in learning. Meanwhile, her mom's interest was getting her hair and nails done or a pedicure.

Now he understood what Mr. Bernard meant when he said, "Can you imagine how that little girl [Marissa] is probably going to end up or turn out with a mother like Meechie?" The old saying "Children learn what they live" was true. Claude knew about his affection for children. He knew if he continued spending this kind of time with Marissa that eventually she would become attached to him, and knowing himself, he knew that soon he would begin to feel obligated. He knew at the end of this shopping trip that he should curtail spending any more time with Meechie—at least in the foreseeable future.

# CHAPTER 27

Meechie's face was now taut, and she had grown solemnly silent. When they arrived at Claude's apartment, he didn't invite them in. He cautioned the females, "Wait here for a minute. I'm going in to check my landline phone for messages, then I'll take y'all home."

As Claude exited the car, he heard Marissa say, "Mommy, I'm hungry. When are we going to eat something?"

Claude shut the driver's side door to run up the apartment steps just as Marissa made her "I'm hungry statement." He stopped, turned around, and came back to the car. He opened the door and said, "Marissa, I'm hungry too. On the way home, we'll all stop and get something to eat for everybody."

"Yeah," said Marissa out loud. Meechie sat there motionless, stoically looking straight ahead, like the pouting child who didn't get anything she wanted. Once again, Claude, now ascending the steps to his apartment, could only shake his head in disgust.

When Claude returned, he took the females to T.G.I. Friday's for a late lunch, and the young Marissa was spellbound, astounded that this new friend of her mother's was kind enough to take her and her mom to a restaurant for the first time in her life. Neither her natural father nor none of her mom's other boyfriends did anything for her. Again, the two females ate heartily on Mr. Claude's coin. When their meal was done, Claude took the ladies home.

Not wanting Claude to know where they lived, the dissatisfied Meechie (really unhappy that she had nothing herself tangible to show for her time spent with Claude) asked him to drop them off more than two city blocks from where the two females lived.

"Mommy, why are we getting out so far from where we live? We have to carry all of my school stuff a long way."

"Cierra la boca, ahora," said her mom tersely to her diminutive young daughter.

"Phewww," Marissa said loudly in disgust as the two exited Claude's car. Claude, loaded with sympathy with regard to what Marissa probably had to endure daily, dealing with her selfish, self-centered, coarse, mannerless mother, promised himself he would pray for the young lass.

As he pulled away, he observed through his rearview mirror Meechie haul off and smack her daughter so hard she knocked young Marissa to the ground. Disgusted, when the traffic allowed it, he immediately made a U-turn and drove up to the pair.

He rolled his window down and said, "Hey, Meechie, what the heck did you knock her down like that for? I saw you. What the heck is wrong with you?"

"Hey, nigger, mind your fucking business. This is my daughter. I'm raising her."

"Oh?" said Claude. "That's what you call it, huh?"

Marissa then yelled, "Mr. Claude, it's okay. My mom is just mad at me being rude. She don't mean nothing."

Meechie had smacked Marissa so hard all of her school supplies were sprawled all over the street. Claude could see that her mom had smacked the young lady like this many times before.

"Look, nigger, get the fuck outta here before I call my brother to fuck your fat ass up. And also fat ass, please lose my fucking number jack," said Meechie.

Claude was astounded. *Why?* he thought. Is that dumb-ass that angry that her daughter and not she received presents today? Is she that fucked up? Maybe she's pissed off that I saw right through her bullshit and called her on it, not succumbing to her attempts to fleece me for her hairdo or nails money.

From Claude's experience interacting with T.A.N. women, Meechie's behavior reminded him of T.A.N. women because if you wanted to see them explode, just call them on their shit. He sat there in wonderment.

"Hey, nigger, you better get going while you still have a chance," said Meechie. She then picked up a rock and yelled. "Keep sitting there, you fucking dummy, and see if I don't bust your fucking window. Get the fuck out of here and lose my number—*now!*"

Claude, of course, complied, and as he drove away, he decided to report Meechie's child abuse to Child Services on the hotline as soon as he got a safe distance away. He felt he had to do something. No, this woman, due to her ethnicity, was not a T.A.N..

*But so what?* he thought. Her daughter was definitely black. Any ethnicity or race, once mixed with folks of African heritage, automatically become black. T.A.N.s hadn't cornered the market on ignorance. Reporting Meechie was something he had to do. This was what was meant by the statement when it came to child abuse, everyone was a mandated reporter.

While heading home, Claude first called information after putting his cell phone on speaker mode. When he received the emergency hotline number, he called it immediately and was instantly placed on hold. He was on hold so long he decided to drop the call and retry it when he made it home. With what he saw resonating in his mind's eye, he was already distracted from concentrating on his driving. He didn't want this call to add to his lack of concentration.

He felt so sorry for the young Marissa. Sure, the child was a bit rude in exposing her mom's lack of manners and ignorance and, most of all, her mom's poor parenting skills. What Claude believed was that, all of Marissa's tattletale rudeness was Marissa's subconscious crying for help. He knew the young Marissa had enjoyed her day and couldn't wait to get home and start opening all her new school supplies. He couldn't make hide nor hair why Meechie had him drop the two of them so far from home, and he didn't really care.

Still, when he made it home, he immediately called the child abuse hotline again and reported the entire incident. He was given a case number and told an investigator would contact him within the next seventy-two hours. Claude immediately received a call from his sister, Carmen, in Baltimore.

"Hey, Kay-Kay [the Paine family's nickname for Carmen], what you know good, little sis?"

"Hey, Claudio. How's everything, bro? Have you been staying out of trouble?"

Claude chuckled his "Sure, sis" answer to Carmen. "What's up, Kay-Kay? What did I do to deserve this call?"

"Well, I was talking to Mom, and she said you were talking about visiting Clarence in prison soon. Can I come too?" said Carmen.

"I don't see why not," said Claude. "I'm driving up after church tomorrow. Can you make it here by then?"

"Hold on," replied Carmen.

Claude then heard Carmen say, "Mommy, he said he's going tomorrow after church. Is that okay?"

Claude faintly heard his mother reply in the background, "Tell him I'll call him back later tonight to let him know."

"Claude," said Carmen, "Mom just said—"

"I know, I heard her," said Claude. "Tell Mom I'll be home all night, to call and let me know if y'all are coming later. No matter what time. We can make a family day of it. I'm sure Clarence would really appreciate seeing us tomorrow."

"Okay, Claudio, what else you doing today?" said Carmen.

"None of your business," Claude quipped in jest.

"Oh, okay, I get it. Up to no good, huh, bro?" replied Carmen in jest as well.

"Look, little sis, I just got in from a date, and I want to make some tea and get a shower and a little nap."

"Oh, you been hanging out with one of your crazy female friends, so now you gonna rush your sister off the phone, huh? I understand. Us people who love you have to take our place on the back burners. Okay, I get it," said Carmen.

"Kay-Kay, you know your guilt trips don't work on me. Tell Mom I'll be waiting for her call, okay?" said Claude.

"Sure, Claudio," said Carmen. "Love you, bro. Talk to you tonight."

"All right, Kay-Kay, y'all take care. Much love," said Claude.

# CHAPTER 28

He made himself a spot of peppermint herbal tea with a dash of honey and a squeeze of lemon. His stomach was a bit queasy and he remembered reading in the book "Back to Eden" by Mr. Jethro Kloss that spearmint and peppermint were good natural remedies for stomach discomfort. He quickly showered, crawled into his bed, turned on the Hustler XXX network, and since his lust had not been sated recently, he started toying with his penis until it became erect. He then masturbated as he watched his favorite porn star, Ms. Roxy, perform. Man, oh man, did Roxy turn him on.

*What a fine, nubile, sweet, ample-butt woman,* he thought as he continued on making love to someone he really loved—himself—until he climaxed. Claude, after a short wash-up, put on another one of his favorite jazz tunes to help lullaby himself. It was Yusef Lateef's love theme from the movie *Spartacus.* He then rolled over and fell into a deep sleep. Claude starting dreaming about what happened to him when he bought his first used car at 18 years old. En route to his home he stopped at Wong Choo's Chinese take out in Patterson, N.J. He placed his order of shrimp egg Foo young, I shrimp roll and two shrimp toast. No sooner did he place his order at the small bullet-proof window wheel then he heard *"Put yo Hanns-up Nig-Kah you know wat dis is."* Claude started to turn around when he felt a hard piece of metal stingingly mash into left cheek. *"Get down now nig-kah try to turn around again and immah bussa cap in yo-ass".* Claude of course complied immediately. *"Gimme yo shit Nig-kah keese and woll it."* As Claude lay face down on the filthy-grimey floor. What a harrowing petrifying life-threatening experience as he yelled himself awake, oh so relieved it was only a dream. Albeit an experience he actually lived through. (He then remembered it took them 3 weeks to find his radio & C/D player torn out with his digital clock from the dashboard car in a Newark N.J. alley) And almost 14 months to replenish his I.D. (Driver's license) and credit.

Actually Claude was awakened by the ringing of his landline phone at 11:30 p.m. It was his mom, calling to tell Claude that she and his sister would not be able to accompany him to see Clarence tomorrow in prison. She had to fill in on the organ tomorrow at church. She had just received (literally) an eleventh-hour call (at 11:00 p.m.), informing her that the organist had a sudden death in his family and that the church needed her to fill in at both the 8:00 a.m. and 11:30 a.m. services.

"Please give Big C our blessings, Claude. Let him know we'll visit him next weekend."

"Sure, Mom, will do," replied Claude.

"It sounds like I woke you. If so, I'm sorry, son," Estelle continued. "If possible go back to sleep."

"Nah, Mom, I think I'll be up for a while. One of my favorite old movies is coming on the Turner Classic Network tonight," said Claude.

"Oh, yeah?" said Mom. "Which movie is that?"

"Lady sings the blues with—"

"Hey, Claude, I saw the movie when it was first run in theaters. I already know who is in it," quipped Mom.

"Well, excuuuse me, dear mother. I didn't mean to insult your intelligence, Mom. Sometimes I forget how really old you are," retorted Claude in jest.

"Watch it, sucker," quipped his mom.

"Okay, Aunt Esther." It was Claude and his mother's reference to the old Redd Foxx TV show *Sanford and Son* and the character Aunt Esther. The two laughed heartily until they ended the call. This time this wretched dream, coupled with Mr. Bernard's advice about Post Traumatic Stress Disorder helped Claude make up his mind to finally start seeing a psychologist. He thanked God he knew Danielle!

A week before, Claude was set to visit Clarence in Rahway State Prison, where Clarence was serving the remainder of a five- to a ten-year term for possession with intent to deliver five kilos of 90 percent pure cocaine.

Clarence had just completed three and a half years of his five-year-minimum term. His initial sentence was eight and a half to fifteen years. However, the Paine family had hired the family friend and lawyer, Ms. Elaine Evans, Esquire, *post* sentencing to represent Clarence in the appeal process, and Ms. Evans got Clarence's sentence reduced.

Clarence had used attorney Albert Rosen, who had the reputation of one of the finest criminal attorneys in the entire east coast. Mr. Rosen had passed four—yes, four—bar exams and was licensed to practice law in New York, Connecticut, New Jersey, and Pennsylvania. This was a move—using Mr. Rosen instead of Ms. Evans—that insulted and annoyed Ms. Evans immensely. Clarence was told to use the best experienced criminal attorney available since the deck was stacked heavily against him, having been under surveillance and wiretapped for six months prior to his arrest. So he decided that Mr. Rosen, not Ms. Evans, was the way to go, and he was wrong.

His number-one man, Alvin Wynnely, had been busted on the New Jersey turnpike with one and a half kilos of heroin (Clarence's product), and to save his own skin, he wore a wire for six months to set Clarence up. He gave the state of New Jersey the entire Clarence Paine organization from the inside out. Alvin served six months and received one hundred thousand dollars and was put into the witness protection program for bringing down the biggest heroin and cocaine dealer in the entire state of New Jersey—Mr. Clarence "Clay" Paine.

Over the last week, Clarence had a running beef with Big Al Short, former hit man, who was serving three life terms, having been convicted for murdering an entire family of three in Margate, New Jersey, some five years earlier. Big Al was 6 feet 9 inches, 330 pounds of massive muscle. His hands were so large; his thumb was 6 inches long and damn near an inch in circumference. When Clarence was in the infirmary for a staph infection, Big Al, who was housed on the same block as Clarence, went into Clarence's cell and took most of

Clarence's toiletries several times at will. He also read Clarence's love letters to Clarence's wife aloud in the day room one day to embarrass Clarence for his own sadistic, humorous pleasure. When Clarence got wind of what had happened, after ten days in the infirmary, he vowed to settle the score with whomever it was who violated his boundaries so egregiously. When Clarence was informed that it was the frightening man mountain, hit man Big Al Short, he was concerned but not frightened at the probability of getting his ass whipped or even possibly killed. After all, Big Al, facing three life terms, had absolutely nothing to lose.

# CHAPTER 29

Big Al was the most feared man in the prison. Everyone knew who Clarence Paine was, and all were well aware of Clarence's reputation as well. Still, not a soul gave Clarence or anyone else a chance of surviving an altercation with Big Al.

Clarence's closest friend in the prison and childhood buddy, Billy White, serving six to twelve years for first-degree manslaughter, told Clarence, "Just let it go, man. I know how you feel, Clay, but in a couple of years, you'll be up for parole. That evil nigger has nothing to lose. What you lost, brother, was minimal. Even if you mix it up with that fucking moose and somehow win, at the very least, you'll come out of it crippled or maimed."

Clarence, who was all of 6 feet 1 inch and 220 pounds and was dwarfed by Big Al, responded, "Look, Billy, today it's my belongings, my personal family business, and my self-respect. Tomorrow it might be an attempt to put a dick up my ass. Billy, I don't care what's at stake. I *have* to let him know his bullshit stops here."

"Well, Clay, that's one nigger I want nothing to do with. I don't want that savage coming after me. So I have to say, my brother, with this one, you're on your own," said Billy.

"Hey, Billy, in all the years I've known you, have I ever asked you to get involved with any friction I encountered from anyone—in the prison or on the street? Huh, have I?" said Clarence.

"No, Clay, but you know I'm not a pussy or someone who would turn my back on you. It's just this time the odds are pretty poor. I've only got four years left to go. I just don't want to have to live every day with my ass in the wind."

"Hey, Billy, it's cool. Don't sweat it."

Billy then asked Clarence, "What are you going to do anyway?"

Clarence shot Billy a glare that no one would want to get a second look of and said absolutely nothing. Billy got the message, and the two went to the yard for their forty-five minutes of yard time.

Clarence, who had several shanks (crude handmade knives) stashed throughout the prison, recently began keeping one on his person at all times, thus risking being frisked and sent to solitary confinement (the "hole") and possibly adding months or years to his already recently reduced sentence. When the two made their way to the yard two or three days later, which was only Clarence's fourth day out of the infirmary, there was Big Al on the weight bench, bench-pressing weights no other person in the prison could even lift.

Clarence approached Big Al and asked, "Hey, Frankenstein, was it you who stole my shit out of my cell and, like a little bitch, read my personal mail?"

"Yeah, motherfucker, so what? You want me to get you more shit from the commissary, or should I give you some shit from my ass? Look, jackass, get the fuck out of my face before I bitch-slap your fucking ass and make you my woman," said the bellowing behemoth.

Everyone within earshot stopped whatever they were doing. They all tried not to draw attention from the guards, but all of the now-encircling yardmates were sure they were about to witness a murder. Without uttering another word, Clarence quickly kicked the supine Big Al on the side of his face, causing Big Al to drop the weight bar on his chest and let out a bear-like bellow.

"I'm going to kill your ass, little nigger!" As Big Al moved the weight off of his chest and tried to rise quickly, Clarence, now aiming for Big Al's face, missed his intended target and caught him in his chest with another work boot kick, this time causing the behemoth to lose his balance and fall from the workout bench to the ground.

Clarence tried to land a quick third kick, but Big Al, holding on to the edge of the bench, grabbed Clarence's leg and wrestled him down to the ground. Big Al then smashed Clarence in his eye with a vicious, tightfisted, squarely landed overhand right, cracking his orbital (eye socket) bone in the process. Big Al then grabbed one of the weight rings—a ten pounder—and caught Clarence squarely in the center of his face, full force, fracturing his nose and busting open both his upper and bottom lips. Immediately, blood started spurting from Clarence's whole mouth and first trickling then pouring from his broken nose simultaneously. Big Al grabbed Clarence in a head-lock and smashed Clarence in his back with the same ten-pound weight ring he used to crack Clarence's nose and cut open his lip. Just that quickly, Clarence was beaten pretty bad.

He yelled a blood-curdling scream when the weight came down on his back, causing a hollow-like, hot, stinging sensation that ran from his midback down his legs, causing a strange pain Clarence had never felt in his life and numbing his entire left leg in the process. Still in a headlock, Clarence then really deeply bit Big Al so hard it seemed to big Al that Clarence was going to bite off a whole chunk of flesh from between his right armpit and chest.

"Oowww, ooohh! Goddammit, turn me loose, nigger! Arrrgghh . . . uuuggghhhhh!" Big Al began to bellow. The next swing from his weight ring-filled hand busted Clarence on the side of his face, on the ear, causing that ear to ring something awful. Clarence was knocked to the ground quick and very hard—all in one motion. Dizzy, having difficulty drawing a deep breath, his ear ringing (ring-ing loudly, steadily), squinting excessively from the eye socket frac-ture, his face now drenched in blood, Clarence was now in a bad way.

"You motherfucking bitch-ass nigger!" Big Al roared as he went to stomp, hopefully to death, the severely beaten-up, sprawled-out Clarence.

Clarence mustered all the remaining strength he had and was able to grab Big Al's massive Shaquille O'Neal–sized foot midstomp. He twisted the foot, causing first his elbow to scrape something fierce on the concrete, and then caused the giant to lose his balance, skip, then futilely reach for the bench to try to steady himself from even-tually falling down in an embarrassing heap. Clarence was squinting and sniffling very hard as he grabbed the gargantuan Big Al's foot as big Al was wriggling about.

Clarence finally pulled the almost forgotten shank from down in his work boot. He had to quickly dig for it. It was a point-sharpened scrawl from the metal shop. He quickly shoved it through Big Al's pants and into Big Al's nutsack (scrotum), penetrating his left testicle with a catlike quickness as hard as humanly possible.

A high-pitched terror-filled scream came out of Big Al's mouth that could be heard throughout the entire D block. "Aaahhhhheeeehhh! Aaahhstah! Uh . . . staah . . . uh, stop it! Stop it! Ahhhh . . . . please, somebody, please get this nah-naaa-niggahh offa me!"

Clarence then started stabbing Big Al, who was now so deeply engulfed in an unusual, unimaginable, abject pain that he could do nothing to stop Clarence from poking him randomly at will. His testicles were simultaneously stinging and burning something ungodly. Big Al, so engrossed in this inexplicable pain that he had to roll into as tight a ball as his six-feet-nine-inch body would allow him to. Now he was clutching his shiv-penetrated testicles and screaming nonstop, a scream so loud, high pitched, and blood curdling it sounded like an ambulance siren had gotten stuck.

Clarence continued to stab the subdued, screaming-for-dear-life Big Al continually anywhere the scrawl could penetrate his side, and then Clarence got a rise out of the dying Big Al when he jaggedly dug into Big Al's left eye, causing the eye to squish-pop out, still dangling from a string like a piece of flesh or skin. As he mercilessly continued to dig the scrawl wherever he could, Clarence emitted a low-toned, baritone growl like a mama bear protecting her cubs. The now pitifully hopeless, fearing-for-his-quickly-ending-life Big Al grimly began to realize that he was in the midst of his final seconds on earth. Big Al now screamed in mortal horror and begged for his life simultaneously.

The loud gut-wrenching screams mixed with moans made his attempt at begging indiscernible. His words now began to sound like muttering gibberish. Still Clarence would not stop stabbing—fourteen, fifteen, sixteen stabs and deeply digging, pinpointing, twisting, jagged digs and pokes. Clarence now grunted and growled even more loudly and ferociously with every poke into Big Al's flesh—in his side, in his chest, in his eyes.

It was so bad that Big Al, apparently dying, had stopped screaming, and he now began whimpering pitifully, begging for Clarence to stop in slow-breath, losing, staggered, stuttered, whining, pleading tones. "Plee—ooh, hoo-hoo. Oh, pah-pul-puleeze, pleeez da-don't kill mah-mah-meee. Pah-pah-pleeez, suh, sta-stop it. Oh, uuggh, huuuuuhl . . ."

Now several guards were running to the two at full speed. Clarence, his vision compromised, then started stabbing Big Al in his neck, penetrating his jugular in the process. The moose-like Big Al was now motionless, inert. Clarence was completely exhausted, spent, and began to suck air like he couldn't breathe at all. Just as he slowly tried to swing stab number 23, a baton came down on his head. *Crrraack*. Clarence went into an unbalanced pirouette—from a wobble to a kind of a shimmy-shake. He went down slowly, his one unbloodied, squinting eye visibly rolling in his head. He dropped the shank and fell, first on a knee then to the side and then on his face.

For sure, Clarence's skull was fractured. Big Al lay motionless in a heap, on a blood-drenched patch of ground. After the initial quick, uncontrollable chill shake, he then seemed to let all the air out of his lungs as death grabbed hold. He was clearly deceased. Clarence appeared deceased as well as he too lay motionless. The fight to the death that seemed to last a half hour took all of two minutes, forty-five seconds—less than a round of a professional Marquis de Queensbury boxing match. Clarence was now in a coma, and Big Al had expired in the yard.

# CHAPTER 30

Even though Clarence was now out of the coma, it was only three days since Clarence's fight to the death with Big Al in D yard. Still, of course, this was unbeknownst to Claude. He made the trip to Rahway State Prison on Sunday afternoon. He arrived at the three o'clock visiting time. His request to see Clarence was denied. The official reason was that the inmate was currently being housed and treated in the prison infirmary. What Clarence was being treated for was confidential.

When Claude explained that he was Clarence's brother, it was explained to Claude that the only people who could see him or had a legal right to demand a diagnosis were his wife or parents. Claude was puzzled, baffled. What could possibly keep Clarence in the infirmary? He knew Clarence had a staph infection, but Clarence didn't say how bad it was.

*Oh well.* There was really nothing Claude could do—at least until he communicated with Clarence. It was not like he could hit Clarence up or text him. This was truly an appropriate time to practice patience. When there was really nothing absolutely at all in his power to do—the true meaning of powerlessness!

Claude decided to stop by his dad's house. Even though it had not been that long since Claude had been at the house, it had been a while since Claude had physically seen his father, and neither had he had one of his long talks with dad either. Claude also wanted to talk to Carter about that idiot T.A.N. Harvey and his threats. Claude was taught, as a young lad, to never ever take a threat lightly or underestimate anyone's ability to do anything at any time, to put nothing past no one. Like they said at the outset of a professional boxing match, "Protect yourself at all times."

Claude hadn't juiced in two days. Part of his weight loss regimen was to juice at least four times a week, using only organic fruits and vegetables, which was why he had so much fruit to offer the coarse Meechie and her daughter. Claude was doing this religiously up until Friday past. He was perturbed that he wasn't able to see Clarence during visiting hours. He knew Clarence had allergies and that he was having an issue with this infection he caught. He felt prison was such a disgustingly nasty and filthy place that anyone could easily catch anything at any time.

Oh, how right he was. Anyway, Claude called his mom and explained to her his ordeal at the prison that day. Mom told him she would talk to Ayisha (Clarence's estranged wife) to see which of the two would contact the prison in the morning.

❦

# CHAPTER 31

The next morning was brisk and very clear. It was quiet in a rising-sun-at-dawn kind of way. Claude started his jog, and every wildlife creature indigent to the area was out stirring about, like they were all gathering sustenance and other items to make sure they and their offspring had enough to eat and to shore up and secure their dwellings in preparation for the upcoming fall and winter months.

About a mile into his run, just as Claude approached the dew-laden, freshly manicured high school football field, a red car came roaring directly at Claude, picking up speed the closer it came upon him. He waved frantically for the car to move left or right, but the driver, for whatever reason, didn't respond. Fearing for his life, and with no sidewalk to escape to, Claude jumped onto the embankment, rolling his left ankle and falling on his face.

His sweat suit was ripped in several places, and his arms and facial and neck skin, which were the only parts of his body exposed to the elements, were scraped and scratched raw by the jagged branches and large loose bark pieces from the tree stumps and long sharp twigs Claude jumped into and landed on. The car in question continued to pick up speed as it sped away much too quickly for him to identify it or get a good look at the driver. The greyish-blue morning sky background didn't help much either with identifying the car as it sped away. The driver had made good his or her getaway.

Claude was wondering whether this was personal or what. *Who the hell was that?* he asked himself. *Maybe that dickhead Harvey, that fat Nigress's boyfriend, husband, or whatever the fuck he is to her. It could have been Mr. Deltoid—recently expurgated from his position in the Human Resources at Johnson & Johnson. Or maybe some drugged-up jerk or racist white man. Oh, well, they are gone and hopefully for good.*

Claude, for whatever reason, could not stop thinking about Clarence. He knew from growing up with him that if anyone was capable of taking care of himself in *any* situation, it was Clarence. Still, Claude knew he wasn't going to be comfortable until he had spoken to Clarence himself. The next day, Monday morning, Claude wanted to go to the police to see what steps had to be taken to swear out a protection order against Harvey. His first move was to go to the Trolley Stop Diner and speak to the manager, Mr. Dibble, who was the gentleman who tasted that bullshit Harvey had prepared for Claude a couple of weeks ago.

Claude entered the diner and had a seat but had no plans to eat there. When he sat down, he asked for a cup of coffee and immediately asked to speak to Mr. Dibble, the restaurant's general manager.

"Hello, Mr. Dibble," said Claude as Mr. Dibble approached his table.

"Hey, Mr. Paine. How's your mom and dad?" said Mr. Dibble.

"Oh, they're fine," said Claude. "Thanks for asking."

"So I take it you're here to take me up on my free-meal offer? I do want you to know that the ignorant cook, for lack of a better name to call him, has been terminated," said Mr. Dibble. "Sir, I don't know what he put in your food, but I assure you he's going to have a difficult time acquiring another job in the food service business. Also, I assure you that nothing like that will ever happen to you or anyone else who decides to take their meals here again, ever! Having said that, Mr. Paine, what can I get you?"

"Oh, I didn't come here to eat, sir," said Claude. "What I need from you is that cook's name and address for the police as I intend to file a protection order. That cook, Harvey, if that's his name, called my parent's home and threatened my brother and myself. To play it safe, sir, I want to go on record with the police."

"Sure," said Mr. Dibble. "I can give you his full name, but I can only give his personal information to the police. That's by law, Mr. Paine. I hope you understand."

"Oh, sure," said Claude. "His full name would be enough to get me started."

"Hey, Mr. Paine. I have one question for you," said Mr. Dibble, suddenly appearing to be wary.

"Okay," said Claude, "what can I do for you?"

"Well, I have to ask you this. Are you planning to sue us because of what that jackass did?" queried the curious Mr. Dibble.

"Oh no," said Claude. "As you're aware of, Mr. Dibble, my family has been eating here for years—long before you became manager. Geez, Mr. Dibble, I remember about ten years ago when you were a waiter and you operated the cash register. That was about ten years ago, right? I was still in high school at the time, wasn't I, sir?"

"It was twelve years and six months to be exact," said Mr. Dibble. "And you were just finishing up middle school, as I recall."

"No, please don't worry about us suing you. I know that that jerk didn't represent what this restaurant is all about," replied Claude.

"Phew," said Mr. Dibble. "Give me a couple of minutes, and I'll get his full name for you. I'll write it down. Also, Mr. Paine, do you plan on honoring my offer for a couple of free meals? It's important to me that you're satisfied and that you don't stay away from here based on your experience with him."

"Well," said Claude. "I have an idea. Instead of two on the house meals for me, why don't I bring my family here for one good meal for the lot of us?"

"Sure, we can work that out. Wait a minute, I'll be right back," said Mr. Dibble as he double-timed it to his office to give Claude some guest cards and Harvey's information. Claude was about to prepare his coffee for consumption. A man approached his table. It was a neighborhood man who had now lived every day begging. Fred, who went to High School (for one year) with Claude.

"Hey Fred," said Claude reluctantly, "How have you been? What's up?"

"Hey Claude," Fred replied, "can you spot a brother twenty bucks so that I can get a quick grub, like you. I'm hungry."

In Claude's entire life he had never seen anyone come *into* a restaurant to beg. Claude had stopped giving Fred a dollar here and there about five years ago, and this 20 dollar request in a restaurant at a time like this really annoyed him.

"Look, Fred, I only have enough for my coffee. Please don't do this right now. This is really rude." Said Claude.

"Oh man," said Fred, "I don't believe you, Claude. I know you got a little something something for a brother. Yo man, I ain't eat nothing today."

"Fred, that is not my responsibility and I'm in the middle of handling some personal business. Please get away from this table. Please, I don't have time for this!" said the severely irritated Claude.

"Hey, you Nigger!" said Fred, raising his voice and drawing attention. "Who the fuck you talking to like that muthafucka, you better have some respect pussy, I aint your damn Son."

Fred was so loud he drew the attention of the security guard-who quickly came to the table and escorted the feather-ruffled Fred out of the diner. Once Fred left the premises, the security guard who also went to High School with Claude came to Claude and said. "Hey Claude, do you know I've had to toss him outta here 4 times this month. If he comes here again we're gonna call the cops on his ass. Sorry 'bout that bro.

*Damn*, thought Claude. Talk about some ignorant crap. The harassment I gotta put up with my own people. When will this shit end! Geez, if you wanna see a T.A.N. get obstreperous, just tell them no!

Claude inspected his coffee thoroughly and added some cream to it (never sugar because of Claude's type 1 diabetes). Just as Claude began sipping his coffee, Mr. Dibble came back with one hundred dollars' (4 twenty-five-dollar cards) worth of guest gift cards and a sheet of paper with Harvey's full name, his start and firing dates. Claude was really pleased at Mr. Dibble's behavior and especially his attitude.

"Hey, Mr. Paine, here's my business card. Make sure you give it to the police and tell them to ask for me personally. I'll comply with anything they want," Mr. Dibble continued. "Also, good buddy, I want to thank you for not suing us because that would fall squarely on my shoulders, you know."

"Oh no, Mr. Dibble. You can rest assured that you have my word on that," said Claude.

"Good, well, Mr. Paine, I gotta get back to work before the inmates start running the asylum," said Mr. Dibble, forcing a smile on his face.

Claude took the Harvey information to the Somerset Police Department, and he was told by the clerk that he had to file his protection petition at the county courthouse. He did, however, fill out a police report about the threat Harvey made. He provided the police with all the information he had on Harvey. He included the time and day Harvey called with his threat and informed the police that the store manager, Mr. Dibble, by law couldn't provide him with Harvey's address or phone number. He informed them what Mr. Dibble told him about the legal problems he'd face if the restaurant gave anyone—save for the police—that kind of personal employee information.

The clerk concurred simply by smiling at Claude when he was finished and saying, "I know." She then provided Claude with a file number for the police report he had just filed. The clerk then told Claude that he could pick up a copy of the report in forty-eight hours.

Claude was pleased he had taken care of this matter as quickly as possible. As he left the police station and headed for the county courthouse to file the protection order, he couldn't stop thinking about Clarence. He planned to call Clarence's estranged wife, Ayisha, to see if he could find out what the latest health update for Clarence was. Claude was again extremely dismayed at this current turn of events, to say the least. Here he was headed to the county courthouse to file a protection order against another *black* man. He had to see a Caucasian to get information about another black man. When done with his legal business, he had to get home quickly to meet with the agent from the Department of Child Services to report abuses heaped upon a *black* child. It was apparent to Claude at times just how poorly he and his own people interacted with one another. His brother Carter wanted to kill a black man (Harvey), and unbeknownst to him, his other brother Clarence had recently already killed still another *black* man.

It brought to mind the classic movie *Dead Man Walking*, which starred Susan Sarandon and the absolutely great actor and one of Clyde Paine's (Claude's father) favorites, Mr. Sean Penn. In this movie, the actor Sean Penn, who was portraying a racist murderer sentenced to death, said, "Niggers shoot one another like tin cans on a fence." This was a reality within the black experience in this country. Blacks were killing blacks or, at the very least, wanting to kill other blacks. This was the kind of problems T.A.N. behavior brought to black people—aggravation on the highest level, to the nth degree. Caucasians as well as other races and ethnicities observed with a keen eye just how difficult it was for blacks to coexist with other blacks.

*However*, Claude thought. *None of those other folks know what we have to endure, why we are so jealous of one another, and why we bear so much angst towards one another. This is our experience, our problem as a people. And as far as I can see, this is a conundrum that we ourselves have to repair.*

# CHAPTER 32

Claude remembered one of his coworkers at Johnson & Johnson—a Haitian named Mr. Joubert (pronounced *show bear*). One day, Claude ordered food from the Red Bull Inn just twelve miles down the road from the plant. As it was night shift it was the only place at the hour to get good food. But he was at work without his car that day, which was having a tune-up, an oil change, and new brake pads installed. He asked Mr. Joubert if he could use his car to pick up the order. Mr. Joubert kindly agreed to allow Claude to use his car.

When Claude returned, Mr. Joubert was nowhere to be found for Claude to give him a few bucks for rendering Claude the use of his car. Claude did find another Haitian named Guy (pronounced Gee like key with a G). Claude told Guy why he was looking for Mr. Joubert.

Guy answered, "Mr. Claude, Mr. Joubert will thank you for even asking to use his car, but I assure you, he will not take any money from you."

Baffled, Claude said. "Are you sure, Guy?"

"Absolutely, he will not take a dime," Guy responded.

Claude found the whole of this very impressive, that this stranger was kind enough to offer the use of his car for free. What was even more impressive to Claude was that Mr. Joubert's countryman had so much respect for his countryman's principles that he knew Mr. Joubert wouldn't even accept money from Claude.

*Geez,* thought Claude. *That's love! That's consideration on the highest level. That's how people behave when they truly respect one another.*

It was what Muhammad Ali was talking about when he went to Zaire, the Congo, Africa, to fight George Foreman. The poor people he met there impressed him. That was why he said they had "dignity in their poverty." Unlike poor blacks in America. Oh, how bad Claude wanted that kind of mind-set for his own people. Everything between the American black man seemed to be in disarray, like the great Nigerian musician Fela Kuti's song "Everything Is Upside Down."

Outside of his immediate family and loved ones, Claude had met many American blacks who behaved the way these two Haitian men comported themselves, but never a T.A.N. A T.A.N. wouldn't even think of speaking about another black man's principles in such glowing terms. All of the T.A.N.s Claude knew would've taken whatever money Claude offered them.

If he offered ten dollars, the T.A.N.s would've said something like "Damn, I really thought you were going to give me at least twenty bucks, *brother*. Shit, that's what a cab might have cost you!" Claude was oh so pleased that these Haitian men were black. He was just sorry that they were not American-born.

When Claude got home, he had a message waiting for him on his landline voicemail. It was from a Ms. Willis at Childcare Services. It said she had an emergency at work and had to reschedule their appointment and that when he had the time he was to return her call. This was a voice Claude was sure he had heard before, but since he never before dealt with Childs Services and he didn't know anyone who worked there, he just chalked it up to coincidence.

About three or four days later, Claude went to buy a new car from a friend of Mr. Bernard's, whose elderly wife had just passed away. The car didn't even have two thousand miles on it. He really didn't want a used car; he wanted something new. His father once told him that when you bought a used car, there was a high probability that you'd be buying someone else's problem. His car was in good shape, but before the repair shop headaches began, he wanted to trade it in for something new—with a warranty. But this was a deal he couldn't refuse. It was a late-model Nissan Altima. Oh, so clean it was, and it still had new-car smell to boot. En route to purchase this car, Claude happened upon little Nickie, a young T.A.N. female from his neighborhood waiting for a bus. When Nickie noticed Claude's car she began waving frantically beckoning Claude to stop and give her a ride.

He looked at her and shook his head negatively as if to say "No can do, Nickie." Just under two years ago, Claude en route to the one stop mini-mart to get some gas and purchase some cigars for Mr. Bernard. He saw little Nickie at the same bus stop. It was freezing cold that night, so Claude pulled over and picked Nickie up to give her a ride, when they stopped at the mini mart, Nickie started to light up a cigarette. Claude stopped her immediately and said,: Oh no, Nickie. I don't allow smoke in my car. If you smoke step outside while I handle my business. Nickie replied, "Okay, Claude, I got you."

When Claude came back to the car it reeked of cigarette smoke. Infuriated, he then said, "Hey, Nickie. I asked you not to smoke in here. Geez, woman! That smoke make me sick. Why the hell did you light up in here!"

"Shit, nigger! It's cold as hell out there. I aint standing in cold freezing my ass off for you and anyone else. My God you damn niggers are always complaining." said Nickie.

Claude was then dumb-founded. He didn't know how to respond. Once they reached her destination and Nickie left he noticed a small cigarette burn on his passenger seat. He remembered saying, "Never ever again." He just couldn't believe his ears or her attitude. When he saw her waving frantically he couldn't believe her nerve. That she would even expect him to stop for her. Again, he thought, such is the attitude of a T.A.N. He knew in his gut from his experience she wouldn't have lit up at all if he was white.

Once he paid for the car, Claude immediately took it to a tag place for new tags and a title transfer. This tag place that he, his friends, and family members had been going to for years had a new black owner. Claude entered the establishment and approached the clerk, who in this case was also the owner.

"What can I do for you sir?" the owner inquired.

"I need to do a title transfer and to apply for new tags," said Claude.

"Well," said the surreptitious owner once he had given Claude the head-to-toe once-over, "title transfers are 250 dollars." He gazed at Claude with an askew glance, waiting for a reply.

"For what?" said Claude. "A title transfer runs between 40–60 dollars depending on where you go. Why are your title transfers so expensive?"

"Oh, okay," said the caught-in-the-act owner. If its 60 dollars you're used to paying, then 60 dollars it is, young man."

"Oh," said Claude, "now its 60 dollars. If I hadn't known better, you would have taken 250 dollars from me. Goddammit, what kind of business are you running here? Good Lord, my people and the shit y'all do to one another."

"Hey, look, brother, either pay the 60 dollars I quoted you or find another tag shop. I just started this business. I'm trying to get on my feet, brother"—*there goes that brother shit again*, thought Claude—"so I'm trying to make an extra buck. What's it to you? Y'all always give the white man what he ask for," said the suddenly aggravated, sleight-of-hand, nervy owner.

"Wow," said Claude. "Talk about horse shit justification. If that don't beat all. Just some more ignorant T.A.N. bullshit. Geez, will you damn black folks ever stop this crap?"

"Hey, look, chubby, either pay the price I quoted or take your black ass to a white man. I don't have all day for a nitpicking nigger that don't know how to talk to people," said the slimy, ignorant owner.

After pausing for about five seconds, drawing a deep breath, Claude then said, "Sir, have a good day." Claude then left the establishment, shaking his head, never to return there again.

# CHAPTER 33

School was just beginning, and with the autumnal equinox fast approaching, but Claude was still out of work. Even though he sent out a great deal of resumés and cover letters that included the employment recommendations that Ms. Evans, the family barrister, had procured for him from Johnson & Johnson, Claude was really tired of having what his mother called idle hands.

Call it coincidence or kismet, but later that same night, he received a call from the state representative. She requested for Claude to please run for the vacant committee man position that had recently become available in his voting district. Claude was overwhelmed that this woman even knew who he was.

*Did Mr. Bernard have anything to do with this?* he wondered. He was caught off guard at the request because she was a lovely, intelligent African American woman who exuded strength and confidence whenever he saw her on the news or heard her campaigning. She definitely didn't fit the profile of the women who usually called Claude's home or the ones he dated. Like Mr. Bernard's daughter, Ms. Sherelle Wright was an African American woman who had that look Claude adored. She was a mocha-complexioned woman with a drop-dead gorgeous, brick house body, and the most beautifully flawless skin. Equipped she was with the most gorgeous, comely mouth with pearl-white teeth. Oh man, did he find her attractive. Now she was on the phone, asking him to devote his time to her. *Wow.*

"Ahh, Ms. Wright, what does the job entail, and what qualifications are necessary?" Claude humbly asked.

"Well, Mr. Paine, I wouldn't have called you if you weren't qualified," said Ms. Wright. "Also, young man, you first have to be voted into the position. I'll stop over your place early tomorrow and whether you're home or not, I'll leave a petition in your mail slot."

"Petition?" Claude queried.

"Oh yes," said Ms. Wright, "you initially have to get ten signatures to have your name on the ballot. On election day in November, once you received the ten signatures, your name will be placed on the ballot and then post election, if you receive enough votes, you'll then officially be our committee man for the next four years."

"Oh, okay," said Claude. "I'm flattered that you even asked me, Ms. Wright. It will be an honor to assist you in any way I can. Sure, I'll pursue it."

"Good, Mr. Paine, you made my day. The materials will be in your mailbox in the morning," said Ms. Wright.

"Okay," said Claude. "One thing, Ms. Wright. I'm curious. What made you think of me to run for this position?"

"Well, you're a registered voter, and you have been for eight years, according to our records. You're a registered Democrat. Also, you're a lifelong resident of Somerset County. Last but certainly not least, you do not have a felony criminal record," said Ms. Wright.

"Oh, okay," said Claude, his ego now soaring. "I'll look forward to the process. But my availability might change in the very near future."

"Oh, why is that?" Ms. Wright replied.

"Because," said Claude, "I'm currently not working, and by the time election day rolls around, I'm sure to be back on the clock, so to speak."

"That's almost two months away," said Ms. Wright. "Let's concern ourselves with what's immediately in front of us and cross that bridge when we get there, okay, young man?"

"For sure, Ms. Wright. Again I thank you for your interest. I'll do the very best I can. Wow, what an opportunity!" Claude replied.

This was news he had to share with both Mom and Dad. No sooner did he hang up his landline phone that it rang again almost immediately. It was Ms. Willis from Child Services, informing

Claude that she would come to his apartment tomorrow morning, Friday, at 11 a.m.

"That's okay with me. I'll be home at the ready, Ms. Willis," said Claude.

"Good, I'll see you then. The whole interview process will take a little more than an hour, okay?" said Ms. Willis.

"For sure," Claude replied.

"Oh, one more thing for my records, Mr. Paine. Is this child in question a child of yours?" Ms. Willis queried.

"Oh, no, not a blood relative, Ms. Willis," said Claude.

"Okay, thanks. See you tomorrow, sir," said Ms. Willis.

When the call was over, again Claude had a strange feeling of déjà vu. He was absolutely sure he knew this woman from her voice; he just couldn't place its origin. *Oh well*, he thought to himself. *We'll meet tomorrow. Maybe it will come together once I see her.*

# CHAPTER 34

He immediately called his favorite woman on the face of the earth—his mother. When his sister, Carmen, answered the phone, he could hear in her voice that something was amiss.

"Hey, Kay-Kay, what's going on? I just got some good news. Is Mom around?"

"No, she just stepped out to get her prescription filled. She should be back in just a few. Hey, Claude, listen. Mom talked to Ayisha about an hour ago. Ayisha told her Clarence was in a fight in prison. She said the social worker at Rahway said Clay was in the infirmary, that he had just come out of a coma and that he was partially paralyzed," stated Carmen

"*What?*" said Claude, flabbergasted at this latest development in Clarence's situation. "Is he a quadra or a para?" Claude asked.

"Well," said Carmen. "That's the good news, I guess. They told Ayisha that his spinal cord is severely bruised, not fractured or separated. Ayisha said they didn't expect his paralysis to be permanent. He doesn't have any feeling in his entire left leg. Also, since he just came out of a coma, he's on a once-an-hour vigil for at least the next twenty-four hours. They said his skull was severely bruised as well."

"Damn!" said Claude. "What happened? Did he get jumped?"

"No," said Carmen. "That's the bad news."

"The bad news? What do you mean?" queried Claude, suddenly dry-mouthed and now quite anxious.

"Well, hold on, brother, let me finish," replied Carmen.

"Oh, okay, Carmen, I'm sorry," interjected Claude.

"It's okay," said Carmen. "I know how close you two are. The bad news Claude is that the guy Clay was fighting is dead. The prison won't release any more information until the investigation is complete. Clay currently hasn't been charged with murder, so once Ayisha gets the news, she said she'd call Mom immediately." Carmen was exasperated.

Claude, though still concerned, starting smiling. He was pleased that his brother wasn't permanently injured and that whoever he was fighting could no longer pose a threat to his big brother again. "Wow, what news. Hey, Kay-Kay, please tell Mom to call me immediately, okay?"

"Hey, Claude, didn't you have some good news to share with us? Ain't that why you called?" said Carmen.

"Oh," said Claude, "it's not pressing. I'll tell Mom when she calls. So you're sure Clay's going to be okay?"

"Well, brother, you have the exact same news Mom and I have. It's virtually verbatim—according to Ayisha," replied Carmen.

"Well, okay, little sis. I'll talk to y'all later," said Claude.

"Okay, bro, fare thee well," said Carmen, mimicking one of her brother Carter's favorite lines.

*Oh, what a day!* thought Claude.

After the bittersweet news about his brother Clarence and the committee-man offer from Ms. Wright, Claude was now exhausted. He sat down and cut on the television. The documentary *Gun Fight* was on, already in session. Claude watched as they filmed young black men in Philadelphia, Pennsylvania. Some had masks on, brazenly talking about how they had to own guns because of who they had to interact with daily. They obviously weren't talking about protecting themselves from or having to shoot Caucasians or any other of the many minorities living in America. Then they (the narrator of the documentary) went to a hospital where the doctor said the predominance of trauma patients were African American males with gunshot wounds. The quote Claude would never forget was that "most gunshot victims die where they are shot on the street."

*Much like Michael Brown in Ferguson, Missouri, in 2014,* thought Claude. The documentary film crew then went to gun shows where right-winged militia's and hate groups—like the Neo-Nazi movement, the modern day Ku Klux Klan, and the Skinhead movements—purchased their guns to make sure they were properly armed just in case. These so-called right-winged groups weren't talking about arming themselves to shoot Caucasians either. Both inner-city blacks and rural dwelling right-winged whites were arming and preparing themselves to shoot black people.

*Wow*, thought Claude. *Just like the subliminal seduction message about black criminals in the television shows I once talked about, whether intentional or unintentional.* After all, like the old saying went, "Good intentions never put an onion in the soup!" He could clearly see the covert message set forth in this. Everybody needed to arm themselves because the black folks might be coming. And like the rogue policeman throughout this country, they all had to shoot some black folks from time to time. He then realized that he himself wanted to shoot some blacks (T.A.N.s) also.

*Geez*, he thought as he immediately became depressed and turned off the television, now extremely tired. Claude then prepared for a shower. He got his Wes Montgomery (African American Jazz guitarist) CD and went right to the song "Bumpin' on Sunset." This was another one of his favorite jazz tunes with soothing, calming effect. All these jazz tunes were introduced to Claude by his brother Clarence, who had learned all he knew about jazz from their father, Clyde. He took an especially long hot shower tonight. Claude then turned off both his cell and landline phones, remembering that his mom was supposed to call tonight. He was really in no mood to converse with anyone else tonight—as he was sure to do every night.

He prayed, got in bed, and said aloud, "God please help save my people. Please help save us all." Then he went to sleep.

— ⚜ —

# CHAPTER 35

The next day, Friday, Claude's plan was to jog four or five miles, take a nice long shower, then go to the Red Bull Inn for some scrambled eggs and some of their delicious turkey sausage links. But he slept too long. He didn't want to interrupt the consecutive days of jogging he had put together (forty-five straight days and counting). However, it was much too late to try to jog four miles, shower, eat breakfast, and return home in time to meet with the case worker from Child Services. Therefore, Claude settled on jogging two miles and skipping the Red Bull Inn for breakfast, which he decided to prepare at home.

*What a day for a run*, Claude thought. There was not a cloud in the sky. The weather was hovering around the low seventies, accompanied by a light, soft, spring-like breeze. He felt so physically good that he just about sprinted the entire two miles. The only difference in the landscape was the dwindling sight of the local wildlife. Since the weather was now cooler, less and less of the wildlife indigent to this area was visible. Yes, the deer were still out and, of course, some of the birds. Every other form of wildlife that dotted the landscape in the summer was no longer visible, at least not daily.

The one thing Claude really began to appreciate was the presence of the Somerset police that rode by when he went out for his daily jog. He had familiarized himself with many of them, and he waved or gave a thumbs-up to them all. One of these policemen used to stop and share a few words with Claude about the wildlife, and this officer would then commend Claude on his commitment and effort. These police officers and their presence now gave Claude a feeling of security, especially since the day some asshole tried to run him over. With the identity of the culprit still a mystery to Claude.

When his two-mile jog was over, Claude came in and prepared to juice. Today's organic juice/cocktail included fresh cucumbers, baby spinach, fresh raspberries, fresh strawberries, bananas, and a heaping teaspoon of both flaxseeds and walnuts. This routine was very effective. It had actually allowed Claude to jumpstart his weight loss program by cutting down his appetite. To date, Claude had dropped just under twenty pounds, and his waist had dwindled ever so slightly from a size 42 to a size 40. His apartment cleaned, his organic juice cocktail complete, and his scrambled eggs and turkey sausage breakfast finished, Claude washed the breakfast dishes and the juicer and waited for the case worker from Child Services to arrive.

Ms. Willis arrived right on time, as if scripted, immediately after Claude dried and put away the last dish he washed. Claude quickly made his way to the downstairs door and let in the case worker.

*Wow*, thought Claude. *Is it any wonder I recognized her voice. Ms. Willis, of course.*

It was Mr. Bernard's daughter, Ms. Betty Willis. Claude was grinning from ear to ear when he offered salutations to Ms. Willis, a grin that wasn't returned.

"Well, well, Ms. Willis, how the heck are you?" said an ecstatic Claude.

"I'm fine, sir. Forgive my ignorance, but I don't recall us meeting before, Mr. Paine," replied Ms. Willis.

"Sure we met, Ms. Willis. I'm a friend of your father, Mr. Bernard . . . eeerr . . . Mr. Saint, I mean. Sorry about that. I met you at his home a few weeks ago," said the still grinning Claude.

"Oh right, right," said the now grinning Ms. Willis. "Carl, right."

"No, ma'am, that's Claude," he replied.

"Well, hello, Mr. Paine. Now, if you don't mind, young man, let's get down to business. I have four other interviews to do after you, and my time is scarce," said Ms. Willis.

Claude told Ms. Willis the entire goings-on (both days) between himself, Meechie, and her daughter, Marissa. Upon completing his story, Ms. Willis quickly interjected, "Excuse me, Mr. Paine, but I must candidly ask you something that might perturb you just a tad nonetheless. It is imperative that I ask you this, sir." Ms. Willis suddenly inquisitive.

"Go right ahead, Ms. Willis," said Claude. "Ask away."

"Well, Mr. Paine, might the reporting of this friend of yours, this Ms. Hernandez, is it possible that this is a case of sour grapes because Ms. Hernandez denied you the opportunity to have intercourse with her?" queried Ms. Willis.

"Absolutely not, Ms. Willis. The narrative I just went over with you about the child not eating properly, the child not having school clothes or supplies when the school year began, the vicious slaps the child's mother hit her with that knocked down all the recently purchased school supplies, and the abhorrent condition of the child's teeth—Ms. Willis, I honestly, humbly submit to you, does any of that sound like I have an ulterior motive, I ask?" queried Claude.

"No sir, I must say they do not. I will follow up with this matter as soon as I complete my report. I need to also ask you, Mr. Paine, if there is a hearing, are you willing to follow through if we need you?" said the comely Ms. Willis.

"Yes, by all means, Ms. Willis," stated Claude.

"Okay, sir, here's my card, and if there's anything you remember or if something else happens to this child that you are aware of, please feel free to contact me immediately," said Ms. Willis.

"For sure, Ms. Willis. Oh, Ms. Willis, one more thing," stated Claude.

"What's that?" said Ms. Willis.

"Well," said Claude, "from the moment I met you at your dad's home, you have been on my mind. I find you extremely attractive, and I'd like to go to dinner with you . . . if that's okay" Claude was nervously.

"Well, Mr. Paine, I am truly flattered," said Ms. Willis. "Really, I am, Mr. Paine. Now I have one question for you, young man?"

"What's that, Ms. Willis? Also, why do you keep calling me young man—with the emphasis on *young*?" queried Claude. "I'm soon to be twenty-six years old. I know I'm a little younger than you,

Ms. Willis. What are you, thirty-seven or thirty-eight? That's not that much of a disparity."

"Wow," said Ms. Willis. "You are loaded with compliments today, huh, Mr. Paine? Well, thanks again. Still, Mr. Paine, I am old enough to be your grandmother. I'm fifty-four years old and a widower."

"You're what?" said the flabbergasted Claude. "Look, Ms. Willis, if you're not interested in talking to me, fine. However, Ms. Willis, absolutely no one is going to believe you're in your fifties. Please forgive me for challenging your veracity, but fifty-four is a bit of a stretch, don't you think?"

Ms. Willis then retrieved her wallet from her Gucci purse. She then took out her driver's license and gave it to Claude to peruse.

After giving Ms. Willis's driver's license the once-over, Claude, his mouth still agape in wonderment, stuttered, "W-w-w-wow, Ms. Willis, I apologize. Geez, please forgive me. I've never seen anyone in their fifties look as good as you. That's a fact, Ms. Willis, not a compliment. *Nubile* is a word typically used to describe young women. Well, it sure enough suits you too, Ms. Willis. Wow, I can't get over this one." Claude was still stunned.

"Well, *young man*, are you still interested in dating a mother figure?" said Ms. Willis between chuckles.

Claude stood there, dumbfounded. Still, he couldn't believe his eyes or ears.

"Oh man, Mr. Paine, you just made my day. Geez, young brother, look at that look on your face! You look like you just saw Casper the ghost. Have you nothing else to say, or do you need a day or two to process what just happened?" said Ms. Willis in jest.

"No, I don't need any time," said Claude. "My dinner offer still stands."

"Well, we can go to dinner, sure. Normally, I don't mix my personal life with my business or work dealings. But you're a friend of my father's, and I think you're safe. My personal number is also on the card I gave you. Call me, and we'll discuss this further, Mr. Paine. Like I stated earlier, I have very much the busy schedule today, and I have to be going. I sincerely thank you for the compliments and the dinner offer," said Ms. Willis as she gathered her belongings. "Well," she continued, "are you going to escort me to the door or just continue to stand there like a statue?"

"Oh, okay, sure," said Claude.

The two made their way out the door and down the steps to Ms. Willis's BMW. Still chuckling, Ms. Willis rolled down her window and said, "Mr. Paine, make sure you call me when you come to, okay?" She then broke out into a full hearty laugh.

Claude, now grinning from ear to ear, responded, "Sure thing, Ms. Willis. Hey, I'm glad you find me comical." Ms. Willis then nodded affirmatively and drove off.

Claude was still somewhat dumbfounded. He had never been romantically involved with any woman almost thirty years his senior. He was rendered quite uncomfortable by the entire experience. The question about whether he was making this report because Meechie didn't give him any pussy. How funny Ms. Willis found his countenance after Ms. Willis stating her age. The one question that haunted him was what the heck she look like under her clothes. Was she sagging in the breast? Were her breasts and belly lying on each other like one entity, or did she have cellulite around her butt and on her thighs or maybe varicose veins somewhere? Did she have wrinkled butt cheeks? Were those her real teeth? Did she wear bikini panties, thongs, or those big, stupid, unsexy bloomers he had seen older women in? Something that he was just curious about was what he thought might be common among older folks. Did she have halitosis? Most of these things he had seen in older women in movies, on TV, and what he had read about. Was any of it true?

"Geez," Claude then said out loud. "Talk about jumping the gun. I haven't even had my first date with her. Wow, look at the effect this woman has already had on me."

# CHAPTER 36

Although Claude had continually told himself that he needed to visit his dad, he didn't commit to it until today. His father (Clyde) worked almost every day at his contracting job. However, being afflicted with severe seasonal allergies that almost always reared its ugly head in autumn, today he decided to stay home, take his allergy medication (which made him woozy, sleepy), and rest. When Claude arrived at his dad's house, after greeting Carter, he made his way into his dad's bedroom and was surprised to see his father glued to the television. Watching TV was something that his father did very little of unless he was watching sports, a documentary, or the news. As expected, his dad was watching the news.

The University of Missouri (commonly referred to as Mizzou) was being covered and discussed on this day because several predominately African American students, including a large number of football players, were demonstrating and planning to boycott the upcoming football game against Brigham Young University, a boycott that would cost the university a loss in the standings because of a forfeit. In addition, the school would've had to pay BYU over one million dollars in forfeiture fees, plus the loss of funds from the television broadcast revenues.

This boycott was demanding the firing or resignation of the school's president, its chancellor, and seven other demands that the African American student body demanded/requested to help quell racial insensitivity and overt racism at the university. When Claude attempted to engage his dad in conversation, he was quickly shushed and told, "Please wait a minute, son." He came in just as CNN was interviewing a young African American male, whom Claude's dad called his newest African American young hero. Mr. Johnathan Butler, some seven days earlier, started a hunger strike that he intended to adhere to until the university took some action with regard to the demands these student activists insisted upon.

*Wow*, thought Claude. *A young man close to my age decided not to eat anything except to drink water until these demands are met. What courage!* This young man obviously wasn't doing this for himself.

"Talk about giving his people some hope. Geez!" said Clyde Paine out loud. "What a commitment." Clyde was fighting back tears. He was so moved by Mr. Butler's commitment.

No one ever stopped taking sustenance for themselves or for some self-serving notoriety. Clyde kept saying, "What a young man, oh my Lord, what a man! I know his parents are proud of this guy!"

Claude hadn't heard his dad say that in years. Johnathan Butler was a name that was going to stick with Claude the rest of his life. What a removal this young man's behavior was from what Claude and his dad had become accustomed to—the incessant backstabbing he had to endure from his own people, the total lack of respect, and the conniving chicanery they both experienced daily. This Johnathan Butler guy exuded hope every time he opened his mouth.

Aside from Mr. Butler, there was also Ms. Naomi Collier. Ms. Collier was the University of Missouri's NAACP president. When she was interviewed, Clyde started grinning from ear to ear at how articulate this young lady was and how eloquently she answered every question put forth. Both Clyde and Claude were both now deeply engrossed in every word this young lion and lioness spoke. The president of the school and the university's chancellor had finally succumbed to the pressure these two, and the dozens of other young predominately black activists (many other Caucasian students and faculty joined in to give solidarity support, like the Quakers did during slavery), put on them, and they decided to resign.

Clyde was now saying, as he wiped away tear after tear, "See what can happen when we as a people unite for a common cause?"

Claude then said, "You're right, Dad. The only thing that bothers me is that it happens too infrequently. And the folks who involve themselves in this kind of civil disobedience are too few."

"That's okay," said Clyde. "It's a start, son. It's a damn good start."

The mayor of Columbia, Missouri, where the University of Missouri was located, Mr. Bob McDavid, also weighed in with some very powerful words with regard to what these young predominately black students accomplished. He stated (paraphrased), "What these youngsters did, their organizing and their protesting, was a seminar in civics and a seminar in democracy. It shows what an *organized* set of students can do when they feel the need to redress wrongs. The fact that they (these predominately black students) stuck together and accomplished their goal says a lot for their organization. That protest itself is American, and it is also a right of democracy."

"Wow," said Claude, "we as a whole can also organize to bring about change within our own culture of violence and inner racial discord."

"You're right, son. These students are a minority at that school. What did they say, about 7 or 8 percent of the school's population? Yet they stuck together, steadfastly, and achieved what they set out to achieve. When we as a people decide that we can do the same thing, then we can achieve inner racial harmony and perhaps bring an end to the vast difference between the true African American and the modern-day, throwback American Negro. These kids just proved it, son. Sure, it's on a much smaller scale, but they did prove it!" Clyde continued, "Hey, son, remember what your mom told you about the difference in prayer in unison at church and prayer alone at home?"

"Yeah, Dad. Of course, I do," said Claude. "She said prayer in unison is much stronger."

"Right, right," said Clyde. "Well, so is protest infinitely much stronger in unison. Just try to imagine what could potentially happen if we as a people united nationally. Let's say there're fifty to seventy-five or one hundred thousand of us in each state. Then we protested about how ignorant we are to continue to kill and disrespect one another, how bad it is for many of our youth to be so disrespectful to African American adults and the elderly. Like that linguistic professor at Columbia University, Mr. John McWhorter, said, start a movement of blacks, stop killing and brutalizing blacks. Just think of how poignantly effective that can be."

"Yeah," said Claude. "My old-timer buddy Mr. Bernard mentioned that a few days ago."

"Wow," said Clyde, "what an accomplishment. The things my people are CAPABLE of doing. The real potential that exist in the black community."

"Yeah, Dad," said Claude. "Not to be a defeatist, but I also remember what you told me years ago about potential. You said potential can be buried.

"Well, if we continue on the path we're on with this inner racial, divisive, cutthroat bullshit and self-hate crap that we go through with ignorant T.A.N.s, our hopes and dreams can be buried as well, just like potential!" Clyde was then silent, for he knew the fatalistic words his son just spoke were right! When the telecast went to commercial, Clyde stood up and gave his youngest son a sincere prolonged hug. "Good to see you son. How the hell are you?" said Clyde.

"I'm good, Dad. How about yourself?" Claude replied.

"Save for these pain-in-the-ass allergies, everything is fine," said Clyde between four or five really hard sneezes. Are you back to work yet?"

"No, Dad, I got a bunch of resumes and cover letters out there though. Hey, Dad, guess what," said Claude. "Ms. Sherelle Wright, the state representative, *personally* asked me to run for committee man."

"Well," said Clyde, "are you going to do it?"

"Sure am," said Claude. "At least until I start working and it begins interfering with my work schedule.

"That Ms. Wright is one hell of a good looking woman, ain't she?"

"Yeah."

Clyde said, "Is that why you decided to run for the position?" He then shot Claude a furtive glance. There were five seconds of silence, then both men started laughing heartily.

"Well, Daddy, that might have had a little to do with me making up my mind," Claude said between chuckles.

"Spoken like a true Paine," said Clyde.

"Hey, Dad, have you heard any more news about Clay?" said Claude about his brother Clarence.

"No, son, I'm privy to the same information you are. Clay got himself into a hell of a jam. But in my heart, son, I feel that he's going to be all right. Just keep praying for him, okay?" said Clyde.

"Sure thing," said Claude. "Hey, Dad, I'm going to holla at Carter. Excuse me for a minute, please, Dad."

After spending a few minutes with Carter, who was in the midst of being washed by his new and very pretty attendant, Claude went to the kitchen for a sandwich. When he got to the kitchen, he made a conscious decision to forego the sandwich, and he grabbed an apple and a banana. He went back to his dad's room to wish him well with his oppressive allergies and bade him and Carter adieu.

Claude had been so caught up in his responsibilities, his legal activities, and other family issues that he felt it was high time to release some of this built-up angst and go clubbing tonight. He had just thought of the Lady Gaga song "Just Dance" and felt that this was exactly what he needed to do. He went home to shower and put on some of his clubbing glad rags and go out and have some fun and maybe meet a new female to cozy up with or possibly get to know one carnally. He told himself that when he left.

Prior to crossing the George Washington Bridge, he decided he was going to stop by his good friend Mr. Bernard's house and see if his elderly buddy needed some stogies or if he needed anything else. He was pleased with the goings-on of the day. He reacquainted himself with Ms. Betty Willis. He caught his father in a good mood. What really pleased Claude on this day were the happenings at the University of Missouri. Every time African Americans did anything positive, it made his heart soar and filled him with hope, like it did his mom and dad. It confirmed to him that the ultimate authority was God.

It seemed to Claude that God was tracking him, always looking out for him. He got himself in trouble from time to time but never any trouble he couldn't handle. Something always seemed to happen just in the nick of time. He refused to believe in luck or circumstance.

*Is this the end result of prayer?* he thought to himself. Maybe it was true what Mr. Bernard intimated. Maybe he really was kissed by angels at birth. He began to think of how easy it was to acknowledge the existence of God when things were going well. No, he was still out of work. However, one of the people from his community that he adored had recruited him to do some political work, something he never dreamed of. What a great way to fill his vacant hours. He again recommitted to Bible study and made sure to keep going as he had to do something, he thought, to thank the Lord for his good fortune.

Again, as he had done so many times in his life, he said out loud, "Good Lord, I sincerely thank you for affording me with the sweetest of kismet." Once he got home, showered, threw on some of his expensive cologne, his dress-up jeans, his gator-skin loafers, and his chocolate-brown cashmere sweater. Just as he made his way to his front door, something prompted him to check the voicemail on his landline phone.

Oh so very much to his pleasant surprise, he had eight—yes, eight—voicemail messages from prospective employers. All left a similar message, stating that they had received his resume and were impressed. They all requested a call back so they could set up an interview.

"Wowee!" said Claude aloud. *Just one more set of circumstances to give all the glory to God*, he thought. Now he really had a reason to party tonight. "Let's go have some damn fun," he said out loud.

One of his apartment neighbors, an elderly woman in her mid seventies, who had her door ajar heard him, yelled out, "Fun? Hey, Mr. Paine, take me the hell with you. I wanna go have some fun too!"

En route to the Big Apple to let his hair down and do the thick man slide and shake while leaving some sweat on the dance floor, Claude wanted to pop in on his buddy Mr. Bernard. He knew Mr. Bernard was privy to the goings-on at the University of Missouri, and he had a few racial-related question to ask his buddy. When Claude arrived quickly, for some reason, he began to think of Ms. Betty Willis, and he wondered whether or not to discuss her with Mr.

Bernard. It just felt a little awkward attempting to date the daughter of such a close friend. And he was still uncomfortable with the gap in his and Ms. Willis's age. He really didn't know how Mr. Bernard would feel about his daughter being out with him either.

"Hey, young buddy, come on in. How's life treating you, junior?"

"Everything is okay, sir, and you, is all as you would have it today, sir?" Claude queried, partially in jest.

"Oh Lord, sounds like a lead-in to a set up. What's that sly Shakespearean shit you're slinging all about?" Both men now laughed aloud.

"Hey, Mr. Bernard, I know you've been keeping up with the protest at Mizzou. Tell me something, sir, please. In all your years of experience and after all your globe-trotting, why is the country and the world having so much trouble with race? I know it's been race problems all the eighty years you've been alive. Mr. Bernard, please tell me, are all white people, in one way or another, racist? You've been on this earth long enough to have an intelligent opinion about that. Please give me what you got."

"Well, good, buddy, let me answer that one without equivocation. Absolutely not! Sure, many of them are. No one can deny that. If you know anything about American history, then you know the vital role many a white person played in assisting Ms. Harriet Tubman and Ms. Sojourner Truth with the success of the Underground Railroad. In the 1960s, as militant an activist as the great Malcolm X was, even he was quoted saying, 'Even white folks are tired of the way blacks are being treated.' Shit, young buddy, personally I don't have to go back that far. I can also answer that question with three words: Mr. Tim Wise! He's a Caucasian who spends his life exposing racism in all its form. In America, Caucasians like Mr. Wise are necessary and appreciated. Read two of the books he's written: *White like Me* and/or *Under the Influence*. Then thank God for him.

"When I was in Vietnam. With ten days left before they sent me home, we had a mission on which I was supposed to be point man, the soldier who was that day's lead man, the lead probing soldier of the platoon. When a firefight, or shooting, broke out, usually the point man was the first to get hit. This Caucasian guy from

Tennessee—*Tennessee*, dammit—told our sergeant that he wouldn't be able to live with himself if something happened to me with me having such a short time to go to see my family again. He then insisted that not only could he go out in my stead but that he be allowed to also serve as point man that day. Believe it or not, young buddy, it was that day that this brave-ass white man earned his purple heart. That's right. A white man took one in the forearm and two in his leg that day, replacing me in the bush. So my personal experience says I know they're not all racist. Claude, that's the real strength of our country and our constitution.

"When Caucasians join hand in hand in any of our battles in this country, then our purpose becomes stronger, our results more effective. That's how America is *supposed to be*! The Quakers, who weighed in during slavery, were a great help to us, just like the Caucasians who joined hand in hand with African Americans during the historical March on Washington, led by the great Dr. Martin Luther King Jr. Geez, Claude, if you've ever been in a situation when your life depended on another man's actions, then you really don't care what color, race, creed, or ethnicity he or she is. That's the kind of camaraderie being in the service creates. No, I'm no lackey or some idiot that thinks we don't live in a racist society. I also know there are many so-called liberal white folks who are liberal until you try to move into their neighborhood or date one of their daughters or sisters. But I know many a Caucasian that is tired of this racist bullshit themselves and those that deplores the way not only black folks are treated. But they don't like to see anyone oppressed—no black person, no poor white person, or any other minority either. Anyway, didn't you tell me that you had an Italian friend, a Darnella or Daniella or something like that? A psychiatrist or something?"

"That's Danielle, Mr. Bernard. She's a psychologist," Claude interjected.

"Well," said Mr. Bernard, "the way I heard you speak about her, sure sounded to me like you trusted her. I could tell by the look that came over your face whenever you discussed her that it was more than lust too. Well, your friendship with her should answer that question for you."

What Mr. Bernard didn't realize was that he had struck a nerve because Claude—who adored her professionalism, how disarming she was, her good looks, her motivational skills, and primarily her *sincerity*—had quite a crush on Danielle. To Claude, Danielle's character was the prototype of what he wanted in a wife.

"No, Claude, young buddy, all white people are not racist, just like all black people ain't what you call T.A.N.s. All black people ain't what you call African Americans either. Still, young buddy, and I've told you this several times, no matter how ignorant, self-hating, uneducated, manipulative, dastardly humble or saintly, if they are of African descent, they're still your people. So when you start concerning yourself with whether or not white folks are racist or not, you just might lose the opportunity to learn about someone's ethnicity, their heritage. Try to appreciate what you could learn from them and about them, what they could possibly have to offer.

"Yeah, racism is a true evil, and it has been around just as long as America has. Just try to treat whomever's path *you* cross with respect and consideration, and you'll experience perhaps just a little more peace of mind as you continue to move forward. I hope that answers your question, good buddy, because my gut and my butt are telling me I have a date with my toilet right now, so I'm going to have to ask you to enjoy your night on this dance floor tonight. If I continue conversing with you, I might soil myself, so good-night, young buddy, and once again, thank you for the stogies."

Claude then said, "Okay, Mr. Bernard, I hope everything comes out okay, and I'll talk to you later in the week."

# CHAPTER 37

Just as Claude got in his car and started it, his glove compartment started buzzing as a text came into his cell phone. Before pulling out of Mr. Bernard's driveway, he checked to see who it was from. It was a photo of Marissa's latest report card.

*Huh?* thought Claude as he commenced perusing it to see what this was about. He thought, *The report card of Meechie's daughter, huh? That's strange.*

The grades were three Cs, two Ds, and two Fs. Claude just chuckled and shook his head. It said underneath the photo: "Hey, Claude, just remember that you promised my daughter a computer. She told me, so please keep your word, brother!"

This was communication from a woman that implored him to lose her phone number and threatened to throw a rock and bust his car window. Then she said her brother would kick his ass. He also remembered telling young Marissa nothing below a C. He refused to let this bullshit destroy his fun tonight, so he erased it, put his phone back in the glove compartment, and made his way to the George Washington Bridge.

He had a long night of drinking champagne, enjoying the intimate company of some beautiful women, who all exposed their shapely thighs, panty lines, cleavages, and more. Two of these lovelies had exchanged numbers with him as they intermittently used his table and champagne as a pit stop throughout the night. When the last call for alcohol was announced, Claude made his way home. It was maybe forty minutes before dawn, and Claude thought about jogging his four miles before hitting the sack for the remainder of the morning. He didn't dance much, so he wasn't really physically exhausted. He did, however, realize how many calories were in alcohol, and he didn't want to sleep on what he had imbibed through the night.

When he pulled in front of the apartment complex where he resided, he reached into his glove compartment for his phone, locked the car, and made his way up the steps to his apartment. En route he checked his phone and saw that there were four text messages—one from each family member, save for Clay, of course.

This was a rare occurrence, so he checked the one from his favorite lady on earth first, his mother. It read as follows: "Praise the Lord and all his glory, my son. Your brother Clay will not have any charges added to his record. His killing of the other inmate, after a thorough investigation, was ruled self-defense. Also, his feeling has returned to his leg. Hallelujah! Call me tonight if it's not too late. Love you! Mom."

"Hallelujah again right back at you, Mom," Claude said under his breath.

He knew that if he went in and sat down for only a few minutes, he would lose his desire to jog. He removed his soiled clothes and readied them for the cleaners. He got dressed in one of his sweat suits and immediately made his way out for his daily (weekday) jog. He had more energy than he had anticipated, and he immediately jumped into a nice rhythm. After about three city blocks, something he hadn't seen in a couple of months happened.

A gorgeous red fox sauntered across the street in front of him. This one was a tad larger than most he had seen prior. Also, it moved just a little slower than the foxes he had seen in the summer, kind of like it had a "Yeah, fuck with me if you want" attitude. He continued on, and the sun had begun to creep up slowly in the sky. The colors this time in the morning were beyond description. A lavender-hued streak was accompanied by the tangerine rays that the sun, peeking over the horizon, emitted, and these morning sunrays seemed to burn holes into the cotton-like, puffy clouds. Lord, lord, lord, the sight of this moved something special inside of Claude. To him, this feeling was true, unadulterated freedom, the epitome of God's wonderful work. Not even a photo of this gorgeous vista could capture how it made Claude feel inside.

*Magnificent*, he thought to himself.

When he reached the halfway point and turned around to return home, a red car was again coming at him, picking up speed as it approached. He went into wave mode and frantically began trying to wave the car aside. Again, as with the first time, his waving was an exercise in futility. This driver seemed to know the landscape because, this being the second time, it only approached him in an area devoid of sidewalks. Again, as it drew near Claude, he had to jump into the thorn bushes and jagged shrubbery.

"You motherfucking asshole!" Claude yelled as the car sped close to him, barely missing him. Then this time, it swerved even closer to him, clearly trying to hit him. Just then, seemingly out of nowhere came one of the police vans he encountered almost every morning; it was in hot pursuit of the driver who just tried to run him over. It's lights were rolling and siren blaring—a scene that totally screwed up the vista he had beheld just moments earlier. Claude was never ever so happy to see the police. He stopped and jogged slowly back to where the policeman had caught up to the car and forced it to pull over. He couldn't wait to see the jackass in this red car that twice had tried to hit him.

As he drew closer, the officer yelled two things to Claude. He barked, "Stay back." It was immediately followed by "Are you okay?"

"A little scratched up from the thorn bushed. Outside of that, officer, all is fine," replied Claude.

"Well, do you know who this is that just tried to hit you?" said the officer.

"No, sir, but this is the second time they tried to hit me," said Claude.

"Oh, yeah," said the officer. "Let's get to the bottom of this."

The driver got out of his car and started to approach the officer. Verily, verily, verily, lo and behold, it was none other than the flaming, butt wipe, fat Negress's man, lover, boyfriend (or whatever), Harvey the jerk.

The officer yelled out vociferously to Harvey, "Turn around. Get back in the car, then produce your license, registration, and your insurance information."

Harvey then replied, "But, officer, I didn't even do nothin'."

The officer than yelled out for the second and final time, 'Follow my instructions—*now!*"

Harvey then said very loudly. "Aw, man, all this trouble over that fucking nigger. All right, let me get my shit for you." Harvey then turned around, walked the four or five steps to his bullshit red car, reached, and opened the door.

Just as he attempted to go into his car—apparently for his driver information—*crack crack crack*. There was the echo of fired shells, and the ejection of the bullet casings filled the morning air. The ominous sound of gunfire was quickly followed by a cloud of fast-dissipating, rancid-smelling gunpowder smoke. Harvey fell against the opened door, then fell over toward the driver's side front seat. As he tumbled, the upper half of his body pitched forward and slumped onto the driver seat, and he then slowly slinked down off the seat on to the ground, coming to rest in a heap inches in front of his opened car door.

Claude, petrified with fear and wonderment, couldn't believe his eyes. "You shot him!" he said aloud in shock.

"You fucking right. You heard him. He said, 'Let me go get my shit." I wasn't going to wait for him to shoot me, my boy!" said the officer.

Claude firmly believed Harvey was reaching under his driver side visor for his driving information. Nonetheless, he knew that if there was ever a time to remain silent, now was that time. Claude was slightly in shock. He was sweating profusely from his jog and growing colder every minute as the perspiration from his jogging began to chill his body. He was told to remain still until the officer's backup arrived.

"First, that bastard tried to kill you. I saw the whole thing. That's why I came to arrest him. He was going to be charged with attempted murder. Then he tried to kill me, and I just saved both our lives," said the officer, attempting to justify the murder he just committed.

"Yeah, well," said Claude, "allow me to go home and shower and change. I'm beginning to freeze from this sweating I'm doing."

"Give me your name and address. You're a witness to this whole thing, and as soon as you're done, you're going to have to come in for a statement, okay, fella?" said the officer.

"Sure," said Claude as he rendered the officer everything he requested. He then began to jog home double time, as they say in the service. He quickly called his father. He told his dad that he just witnessed a police shooting—a murder, as far as he could tell—and that it was a story with many layers. He told him that he just got home from jogging and that he didn't have the time to go over the entire story because the officer had asked him to come in immediately to give a statement.

"Do you want me to come? Do you think you're in any danger?" said his dad.

"No, Dad," said Claude. "I'm pretty sure this is going to be okay—at least for me."

"Well, okay, son. Call me immediately to update me, okay?" said his dad.

# CHAPTER 38

Claude was now confronted with a problem of immense magnitude. Something he never experienced before. He had no idea what awaited him as he dressed, hurriedly made his way to his car, and drove to the police station. He considered driving by the scene of the shooting, but something in him told him that to do so might add insult to injury. Just then it dawned on Claude that he had eight—yes, eight—job-related calls to make to set up interview dates. All of a sudden, he began to feel really tired.

"Damn," he said aloud to himself in his car, "I haven't been to sleep yet. Now I have to deal with this bullshit. Damn! That stupid-ass Harvey is dead." Claude did not realize until now that hate was not the feeling he harbored for Harvey. He felt horrible that the dumb-ass had been killed. Yes, some several weeks earlier, he himself wanted to kill Harvey. But now this new set of circumstances brought on feelings of sorrow, of pathos and empathy that another unarmed black man had been gunned down. Even if it was the witless Harvey. He then started to think about whether or not Harvey really did have a gun in his car. Save for the movies and the news, Claude had never seen anyone killed or even shot for that matter. He was now in the middle of quite the conundrum.

He had witnessed a fatal shooting. A shooting that was initiated by someone who tried to hit him or at the very least terrorized him. Yeah, he had a brief troubled recent history with Harvey, but until the moment he saw the jerk gunned down, he didn't realize that anything could happen to the same guy that contaminated his food and threatened him and his brother that would eventually make him feel sorry for him. Now, all these things were running through his mind and confusing him because, with each passing moment, he grew more and more drained, exhausted, and in need of sleep. Now his motor movements had become somnambulant.

*Wow*, he thought to himself. *What the heck is this cop going to say?*

Geez, what the heck were they going to ask him? What answers was he going to give them? Could he mention that he didn't believe Harvey was behaving in a threatening manner and that there was absolutely nothing about his behavior that warranted the officer's brutal, heinously arrogant response?

Immediately going to the police station might not be a good idea. Perhaps he should've spoken to a lawyer first. He then thought of the lovely, powerful Ms. Evans, Esquire. Did he still have time to do so? After all, he did give the officer his word that he would return immediately. He knew the officer could have demanded he stay at the scene until his backup and/or the meat wagon arrived to take Harvey's lifeless, limp body to the hospital for the morgue. Did this officer let him go so that he could plant evidence on Harvey's person to solidify his assertion that Harvey really was attempting to shoot him? Wow, it had all happened so quickly.

He continued on until he arrived at the Somerset Police Department. Damn, he had seen other black folks in the news and online play into this kind of behavior from wanton killer police before. They, like Harvey, didn't respond to the police like, "This cop has a gun and could kill me." If Harvey had just remained in his car and followed proper get-stopped-by-the-police protocol, perhaps he'd be alive right now. Claude failed to get the officer's name or badge number. Nonetheless, he knew that by the time he got to the police station, they would all know exactly who he was and why he was there. Now, he was so confused and conflicted he knew he could adequately answer none of the questions he was asking himself. However, Claude knew in his heart. It was time to pray. Oh good Lord, if ever there was a situation that demanded prayer, it was now.

# CHAPTER 39

When he entered the police station and approached the information desk, the look on the attendant's face assured him that all were apprised of the recent shooting/murder of Harvey and that they, as he had expected, knew exactly who he was.

After quickly verifying Claude's ID, the on-duty desk attendant said, "Have a seat, young man." After summoning a Detective Boerwinkle, the attendant then said to Claude, "Someone will be with you in a moment to take a statement, young man."

At that very moment, Claude's cell phone was abuzz with call after call. First, it was the gorgeous politician Ms. Wright, followed by Estelle, his mother. Then a call came in from his brother Carter. Following Carter's call, Dad called to catch up on the status of this police issue his son was witness to. Claude, of course, answered none of the calls. The final call came from Ms. Evans.

*What?* thought Claude. *Why the heck is she calling? Does she know what happened and where I am right now? If so, who called her?* Still, he didn't answer Ms. Evans's call either. Her call was quickly followed by a text message which read as follows: "Claude, U hav a rite nt 2 ansa any questns or mke any statemnts without a lawyer present. This is your constitutional rite! Pleez call me immediately."

Of course, Claude complied.

When Ms. Evans answered, she immediately asked Claude to allow her to speak to the detective before he said a word. When Claude told the desk attendant of his intentions, the desk clerk said to him, "Well, who's your attorney?"

He replied, "Ms. Elaine Evans."

The attendant's face grew long, and he inadvertently said, "Oh my god!" He then told Claude, "Please wait a moment, Mr. Paine. I'll be right back."

When the Detective Boerwinkle came to the front to meet with Claude, he too carried a long face. "So you don't want to make a statement without your attorney even though you witnessed the entire event, Mr. Paine?" said Detective Boerwinkle.

"That's right, sir. Here," said Claude, handing the phone to Detective Boerwinkle after first shaking the detective's hand. "That's her on the phone now. She wants to speak to you, sir. Per her instruction, I'm not going to say or sign anything until she is present."

"Okay, have it your way, Mr. Paine," said Detective Boerwinkle. After a brief conversation with Ms. Evans, Detective Boerwinkle gave the phone back to Claude. He then said, "Return with her as soon as possible. Our investigation will remain suspended until we get a statement from you. Please have her contact our office when the two of you are ready. Just remember, Mr. Paine, time is of the essence. You really have nothing to be concerned about. All we're requesting is an honest witness statement. But like your attorney said, waiting for her is your legal right."

"Okay, sir. Thank you, and I'll return with Ms. Evans as soon as possible," replied Claude. He then left the police station for home.

As he drove home, this whole unexpected incident was unnerving to him.

*Damn,* he thought. *Why didn't Harvey just stay in the car and follow the officer's instruction? If you don't listen to the cops at a time like that or don't do everything they ask or tell you to do, chances are you won't get the benefit of your humanity even if you do what they want — you still might catcha bad one. It's always best to do all they ask, and slowly. The sentence for ignorant arrogance should not be death. They kill black folks so easily because apparently some of them really don't see a human being, forget about them possibly seeing an equal. Yes, Harvey was an idiot, but in order to be an idiot, you first have to be human. Obviously, to many of them racist and rogue cops, black folks don't qualify. Maybe — just maybe — the officer was really intimidated by the witless Harvey. Perhaps he sincerely did feel fight or flight at that moment. That's a hell of a thing to feel when you have the law on your side and you're strapped! When Harvey said aloud "Okay, let me get my shit. Claude knew he would've taken that to mean – Get his credentials. But, Claude said to himself my Mom used to always say "Everyone didn't grow up around you, or like you son! Yes, there is a vast difference between the African American and the throwback American Negro. However, that's our problem—an inner racial issue. To the overtly racist portion of the Caucasian population in America, we are all one entity. When they see the witless Harvey or the extraordinary strong African American, they see one in the same, a nigger animal! That's why it is up to us as a people to shrink the chasm that exists between the African American and the throwback American Negro. Because like the former governor of Texas, Governor Connelly, said the day he rode in the same limo as former President Kennedy as he too took a bullet, "My God they're going to kill us all!"*

Now Claude finally understood. He could finally feel what Mr. Bernard meant when he said with regard to T.A.N.s, "Yeah, they're ignorant, but they're still your people." Claude had a great disdain for Harvey. However, the manner in which Harvey died made Claude realize that he really didn't *hate* Harvey, that it could have just as easily been him or a close friend or family member in Harvey's stead. Yes, Mr. Bernard's words about not hating T.A.N.s finally resonated in a way they never had before today. All in all, the killing of Harvey today was ultimately an unjustified execution.

Claude needed sleep. When he arrived at his apartment complex, it was inundated with five or six news vans accompanied by about twenty to twenty-five members of microphone-wielding, boon-carrying, members of the press.

"Good Lord!" said Claude under his breath. He parked and hurried past the throng of reporters and other members of the press with camera's rolling. "No comment," he said ad nauseam. This "no comment" statement and desiring to be left alone at this moment was a nugatory request as question after question was blurted out aloud as he tried to avoid everyone. "No comment until I meet with my attorney" were the final words he said as he ascended the steps and entered his apartment.

His landline phone had so many voicemail messages it was full and could accept no more. Claude was exasperated and truly exhausted beyond comprehension. He shut down his landline and completely turned off his cell phone.

"I'll deal with this shit later," he said to himself as he showered, made a quick sandwich, and got in his bed. In a matter of seconds, he fell into a deep sleep. When Claude awakened, it was just after 1:00 p.m., which meant that his slumber lasted a little under four hours. Still, he felt adequately rested. Both his phones were inundated with messages. Just as he got out of bed, en route to the bathroom to brush his teeth and wash his face, his doorbell rang.

He slightly pulled back his drapes and saw his dad's car, so he buzzed him in and went to the door to unlock it.

"Hey, son, we've all been trying to contact you for the last three or four hours. Where the heck have you been?" said Clyde. "Are you okay?"

"Yes, Dad. I was exhausted, so after the police station, I came home and wanted to nap so that I could have my wits about me," said Claude.

"Yeah," said Clyde. "I talked to Ms. Evans right after you and I talked this morning because you had stopped answering your phone. I'm glad she got to you in time. Look, Claude, the suspense is killing me. Please tell me the entire story. Take your time, and, son, please omit none of the details."

"Oh, sure, Dad," said Claude. "Let me put on a pot of coffee. Are you hungry?"

"Who could eat at a time like this? But I would appreciate a rather large cup of coffee," said Clyde.

Claude got the coffee going and commenced to bring his dad up to snuff about the entire Harvey story—from the fat Negress at their home right up to Harvey's last minutes on earth. Clyde was spellbound, flabbergasted to say the least. If it wasn't his son telling him this story, he would've had a difficult time believing him.

He said, "Son, right now you're caught between a rock and a hard place. That officer is going to use you for his own agenda. There isn't much breathing room for you right through here. That protection order you filed on behalf of you and Carter will play right into his hands like the cards in a royal flush. Harvey's final words are also going to fuel the flames of this cop's defense. I'm no expert legal mind, so I suggest you wait until you speak with Ms. Evans. Still, the incident at the Trolley Stop restaurant, the involvement of Mr. Dibble the manager, you confirming to the officer that this was Harvey's second attempt to run you over, the protection order, and the charges of terroristic threats—all these things will solidify the officer's so-called righteous shooting of Harvey as justified. Did you know they're saying that Harvey had a pistol in his hand? Did you see him reach for a pistol?"

Just then, Claude's mind started racing again, and he inadvertently started mumbling under his breath, "My god! That's why that cop allowed me to go home. He did plant a stinger, an illegal gun, on Harvey."

"How's that, son?" said Clyde.

"Oh, I was just thinking aloud, Dad, that the cop let me go home just to give himself enough time to plant a stinger on Harvey before any other cops arrived," said Claude.

"Yeah," said Clyde, "Carter told me about that Harvey guy calling the house and threatening the both of you. You really don't know what he did to your omelet? Well, I have a good idea. That's a jail house move. He probably cleared his throat or cleaned out his nose on to your food. That's what they have been known to do in jail when a convict works in the kitchen or has a comrade that works there. Instead of crushing and grinding up a light bulb or putting a cleaning solution or any other kind of chemical on your food, to avoid being charged with attempted murder, he threatened you, screwed up your food, and then tried to run you over twice. And you feel sorry for him, huh? Well, your mom and I obviously did a hell of a job raising you if you're that forgiving. I really commend you, Claude. I'm not trying to antagonize you, son. But had anyone done those things to me, I wouldn't give two shits whether or not he was dead or alive. I mean, how do you know he wasn't trying to kill you on the road? From where I sit, that cop has an airtight case for a justified shooting. He apparently chose to dispatch the right person.

Claude, are you sure he didn't have a gun when the officer cut loose on him?"

"I'm as sure as there is shit in a goat, Dad. From what I could see, he was reaching under the driver side visor for his driving information, and I'm absolutely positive that he didn't have a gun in his hand when the fireballs tore through his flesh either, Dad," said Claude

"Tell me something, Claude. When have you seen a cop let his only witness go home after a fatal shooting? Do you really think he gave a fuck about how cold or wet from sweat you were? Geez, son, you're probably going to catch a ton of smoke when you tell the truth too—from both sides. The police and your people are going to bust your balls with this. You were on all the network news stations at noon today. All of America witnessed your 'no comment' response to the media as you walked up the steps this morning. Well, I think I've said enough. Listen, Claude, before you contact anyone else, get in touch with Ms. Evans as soon as possible. Then call your mother immediately afterwards. Keep your mouth shut in the interim also."

The smell of freshly brewed coffee suddenly permeated the air in Claude's apartment, and that confirmed to Claude that the coffee was ready.

"Hey, you can come stay with me and Carter until this thing blows over—if you want to avoid the media hordes," said Clyde.

"Thanks for the offer, Dad. I might just take you up on that. Let me make my return phone calls, and I might stop over around dinnertime, Dad. I might just come to eat with you guys tonight. Right now, I think I'll be okay," said Claude.

"Okay, son, now I can go home and get some sleep. This whole thing has rendered me very anxious also. You wait until you have kids, then you'll appreciate how I'm feeling right through here," said Clyde.

"Oh, Dad, I can imagine," replied Claude.

"Well, I'm going to hat up son," said Clyde as he guzzled his spot of coffee, then made his way to Claude's front entrance. "Love you, son."

"Love you back, Dad. Talk to you around six, okay?" replied Claude.

"Sure," said Clyde.

# CHAPTER 40

Claude made himself a toasted bagel, which he prepared with his low-fat cream cheese. He then called Ms. Evans.

"Hey, Ms. Evans, how are you?" asked Claude.

"I'm alive and awake, young man, so all is well. When can you come in?" queried Ms. Evans.

"Oh, you don't want me to bring you up to snuff right now?" asked Claude.

"Oh no, young man. On the phone—never that. That's not something I do, Claude. The phone is the second most compromised means of communication there is—second only to the computer. You never know who's listening or observing on either one. Anyway, can you be here by 3:00 or 3:30 p.m. at the latest? We're going to have to get our ducks in a row before we go to the police station. I absolutely wouldn't wait until tomorrow if I were you, and I never do anything without the proper preparation either. So again, young man, I ask, what time will I see you?" said Ms. Evans

"Oh, three o'clock is cool, Ms. Evans. I have some return calls to make. I'll get dressed and stop in as soon as I'm done, okay?" queried Claude.

"Sure is," replied Ms. Evans. "One more word of advice, young man. Don't say anything to anyone before we meet, okay? *Especially* the media."

"Sure thing," replied Claude. "So long."

Claude hung up the call and immediately dialed his mother. He spoke briefly to Estelle, telling his mom that he couldn't go into detail until his visit with the police was over. He then called Ms. Wright, who told him about the ad hoc meeting all of the area's committee people were scheduled to have at 7:00 p.m. tonight. Confirming his intended attendance, he quickly made short work of his call to Ms. Wright as well. No sooner did he hang up on his call to Ms. Wright than his phone rang. It was a Ms. Ann Sheppard.

"Ann Sheppard?" said Claude. "I'm sorry, Ms. Sheppard, but I don't recognize your name."

"Well, Claude, you were certainly interested in my name last night."

"Oh, Annie," replied Claude, now smiling widely. "I'm sorry. How are you?"

"Me? I'm fine," said Ann. "The question is, how are *you*? I saw you on the news at noon. I was shocked. I couldn't believe anyone would go jogging after drinking and partying all night. Did you get any sleep at all?"

"Not until I got home from the police station."

"Police station?" queried Ann. "They took you in this morning?"

"Not really," said Claude. "Hey, listen Annie, I'm really busy right now. I have to go meet with my attorney and make some business-related calls. Can I call you back a little later?"

"Sure," said Ann, "I'll be home all day. Okay, I'll await your return."

While he ate his bagel and the nasty, disgusting, low-fat cream cheese and got dressed, Claude considered contacting the prospective employers and setting up interviews, but his mind again was all over the place. So he decided to wait until after he dealt with this police-shooting-Harvey mess. When Claude arrived at Ms. Evan's office, he was pleased that he was going to see her. As usual, prior to going to her office, he wondered what she had on today. While he waited in the waiting room, for the first time, he perused the office and was shocked at the ethnic artwork and the curios that filled the office.

She had photos of the great Thurgood Marshall, an African American artist's rendition of Mr. Nat Turner, and photos of the prolific Martin Luther King Jr., Dr. Ralph Abernathy, and Mr. Andrew Young. And there was a photo of herself standing next to Mr. Nelson

Mandela. There was a classic photo of Ms. Lena Horne, and there, in one of the corners, was a glorious artist's rendition of Beyoncé Knowles adjacent to a photo of the iconic Ms. Diana Ross during one of her concerts, which was placed directly underneath a classic photo of Ms. Ella Fitzgerald. Directly behind her secretary's desk was an artist's rendition of the courageous Ms. Bessie Coleman, aviator, which was to the right of a photo of the versatile actress Ms. Whoopi Goldberg.

Claude's face seemed to be now stuck in grin mode. "Wow," he said and continued to say it about four or five times, "talk about class!"

This Ms. Evans was truly a hip and historically informed African American woman. She clearly delineates the difference in the attitude of a real African American female as opposed to the stank-ass attitude and behavior of a well-dressed, physically attractive T.A.N.. If you were black, you could feel the difference. You could even see how much love of self she had, especially when it came to her people. Talk about being grounded. There were African tribal masks and miniature busts of people like Ms. Angela Davis, Ms. Sojourner Truth, and Ms. Jane Pittman. The photo that brought the largest smile to Claude's face was the photo of Ms. Nicky Minaj in concert.

"Wow," he said for what must have been the sixth time.

This woman has really spanned several generations of appreciation for her own people's history, arts, and culture. There were treated newspaper and magazine articles of the assassinations of both Mr. Patrice Lumumba and of Malcolm X and an article of how the once great Mr. Huey P. Newton died. Talk about being in touch and truly loving her own African American heritage. Side by side and close to the door were treated book cover photos of the great Mr. Toussaint L'ouverture's biography *Citizen Toussaint*, and Mr. Richard Wright's *Native Son*. Just above those was a blown up replica of the book cover of *The Invisible Man* by Mr. Ralph Ellison. The last miniature bust that caught his eye was a bust of Mr. Marcus Garvey.

"Geez," he said right before being called into her office, "this is a museum, a shrine of appreciation for the struggle and accomplishments of people of African descent from all over the world, covering more than over three hundred years."

His respect and appreciation of Ms. Evans just jumped tenfold.

Ms. Evans stepped out and greeted Claude like he was her own son. "Hello, Claude! Well, how the heck are you?" said Ms. Evans.

"I'm okay, Ms. Evans. I guess you're thinking this guy stays in some kind of trouble, huh?" said Claude.

"Well, young man, you know what the Russians say, "Shitsky happens." The retort brought a smile of appreciation from Claude. "Well, before you say anything, let me tell you that Officer Hooven, the officer that murdered Harvey, has been behaving in front of the media like he was put on earth as your savior, your knight in shining armor. Let me apprise you of all I've been able to glean from his comments and what has been set forth by the press." After giving Claude an earful, Ms. Evans then said, "Now it's your turn to tell me how much of what I just said is true."

"Well, save for Harvey Boone having and reaching for his gun, the rest of it fits the officer's point of view, that's for sure."

"Meaning?" said Ms. Evans with a quizzical look on her face.

"Well," said Claude, "it's more accurate than true. I mean, Mr. Boone—as you call him—did run me off the road twice. Yes, he did contaminate my food. As a matter of fact, he did that the same day you settled my case with Johnson & Johnson."

"Oh, that's why you looked so forlorn, so agitated that day when you arrived here," interjected Ms. Evans. "I'm sorry, continue please."

"Well, also he did call my dad's house and threatened both me and my brother Carter. Still, Ms. Evans, that guy was not reaching for nor did he have a gun in his hands when that officer gunned him down like a rabid squirrel," said Claude.

"You know, young man, your attitude with regard to Mr. Boone is extraordinary. I must say, not I nor most people I know would give a horse's balls what happened to this guy. But obviously you do. You're a firm believer in the Bible, like your mom, aren't you?" said Ms. Evans.

"Sure am, Ms. Evans. What makes you say that?" replied Claude.

"Because only someone who believes in the words 'Vengeance is mine, sayeth the Lord' would be this concerned about the fate he met and be that sympathetic or that forgiving, especially after he screwed up your food. Geez, I would've wanted to kill him for that alone! Nor do I know if that anger I harbored would've dissipated so quickly, especially if he continued to take the scab off the wound by continuing to harass you, like this guy kept doing to you. So let me get my coat, and we can head on down to the police station, and you can give your written statement to Detective Bull Wrangler," said Ms. Evans.

"Ah, Ms. Evans, that's Detective Boerwinkle," said Claude.

"Hey, Claude, don't you think I already know that? Aren't I allowed a little comic relief from time to time? What, do you think I'm really a staid cunt with a stiff board up my butt or that I wear a heavily starched corset? Geez, a little levity is sometimes great medicine! Lighten up a little, okay?"

Claude was now grinning from ear to ear.

To be his mother's contemporary, this was one really attractive, sharp lady. All her clothes were very formfitting and were of the finest quality. You could clearly see the way her clothes fell over her body, like a runway model, that they were all tailored just for her. What a shape this lady had also! Her panty line was clearly visible in the slacks and skirts she wore and those 100 percent Egyptian cotton and Italian-cut silk blouses she wore. How they accentuated her shapely breasts! Like Ms. Betty Willis and Danielle the psychologist, this woman really turned Claude on intellectually as well as physically.

"Well, one more thing, young buddy, before we get there. Answer absolutely nothing quickly, and keep your eyes on me for a 'yay, you may answer that' or a 'nay, don't answer that' response from me. Do you understand me?"

"Sure do, Ms. Evans. Oh, another postscript statement, Claude. You and your brother please kill that fat Negress stuff. That *Negress* word is steeped in slavery, Jim Crow, and oppression. Please find another derogatory epithet to describe her. I can understand she inspired you and your brother's ire. However, when you use that word, you tend to insult *all* black women—African Americans and ignorant black women alike. So like they used to say in Patterson when your mom and I were growing up, please kill that noise about Negress, okay?"

"Sure will, Ms. Evans, and I'm truly sorry if I offended you in any way," said Claude.

"Apology accepted, my good man."

# CHAPTER 41

After an hour and fifteen minutes of the most annoying questioning, Claude and Ms. Evans left the police station to make their way
to their own respective destinations. Claude went to his father's
house to have dinner with his dad and his brother Carter before he
attended his first committee person meeting. Election day was but
a week away, and he was informed that he would have to first work
the polls and then see whether or not he was voted in before he could
actually start doing his committee person duties.

The questioning made clear to Claude what the police's, in
particular Officer Hooven's (who had shot Harvey to death), intentions were. They were privy to everything that had gone on between
Harvey, Claude, and Barbara the beast. They had procured copies
of the protection order and the criminal complaint Claude had filed
against him. They had tried (unsuccessfully) to contact Carter several
times but—*of course*, thought Claude—to no avail. As Ms. Evans had
put it, they had all their ducks in a row, lined beak to tail.

After Ms. Evans's comments about what Harvey had done to
Claude and his dad, he was now severely conflicted about how to
move forward with this matter. Should he tell the truth, the whole
truth, and nothing but the truth? Should he just let sleeping dogs
lie? After all, the crap Harvey pulled on him was enough to make
anyone want to kill him. If he left the whole issue alone, wouldn't he
being playing into the hands of a white man that just wanted to kill
a black person? Had Officer Hooven done what had to be done that
he himself couldn't or wouldn't do?

*Damn, all this shit because that ignorant Barbara the beast couldn't do her damn job!* This was exactly the kind of stuff that happened when T.A.N.s worked their magic, infiltrated the everyday goings-on in an African American's life, and caused nothing but discord. If only Harvey had remained in his car and just followed the law . . . Again, interacting with a small populace of T.A.N.s would screw up your whole life for days, weeks, and months just because they really hated their own stations in life. If, if, if . . . "If ifs and buts were cookies and nuts, everyday would be Christmas." It was a saying Claude's dad used to use a lot when he was growing up. It was a way of saying you had to deal with life's impediments as they came. Complaining and wishing would avail you nothing.

Thank God he was skilled enough to employ himself when circumstances demanded it. Thank God he was capable of earning enough money to save. Thank the Lord that both his parents were in his life at the most crucial times. Thank God that, due to the time his parents and loved ones devoted to him in his formative years, he didn't grow up ignorant. Thank God there were *real* African American women and men in his community, like the ones— *what's their names, the two women? Ahhh, Marsha and Queen. Yeah, that's them*—who worked at the ShopRite supermarket, the lovely Marshada who worked as a pharmacist assistance at the Walgreen's Pharmacy he used for his diabetes and blood pressure medicine, the brothers Reds, Haru, Frank, and Marc at Red's Creative Cuts (the barbershop he frequented), and the women (including the gorgeous Rochelle and Shanae) who worked at the post office he used; they were cordial, courteous, and very professional in the discharge of their duties.

What he had come to realize was that T.A.N.s were a minority in the black experience. Even though they were a minority, their bullshit was very powerfully disruptive and virtually intolerable. Therefore, what did Harvey's death really mean? The things Claude had learned about telling the whole truth conflicted him immensely. The sayings he knew were "Evil flourishes when good men do nothing" or "To sin by silence makes cowards out of men."

*Do I have to tell the truth? I know myself. I really won't be able to forget about that if I do lie or remain mum. If I do tell the truth, am I putting my life or my safety in imminent peril? Will I have to move if I tell the truth and the officer gets charged and goes to jail? What if he gets charged and then acquitted? Will I be able to continue to go jogging safely? How will I be viewed by my people, whom I eventually have to look in the eye every day? Yeah, like my dad said, I'm really caught between a rock and a hard place.*

Claude knew the police would be in touch with him through Ms. Evans at the culmination of their investigation. Therefore, might as well start living again. At the political meeting, he met other committee people and familiarized himself with the process. He was getting to know Ms. Sherelle Wright personally, and that was fine with him. They served some sorry-ass food, and after ninety minutes of introduction and instruction and after enduring quite the elongated, unnerving day, Claude knew it was time for a hot shower, a meal, and the comfort of his queen-sized bed.

The very next day, Claude woke up with an agenda. He set out to contact every agency and/or company that left him messages to set up an interview. Two were apartment buildings, not complexes. These two were looking for a porter or just a maintenance man, a job that really didn't interest Claude because he did that kind of work on his own. If an employer couldn't offer benefits, in particular health care and life insurance, then he quickly bowed out gracefully.

He chose a social service agency that sought a custodial supervisor. This agency was named after Dr. William E. Smith, a rich (multimillionaire) African American physician. They employed primarily African Americans and were a fledgling agency. Only in business for less than three years, they were recruiting people to shore up the professionalism of their staff and management personnel. Many of their management people were there when they opened as a private organization, and most were not degreed individuals.

However, over the last two years, they had applied for and had been granted funds from both the state and federal government, and because of that, their criteria for management personnel had changed. The people who were managers there had to enroll in school within ninety days, seeking at least a bachelor's degree, or be demoted to positions that didn't require a degree. It was either that or leave the agency altogether. The supervisors in their maintenance department had to be licensed in whatever positions they held.

That was where Claude came in.

Life is very similar to riding a bicycle. In order to maintain balance it is necessary to keep moving.

—Albert Einstein

 

# CHAPTER 42

Being licensed in both carpentry and plumbing, having his own business, and being incorporated and bonded made Claude a valuable commodity. He was interviewed by the William E. Smith organization and was made an offer that dwarfed what he made at Johnson & Johnson by almost half. Now, he would supervise his own department, and that was fine with him. He accepted and made plans to start two days after next week's election. He chose two days because he was told his work at the polls would require long hours—at the very least twelve hours—and he didn't want to start work the next day tired. His secondary reason for starting later in the week was not to have to work an entire five straight days his first week.

Claude was again very happy to seemingly be starting a career. He knew he had some things to straighten out, and now that he was back in the workforce, he was more than happy to once again be in the midst of a productive routine.

His work at the polls on election day was draining. He worked from 7:00 a.m. on election morning until the polls closed at 8:30 p.m. He was oh so pleased that he won. He just hoped the position of committee person didn't interfere with his new job, which he was excited to have, having never supervised before. What he didn't realize was that this committee-person is a paid position. He was shocked to be receiving funds for working the polls. What Claude learned that day was that many of the other committee people would disappear an hour or two at a clip. He didn't know where they went, but he knew per his instruction at the meeting he attended that he wasn't supposed to leave, save for an emergency. Food (lunch) was also provided for the people who worked the polls, so food wasn't an excuse to leave either.

Notwithstanding, these were some cordial, well-intentioned people. Their goal was to meet the political agenda of Ms. Wright, and they worked tirelessly at it. Maybe after a few years of devoting my time and effort, he'd be able to feel when respite time was available. But right through here, he did what was asked of him. When the day's work at the polls culminated, he was thoroughly spent—physically as well as mentally. He'd had to endure so much anxiety the last few days over the shooting of Harvey, the in-depth questioning by the police, the tension of the interview process. All these things wore on Claude, and he really needed a day to relax and get things in order before he began his new job.

At the orientation Claude attended, he realized how much responsibility he had. The agency was located in a very large building, and Claude was not only responsible for the maintenance personnel at the main building, but he was also charged with all the custodial and maintenance personnel at the two other buildings as well—twenty-four workers in all. Was it any wonder why his pay was doubled from the last position he held? He also had to be on call during the entire second shift and alternate weekends. This he knew would completely change his leisure schedule. No more ad hoc partying/clubbing dates.

There was a problem that Claude knew would eventually rear its ugly head sooner or later. The person he was replacing was the same person who was instructed to train him. He knew from the look on this gentlemen's face that this would be a problem. Mike Goss, who had been with the agency since it began, was not going to school anytime soon to get his licenses now required by the agency. Therefore, the only work available to him was as a laborer working *for* Claude, the same guy he was instructed to train. Even though the agency was keeping Mr. Goss's salary the same, it was still a loss of prestige, and Mr. Goss now had very much the resentment with Claude.

He tried to be diplomatic, but his face and countenance belied his amicable presentation. Whenever possible, he made things difficult for Claude. He didn't give Claude the proper instructions, or he misled him whenever possible. He would invite Claude to have lunch with him and then try to talk Claude into having a beer or two before returning to work. When that didn't work, he would change the lock on Claude's locker or give him the wrong combination. He continually tried to talk Claude into firing folks he didn't like.

After firing two employees that worked under Claude, he told Claude that he had to sign their exit sheets and letters of termination because he was officially the new supervisor.

Then he went to the maintenance manager and said, "This new guy just comes on board and fires two people as his first discharge of duty. Who the heck we going to be working with now? Don't you think he should've at least waited to get to know people first?"

When the maintenance manager called Claude in to quantify why Claude fired these folks so quickly, Claude replied, "Mr. Langston, I didn't fire anyone. Mr. Goss did. He is training me, sir, and he instructed me that since I was the new supervisor, I had to sign their termination papers. As I'm sure you are aware of, Mr. Langston, I barely knew those two employees."

"Well, Mr. Paine, let me remind you that you are the supervisor. All those decisions of hiring and firing are in your hands and are to be made at your discretion. Remember, anything you sign is your responsibility from that point on. I'll speak to Mr. Goss about this mix-up." Mr. Langston continued, "Now, before you return to work, are there any other issues you'd might like to discuss with regard to your job?"

"Well," said Claude, "there is this issue about having Mr. Goss train me, the same man who's position has been replaced by me. I don't feel he is at all comfortable training the person who is replacing him. The instruction I'm receiving from Mr. Goss leaves a lot to be desired."

"Oh, is that so, Mr. Paine? Mr. Goss, myself, and Human Resources discussed this issue at length, and Mr. Goss assured us that as long as his pay remained the same, he would have no problem training you or stepping down. I must say, Mr. Paine, that Mr. Goss has done an excellent job for us. I have known him the entire three years he and I have been here, and I have never known him to be a vindictive sort or to have a veracity problem. Still, if you say you haven't received thorough instruction, I have to believe that perhaps it's just a problem of style or a lack of communication. Go back to work, Mr. Paine, and let me discuss this issue you two are having," said Mr. Langston.

The next day, when Claude laid eyes on Mr. Goss, he could see immediately that Mr. Langston had indeed spoken to Mr. Goss about Claude's issues with the poor training he was receiving. He was as tight-lipped as if he continually walked around, sucking on a lemon. He only spoke when spoken to, and he answered every question Claude asked facetiously, as if he were talking to someone for whom English was a second language—in slow, methodical, calculating terms.

Claude kept thinking, *All I did was apply for a job and get hired. I meant not to get involved in anyone's personal employment and lack of educational issues. If I were a manager, I would expect this kind of friction if I too gave someone the task of training the person who'd soon be replacing her or him. To me, that's just common sense, appreciating the human condition. Well, like my dad used to say, it's a shame you aren't the one hiring you. You would automatically be your own first choice.*

Still, Mr. Goss treated Claude like Claude was a leper. And most annoyingly, he never again looked Claude in the eye. He behaved overtly and intentionally like the absolute worst part of his day was the time he spent in Claude's company—just some more crap to endure interacting with my own people. After the first eight or nine days, Claude had developed his routine and was now more comfortable. He no longer needed Mr. Goss's tutelage, and that was fine with him.

$$\text{\footnotesize ——————————}\ \text{❧}\ \text{\footnotesize ——————————}$$

# CHAPTER 43

Having to oversee the everyday goings-on at three buildings and to supervise eighteen employees was time-consuming work that required attention to detail. He really liked the autonomy and appreciated the ability to have lunch when and where he wanted to. He had stayed in touch with Ms. Willis (Betty), and the two of them had lunch twice. He really enjoyed her conversation and her company. She invited Claude to her home for a home-cooked meal.

"You eat out too often, young man," she had stated on several occasions. "That's not always a healthy thing to do. Too many hands are handling your food all the time."

That was when he received a dinner invitation from Betty, and he, of course, accepted immediately. There was one thing that Betty told Claude that he didn't know how to take, whether or not it was said in jest, or just really what to make of it altogether.

On their second lunch date, Betty queried, "What exactly are you looking for with me?"

"Wow, that came outta left field," said Claude. "I haven't given that much thought. I mean, our age difference is significant. Still, I find you very sexy and quite attractive, Betty. I enjoy this. Why? Do I annoy you?"

"No, young man, not at all. I asked you that because I pretty much know there will be no hanky-panky or shenanigans between us, and I just wanted to make sure you weren't being misled," stated Betty.

"Hanky-panky," said Claude. "I don't think I heard that one before. Okay, okay, I got it, Betty."

And she and Claude enjoyed a good hearty long laugh. Was she serious or just expressing doubt aloud? Either way, it did not impede Claude's desire to develop a close friendship with Betty. Claude meant to query Betty about what she thought about her dad and if he would mind the two of them developing a friendship. For some reason, the one thing Claude and Betty never did was discuss Mr. Bernard.

Claude had a date this upcoming weekend with Annie. She had met Claude that night he went to the club, and they had stayed in touch sporadically in the interim. She, like Claude, had just begun a new job, and she too was experiencing the doldrums of orientation—the initial learning curve, so to speak. When everything everyone else was doing their everyday routines, it seemed so hard for you to grasp at first.

Annie was an English teacher, and she was recently hired to head the entire English department at the high school she worked. This weekend's date would be the first time either one of them had been out since the night they met at the club. Things were now settling in. The investigation of Harvey's shooting was drawing to an end any day now. This was not an event Claude was looking forward to. The date with Annie was something Claude *was* looking forward to.

She appeared to like Claude, and at this point, he could see no ulterior motive. Annie was two years Claude's senior. She didn't have any children and owned her own home. Annie had a BA degree in education with a minor in English. She was beginning her first semester of her final year in seeking her master's degree in education. She had already been accepted to Seton Hall grad school in their doctors of education program. However, her goal was to get into Rutgers main campus so she didn't have to travel far as she lived less than a mile from Rutgers.

She was attractive, and her behavior contradicted the woman he met that night at the club who did the fast-moving dance all night (and man, oh man could this woman dance!), sweat up the dance floor, and drank champagne all night. Claude was overwhelmingly pleased to have met an African American (he hoped) woman who was well read and had an appreciation for the arts. Still, between the time he spent with Betty and dating Annie, Claude was more than content when it came to the women whose company he was now keeping.

Claude had missed only two days of his jogging routine in the last three weeks or since beginning his work at William E. Smith. This morning was a dreary, damp, chilly morning with very poor visibility. He was a bit sluggish throughout the jog, and he pulled in much slower than usual. Still, he got it done. The one thing his jogging always did for him was to give him a feeling of accomplishment at the outset of the day.

*Most people are just waking up, while I already accomplished something productive*, he thought. After his shower and some dry rye toast and coffee, he was off to work. Once again, he was low on gas, and he hadn't been to see Mr. Bernard since Harvey was killed. He stopped by the one-stop gas station he frequented to purchase both. When he pulled in, there sat Herbie the hobo next to a filthy face that was spotted and cruddy with grime and lips encrusted with dried saliva—female.

*I guess you can call her that*, thought Claude. He pulled in next to a pump and made his way inside the store, hoping Herbie wouldn't ask him for any money.

"Hey, thick!" yelled Herbie. "Come and meet my new lady."

Claude looked at the woman and thought to himself, *Your lady, huh?*

"Hey, hello, miss!" said Claude.

"Is that Claude Paine?" said filthy lady, much to Claude's amazement.

"Yeah, that's me," said Claude. "Did Herbie tell you my name."

"No. Hey, Claude, it's me, Diana? Your friend from elementary school? Don't you remember me?"

"Diana," queried Claude. "Diana Maximum? Oh wow. Hey Diana, how are you? Geez I haven't seen you in about seven to eight years."

"Oh, y'all know each other, huh?" said Herbie.

"Yes," said Claude. "I've known Dee Dee all my life. Hey, look, I'm running a little late for work. Let me handle my business and get going."

"Well, wait a minute, Claudio," said Diana. "Remember, we used to call you that? Hey, look, Claude, could you help a sister out with a couple of dollars? It ain't like I ask you for money all the time."

Claude said, "Just a minute, Dee Dee. I'll be right back."

Claude got his coffee, a *New York Post*, and fifty dollars' worth of gas. When he finished pumping his gas, he walked over to Diana and began to smell her while he was still fifteen feet away from her. Damn, did she stink! The few teeth she had were rotted something fierce, and Claude could not hide his disgust.

"Wowee," he said aloud. "Damn, Diana, it's time for a shower, don't you think?"

"I know, I know, brother. As you can see, life ain't been too good to a sister. I'll get a shower sooner or later," said Diana.

"Hey, Diana, have you seen or heard from Benton?"

"Who?" asked Diana.

"Benton Buck who grew up with us?"

"Oh," said Diana. "You mean Bee Bee?"

"Yes," said Claude. "How is he?"

"Oh, he's on the plantation—cotton field."

"Huh," said Claude. "Again, is that where he works? It was where he works, eats, sleeps and lives?"

"You know, Claude, the stationary slave ship."

"Hey, Diana, you lost me," said Claude.

"He's in the penitentiary, doing double life," stated Diana.

"Wow," said Claude. "Sorry to hear that."

"Well, Diana, here's ten. As a matter of fact, here's another ten. I'm doing this to let you know to never ever ask me for money again. That's something I just don't do. You can have this money this time. If you ever ask me again, you're going to be embarrassed. I hope you're listening to me. The buck stops here. Take care of yourself."

As Claude drove to work, he was almost in tears. With all the crap he had to endure, thank God Diana and Herbie's fate was not his own. That odor that emanated from Herbie's and Diana's person stayed in his nose for the entire ride to work. Lord, they didn't wash, eat, and change their underclothes or their clothes. They slept wherever—in the park, in the train station, in the fast-food bathroom.

*Geez, what a way to live. Well, not live, survive . . . eerrr . . . exist, I mean.* Just before exiting his car at work, he said aloud while still thinking about Herbie and Diana, "There but for the grace of God go I."

The ultimate measure of a man is not where
he stands in moments of comfort and convenience, but where he stands in times of
challenge and controversy.

Dr. Martin Luther King Jr.


Be in the heat of battle—it's no rest for the
weary—you snooze, you lose is the theory.

—Mr. Mark Curry,
rapper (from Notorious B. I. G.'s
song "Dangerous MC's")

⌒⌒✦⌒⌒

# CHAPTER 44

Saturday night couldn't come quick enough. That was how anxious Claude was to go out on the date with Annie. With his new schedule at work dictating that he'd be on call next weekend, he reshuffled his dates with Annie and his dinner date at Ms. Betty Wilson's house. Ever since Betty laid down the no-hanky-panky, no-shenanigan rule, Claude set his serious romantic goals on Annie, and now Claude knew Betty would only be a good plutonic relationship, a dear friend. He was really checking Annie out to see if she liked the arts and also to see if she had been honed on things of culture. This was what he truly wanted in a woman he was to get serious with.

The two went to dinner at a small, quaint Italian restaurant that seated about twenty max. The waiter waited on him and Annie like they were his only two charges for the night (the kind that stood there, towel draped over his arm, looked at you with that "Your wish is my command" look). After dinner, the couple went to the Blue Note cafe to catch the masterful jazz trumpeter Wynton Marsalis. It was a very nice night for prospective lovers who were still in the "just friends getting to know each other" stage. Claude wanted to see if Annie appreciated jazz and, if not, if she was opened minded to learn about something new and if she didn't, if she was at all interested in what he liked.

The two enjoyed each other's company and parted ways with an insecure, abbreviated kiss and an "of course" response from Annie when asked, "Can we do this again?" Claude was enjoying his job, in particular, the responsibilities he incurred when he accepted the position. It kept him really busy, focused. He looked forward to staying there for a while as the money was much more than he ever made or expected.

The next day, Sunday, Claude prepared for church that morning, but he couldn't keep his mind on tonight's dinner date over Betty's house. After church, he decided to make pasta seafood salad consisting of two kinds of pasta, lump crab meat, bay scallops, cherrystone clams, and diced oysters to take with him to Betty's house to include with their dinner. She lived in a kind of a rough neighborhood for someone as educated and as well-off as she was.

It was her father's house that she grew up in. Through the years, the neighborhood had taken a turn for the worse, and instead of selling it, she decided just to reside there. Church was really filling on this day for some reason, just a little more filling than usual. Claude was more relaxed today than he had been for a while. For some time, he wanted to feel the sense of hope he had been feeling lately with Annie in his life, his new job, and his interactions with both Mr. Bernard and his daughter, Betty. That afternoon, at 4:45 p. m., Claude arrived at Betty's home for a 5:00 p.m. dinner date. After getting his large dish of pasta seafood salad from the passenger's side back seat, Claude neglected to lock the back door of the car.

As he entered Betty's house, he was greeted by the appetizing aroma of homemade tomato or marinara sauce. In visually perusing the house, he noticed that the house was immaculately clean, yet sparsely furnished, much to his surprise. In his life, he had never been to a woman's house or apartment that didn't have a whole lot of little curios, trinkets, photos, posters, stuffed animals, or some kind of decorative wall ornament. None of the above existed here. There was a beautifully crafted book shelf loaded with all kinds of books, magazines, poetry, and newsletters. The house still had a real homey feel to it and a really nice, pungently sweet aroma.

Dinner was simple and filling: spinach and mozzarella lasagna, steamed asparagus, and garlic bread. She followed dinner with coffee; he with herbal tea with lemon. There was no dessert to be had by either. Claude immediately subconsciously thought, as he consciously engaged in post-dinner titular conversation, *Is this woman cheap or what?*

Nonetheless, he really enjoyed the evening, and as with Annie, he was told, "Of course" when he requested an encore. Claude, after a short hug, made his way to his car. It was time to go home, watch some television news, and prepare for the work week. He started his car, and the growl-like purr of the starting engine drowned out the heavy footsteps that were running full speed down the street towards his car. Just then, someone opened the unlocked passenger's side rear door and jumped in, breathing heavily, sweating profusely.

"Yo, man, you better get going now!" the intruder yelled.

Claude, of course, was in shock. "Hey, man, get the fuck outta my car!"

The guy then brandished a gun and said, "Hey, let's get going now, motherfucker!"

At that very moment cops, with guns drawn, were on both sides of the car. Claude didn't know what to do or say. He made only one judgment call—do exactly what the police said. The intruder quickly slid his pistol under Claude's seat. The police on the driver side of the car had clearly seen this.

He yelled a second time, "Don't move! If either one of you move, I'll light you the fuck up!"

Both men followed the police's instruction to a T. They lay face down on the ground, were cuffed and shackled. Then three more backup cars arrived. A police officer had just been shot as he happened upon an armed robbery, and the number-one suspect had just jumped into Claude Paine's car.

Claude spent close to nine days in jail while this mess was straightened out. Again, of course, he called first his mom and then his dad. He cautioned both not to call Ms. Evans as he wanted this one to play itself out. Only someone who was completely innocent would even think that way. The policeman who saw the bandit slide the gun under Claude's seat was Claude's biggest ally. There were none of Claude's fingerprints on the gun. None of the witnesses could identify him. The culprit had no idea what Claude's name was either. This was made manifest during questioning. Claude had no felony criminal record and was gainfully employed. Nothing about him fit the profile of a would-be armed robber / cop shooter. Still, even though Betty provided him the perfect alibi, it still took nine days to release him. Once again, Claude had dodged a bullet that someone black of lesser means might not have been able to dodge.

# CHAPTER 45

During his nine days in lock-up, Claude experienced some amazing things that had a resounding effect on him. The conversations he listened to were so appallingly hopeless. Guys whose bails were less than five hundred dollars couldn't come up with fifty dollars. Some were there seventy-eight-ninety days because they had burned so many bridges they weren't able to procure a fifty-dollar pledge. What annoyed Claude the most was that all the inmates were people of color, even the immigrants. Several men who had accepted their fate of having to be there for a while were wondering whom they would have to bribe to get the inside track to their old jobs in the kitchen or the cleanup crew. The one job that most inmates would kill for was the forty-one-cent-an-hour (wow!) laborer position in the steamy hot boiler room. What a thing to aspire to!

Life had gotten so hopeless that a step up was to be looking forward to forty-one cents an hour. This was a job upstate for folks in prison—not jail. However, these men had such a bleak outlook into the future that they assumed and accepted they were soon to be shipped to prison.

Claude vividly remembered the first night in lockup. The guys in the dormitory-like intake pod were engulfed in a Sunday night football game. He was so drained and disgusted that he wanted to do nothing but sprawl out, stretch, and sleep. Before he passed out, one of the inmates said, "Hey, buddy, this is something new to you. The look on your face—shit, your whole body says, 'What the fuck is this?'"

Immediately, Claude thought of saying, "Well, I can tell that you *are* used to this shit." But he said nothing. He knew to avoid warming up to or having a confrontation with anyone so quickly or to joke and get familiar with no one. He knew that, although they were quiet and withdrawn at the moment, behaviors in jail were very unstable. To be in plot mode here was commonplace. Everyone wanted something from someone.

He could hear that most of the males here have been in the system for decades. The T.A.N. stick-up man cop shooter that Claude was arrested with was being held in another pod on the other side of the prison compound. He was lying by the boatload to make himself look like some kind of folk hero, placing a noose around his own neck, embellishing his story about the cop he shot.

These stories from his own mouth, the recordings of the calls he made, his inability to adequately explain how he knew Claude and from where, then the officer who saw him slide the pistol under Claude's seat—these things plus Betty's notarized affidavit swearing that she and Claude had dinner that night and at the time of the shooting freed Claude none too soon.

He held on to his job, but Annie was at her wits' end. Still, after a few days with some long looks at the facts, Annie acquiesced, and she and Claude continued to woo one another.

*How much more of this my-people-are-killing-me-shit can I take? Sure, racism is bad,* he thought. However, the most harrowing moments and days of his adult life happened when he was in the company of or interacting with black folks. Claude could see no end in sight to the crap that happened to him every so often. He refused to just accept this kind of thing as the norm in his community, among his own people. If he'd had a weapon on him that night, if he had a felony police record (like a great deal of men of color), if he didn't have the support in place that he had . . . he just continued to think of all the things that could have been.

The old religious saying "The Lord never puts more on you then you can bear" was definitely true in Claude's life. Sometimes he felt like a martyr, like he was placed in a situation to put up with pain and terror because he was equipped with enough wherewithal to circumvent the worst of it. All this unsavory crap he had recently endured would've devastated most black people. Most would still be in jail, unable to come up with bail money, waiting on a hearing, and hoping to be freed in a few months or so. How about that? A few months or so—like adults had enough time to be arrested unexpectedly and then all of a sudden and out of the blue had to give up two to six or ten months when they might be totally innocent.

# EPILOGUE

All Claude could think of was *We don't have time to be at one another's throats. Our condition is such that things need to be turned around much sooner than later. We have to do what Mr. McWhorter (the linguistics professor at Columbia University) said—start a blacks-stop-killing-blacks movement. Our children need support, love, and nurturing—not abuse and neglect.*

Claude could definitely see that there was such a difference in the direction his people were heading. Even though there were many that didn't want to hear it, there was very much a *vast* difference between the African American and the throwback American Negro.

*Yes, I can think of ten excuses that could adequately define our people's wretchedness. But like his doctor once told him, "So!"*

No matter what reasons or excuses there were, it was past the bewitching hour for black people. The time to address *all* of our issues was *now*! That whole nine-day jail experience changed Claude's opinion about the wretchedness of T.A.N.s. He could now see where the predominance of their "Lets fuck one another" frame of mind came from. In jail, you didn't live; you existed, survived. Everyone was wary of everyone else all the time. The only thing that brought respect and consideration in a place like jail was fear of reprisal. That was what was known as respect in jail. If anyone spent most of their lives living like this, was it any wonder that their social skills were lacking?

There were no adults to look out for you. When you were raised in the system, or in foster care, a place where finding decent folks who really care about you is a crap shoot. Then after being raised by folks who only really wanted money, you go to jail. Then if by chance you didn't kill or rape anyone or didn't commit any other capital crime, you'd finally get out. After years of dealing with grown men who would never even sniff a pussy again so they'd go around, trying to have sex with as many frightened males as they could. Released, now you'd be on the street. You would not be employable because you'd be devoid of any employable skills. You really didn't have any social skills because you hadn't been raised or taught anything by the adults whom you'd interacted with. The T.A.N women are even more diabolically antagonistic that the T.A.N men because they're usually smarter. Their evolution into T.A.N womanhood is as follows: They get honed and nurtured in their nefarious behaviors by their mothers (if they're still around during the formative years). These so called mothers model a whore-ish-get all you can from a man behavior either with their pussy or by learning the behavioral tendencies of a man, than manipulating him. They don't really know how to be a mother of children or a motivator of men, nor do they really want to do either. When the men leave them they ruin their children's outlook and hope by telling their children, "He doesn't want to be around *us*."

They say undermining things to the men in their lives; like you're lazy, you're spoiled, or you're selfish, so that the men will feel bad enough to give them what they want. If these women ever see a black man forget anything they now have the ammunition they need to rob him. They'll steal his money or any valuable they can use as barter or pawn. Once these men notice their valuables are missing and he confronts them (his T.A.N female aberration of a lover). She'll respond with "You're the one who forgets all the time, maybe you forgot where you left it! On the other hand African American women use their intuition to better the lives of their friends or themselves or to avoid trouble.

T.A.N women use their women's intuition to get what they want, or to take advantage of their sucker lovers. They are wont to use this intuition to make a stranger male or authority figure that they know wants to have sex with them to hurt the black man they've either grown tired of and don't want to be around them any longer or who they've robbed and now they want to make an ally out of these men (who want to fuck them) to stop themselves from getting hurt, for the lousy deeds they perpetrate. If this is all you've learned as a woman then it's difficult to teach these T.A.N. women anything else. Until hopefully she grows tired of herself. Maybe with prayer they find the lord then realize her ch'i (or spirit) will benefit even more if they just try to be decent.

All you had done was be fed and taught how not to trust or how not to be trustworthy. You'd gotten older, but you were now a repulsive, ignorant human being with a repugnant attitude and sent back to live around African Americans who were community minded, struggling, decent people trying to get educated and live and enjoy life. And you, who never had an opportunity to learn anything productive or a chance to develop any skills, would be perpetually pissed off and mad as hell at them because they were reasonably happy. So you'd fuck with them or fuck over them because that was all you know. No wonder there was a difference in African Americans and the poor, neglected-all-their-lives T.A.N..

Then there was the well-to-do, totally integrated, fully assimilated T.A.N. that hates his/her own people, like the aforementioned Charles "Chuck the Fuck" Fakirr and devilish cohort Willis "Poco Diablo Blanco" Gate. They were more dangerous and undermining to the growth of African Americans than the KKK, Skinhead, or Nazi movements even though they were people of color. And like Claude's dad used to say that when those creeps said, "Carter, he's my boy," they meant it in its most derogatory form. That was why it was highly unlikely that they'd ever change their disgusting Holier than thou – entitled to anything the Ghetto dweller has mind-set. So sorry were they that the world looked at them and saw just another nigger. They were educated. They were affluent, and they damn sure didn't want to live around any black folks.

"Be they African American, T.A.N., or whatever, just don't compare their black asses with me. I may be of color, but I damn sure ain't like any of them." That described the attitude of those two butt wipes Chuck and Willis to a T. "How dare anyone think we're not different?"

The female well-to-do upper middle class T.A.N.s are usually employed as managers of Human Resources, or Department Managers and Supervisors in industry or the corporate world. These are the colored women who came to work to break a black man's balls. They speak to black men condescendingly like an unruly child usually unprovoked or contrived. If they previously experienced pain or had ever been jilted by a black man then every black male employee in their path has to pay, and/or they are eventually terminated.

Now another black family is strained or destroyed. The higher up these T.A.N women climb in the corporate or industry worlds the more black families they tear apart. Conversely the African American women in these position are usually focused and extremely proficient in the discharge of their duties. Their hearts, conscience's and experiences wont allow them to be complicit in destroying any family, no matter what race especially their own. When an African American woman is at the helm in any capacity in any business then everyone prospers. The company/business, all of the employees in particular the black ones, its's because of them that we have an equal chance.

Like it or not, might it be repulsive or not, but within his own race, there were people who thought, behaved, and lived differently. That was why Claude got so angry at white folks or any ethnic group or race who thought black people were a monolithic race. If Michael Vick was convicted of killing animals—then all blacks were animal abusers. If Ray Rice punched his fiancée (now wife), then all black men were domestic abusers. If Michael Jackson was accused of child molestation (and he was never convicted of that), then all blacks were child abusers.

*Don't y'all smoke weed and like chicken and watermelon? Well, don't y'all? Isn't it true that y'all don't give a shit about birth control?*

What Claude saw about that monolithic theory that was so amazing was that black folks were always equated with the negative and criminal things other blacks did. It was never "Ooh, a black man performed the first open heart surgery, so they all must be brilliant and medically inclined." No, you'd never hear "Buion Guilford was an astronaut. Wow, I guess all black people are as brilliant as him." No, no, you'd never hear that.

*So, Americans and all other ethnic groups who believe all black men have gargantuan penises, please, that plays right into my hands, so continue to think that!* thought Claude. *So go on, believe what the hell you want. Just try to believe that all of us—T.A.N.s and African Americans alike, cultured, educated, affluent, ignorant, poor, or not— we are all human beings. Try to get a grasp on that. Then perhaps, just maybe, you'll stop killing us so wantonly.*

It had been weeks since Claude had laid eyes on his old buddy Mr. Bernard. He had a couple of boxes of Black & Mild and a boatload of stuff to bring his old buddy up to snuff with. Claude met with Mr. Bernard, and the two men talked for what must've been four to five hours.

Mr. Bernard weighed in about the shooting of Harvey as an "eventuality." He said that he brought it all on himself. When Claude asked Mr. Bernard about the officer's moral culpability, Mr. Bernard said, "His day will come also. Young man, I'm astounded at how you've handled every test set before you, and I'm oh so serious about that. Then that shit with the robber / cop shooter. Do you know there are folks who have spent twenty to twenty-five, thirty years in jail for stuff like that—being in the wrong place at the wrong time? Geez, was that ever a test. I don't know, young man, but the Lord has something big planned for you. He's definitely preparing you for something extraordinary. You mark my words. No one has to tell you to be more vigilant, more careful. When interacting with folks, especially your own people, based on your experiences, you have to be acutely aware of everything and everyone around you at all times. Look, Claude, to paraphrase the beautiful Ms. Michelle Alexander of Ohio State: "All of us are flawed, but all you and I want to do with T.A.N.s is to see one another as we really are. With all the baggage and the beauty that we bring and still love one another, still try to care about one another", not be jealous of or undermine and/or kill one another. Another big mistake that a lot of black people make is thinking that white people are automatically the evil enemy. Enemies, beast, humans, devils, and living monsters come in all races, creeds, and colors. That might sound like a paranoid state of being. You can't let that stop you from being vigilant. These things have happened to you for a reason, and you've weathered each storm like a champ. The reason why might not be made manifest in your life for years. Still, it has toughened you up and educated you about what really exist amongst you. Who your people *really* are and what they're capable of doing, both extraordinarily good and destructively bad, like it or not, that's a fact of life. Yes, you and I have provided T.A.N.s with a great deal of excuses about how they've come to be. However, my young friend, let your empathy be the very thing that keeps you separated from people who think and behave like they do.

"Yes, I know they're troubled, but if I'm sympathetic, and if I show it, they'll eat me alive. If I'm generous, they'll think I'm gullible, and they'll try to take advantage of me. If I try to teach them anything, they'll say, 'You think you so damn smart!' Realizing this, my young friend, you just have to tread lightly, be extremely vigilant. I mean watch your back and front at all times, and pray good, buddy—lots and lots of prayer. Only God can close the hole, the chasm, the vast difference between the African American and the throwback American Negro!!!"

….But we also rejoice in our sufferings, because we know that suffering produces perseverance; perseverance character; and character hope.

And hope does not disappoint us.

The Holy Bible
New Testament
Romans, Chapter 5
Verses 3, 4, 5

At the culmination of this novel, I would be remissed if I didn't thank
the following people:

<table>
<tr><td>Mr. Greg Edelman</td><td>Mr. Mack Graves</td></tr>
<tr><td>Mr. Eric LaBohne</td><td>Mr. Dexter Morris</td></tr>
<tr><td>Mr. Winston Morris Sr.</td><td>Mr. Peter LaBohne</td></tr>
<tr><td>Mr. Winston Morris Jr.</td><td>Mr. Michael Lindsay</td></tr>
<tr><td>Mr. Mike 'Baltimore' Lewis</td><td>Mr. Alfred Jones</td></tr>
<tr><td>AND</td><td>Mr. Jay Rogers</td></tr>
</table>

<table>
<tr><td>Mr. Percy LaBohne</td><td>Miss Natalie Baker</td></tr>
<tr><td>Mr. Gerald K. Williams</td><td></td></tr>
<tr><td>Mr. John Lee</td><td>Mr. Harold Jackson</td></tr>
<tr><td>Mr. Emanuell Baker</td><td>Mr. John Ricketts</td></tr>
<tr><td>Mr. Jerome Baker</td><td>Mr. Lloyd Romero</td></tr>
</table>

My only Son Mr. Haszaan E. Dicks

Mr Michael LaBohne: You left too soon brother!
God rest your young soul!

# About the Author

Martin J. Lee with youngest Daughter, Ayisha Theresa Hunt

The only surviving member of a family of nine siblings, Martin Lee's personal, social, educational and professional experiences within the Black, Latino, and Caucasian communities are plentiful, having been born and raised in a melting pot like Brooklyn New York. After a career as a locomotive engineer, Martin worked as a Social Servant with Wayward Youths of all races and ethnicities. He helped place parents who wanted to be reunited with their children that were placed in foster care—quite the trying, emotionally charged experience to say the least. His interactive experiences are drawn from and made manifest throughout this novel.